Fish

WITHOUT
A DOUBT

RICK MOONEN
AND
ROY FINAMORE

PHOTOGRAPHS BY BEN FINK

Houghton Mifflin Company

Boston · New York

2008

The Cook's
Essential Companion

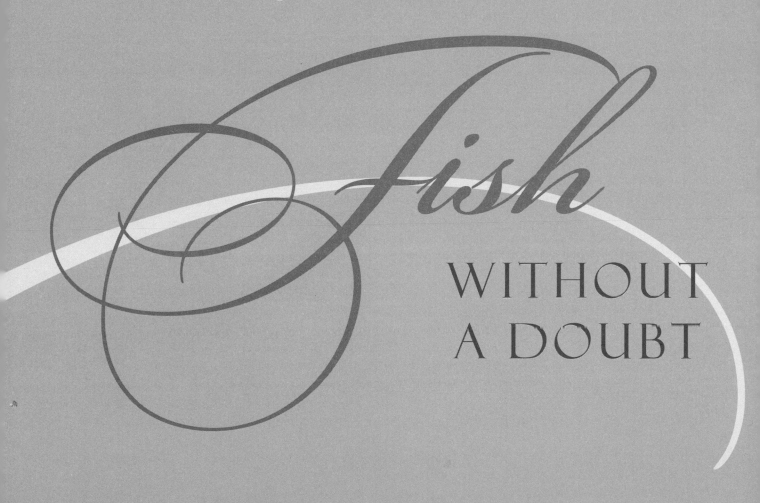

Fish

WITHOUT A DOUBT

For information about permission to reproduce selections from
this book, write to Permissions, Houghton Mifflin Company,
215 Park Avenue South, New York, New York 10003.

www.houghtonmifflinbooks.com

Library of Congress Cataloging-in-Publication Data
Moonen, Rick.
    Fish without a doubt : the cook's essential companion /
Rick Moonen and Roy Finamore ; photographs by Ben Fink.
        p.   cm.
    Includes index.
    ISBN-13: 978-0-618-53119-6
    ISBN-10: 0-618-53119-X
    1. Cookery (Seafood)   2. Cookery (Fish)   I. Finamore, Roy.   II. Title.
    TX747.M66   2008
    641.6'92—dc22   2007052084

Book design by Ralph Fowler / rlf design
Typefaces: Dante MT, Felix Titling, Bickham Script
Food styling by Rick Moonen
Prop styling by Roy Finamore

Printed in the United States of America

MP 10 9 8 7 6 5 4 3 2 1

This book is for my brother Bob,

with whom I had the pleasure

of sharing my childhood.

—R. M.

ACKNOWLEDGMENTS

FROM RICK AND ROY

Thanks first to David Black, for setting us on our way and for his enthusiastic support all through the making of this book. Thanks second to Marian Young—our favorite critic, motivator, and friend—who has an amazing palate and the opinions we lived to hear.

We are deeply grateful for the support of our editor, Rux Martin. Thank you as well to Mimi Assad, Anne Chalmers, Alia Habib, and Clare O'Keeffe at Houghton Mifflin.

To Ben Fink, thank you for the beautiful photographs and your ever calm and cheerful presence on set. Thank you as well to Benjamin D. Kronick and Meggin Juraska for work in the kitchen and to Jeff Kavanaugh for keeping the shoot running smoothly.

To Ralph Fowler, thanks for a great design.

Special thanks to Tim Fitzgerald and Rebecca Goldburg for reviewing the manuscript and setting us straight when we erred.

Thanks to Mike Cioffi and the crew at Pisacane, to Chris Lazicki, and to Carol Devine of Australis for consistently coming through when we needed fish to cook and photograph.

Raissa Lopez provided invaluable support as a taster, cheerleader, and dishwasher.

Elise Ehrlich graciously opened the door to her kitchen and turned on the air-conditioning for a week of summer testing.

To our tasters and testers—Pat Adrian, John Curtas, Deborah DeLosa, Steve Geddes, Victoria McKenzie, Tom Pearson, Jamie Smith, Sean Tupper, and Steve White—many thanks.

My late parents taught me respect, the importance of integrity, and the focus of desire. My family — Lynn, Christopher, and Geoffrey — have given me years of support, love, and understanding.

I have to thank the many people with whom I have shared a kitchen over the years; they've all had an influence on the chef I am today. Chef Eugene Bernard, my mentor and direct link to the classical cuisine era, taught me the meaning of the foundation of cuisine and the passion of the kitchen. Chef Claude Guermont was a significant inspiration from my school days and allowed me to use his kitchen as a playground for experimentation and development. Chef Jean Morel was my teacher for an important part of my formative years; chef Leon Dhaenens, an inspirational mentor; chef Jean-Jacques Rachou, a chef with a clear vision; chef Alain Sailac, a passionate teacher and mentor; chef Jean-Louis Palladin, the most talented chef I ever worked next to. Sam Correnti taught me a priceless lesson about wine: balancing flavors and pairing food and beverage. Matt Accarino, Anthony Amoroso, Kirk Avondoglio, Frank Crispo, Greg Gilbert, Gerry Hayden, Rad Matmati, Neil Murphy, Charlie Palmer, Don Pintabona, Michael Schenk, Brad Steelman, and John Tesar have all been there for me over the years.

My staff, past and present, at rm seafood in Las Vegas has been a great help, and I thank them all. Brian Rae and Matt Griffin have been outstanding.

Deep thanks to my friends in the realm of environmental responsibility: Rachel Hopkins, my go-to person for anything to do with the ocean and beyond; Tim Fitzgerald, an avid supporter and my contact at Environmental Defense; Becky Goldburg, with whom I have had several thought-provoking discussions about sustainability, fish farming, and health concerns surrounding our oceans' bounties; Jeremy Rifkin, the first truly focused activist I met during the pure food campaign days; Alexander Morton, the scientist who opened my eyes to the impact of the fish farm on the wild environment; Vikki Spruill of SeaWeb, who supported me long before environmental involvement was in fashion; and the Monterey Bay Aquarium's Seafood Watch Team and everything they stand for.

Thanks to Roy Finamore, my coauthor and friend, without whom I would never have stayed focused on the project at hand. We kept a lot of pots and pans moving in tight New York City apartment kitchens.

Finally, I dedicate this book to my brother, who passed on years ago and whose memory lives with me, but my appreciation of him goes way beyond that.

FROM ROY

Thanks to Rick Moonen, who invited me to share in this book, for his passion and enthusiasm and for making my work as coauthor so much fun.

My sister-in-law, Donna Rossler, has led her family (Marie, David, and Hannah) in urging me to finish the book because she couldn't wait to cook from it. My parents, Roy and Marie Finamore, are always ready with encouragement.

I must offer particular thanks to Judith Sutton, whose work as a copyeditor is all an author could dream of. Molly Stevens is a great pal and a terrific source of support and encouragement.

I thank them all.

CONTENTS

INTRODUCTION

Cooking fish at home can be a very satisfying experience. We can all tick off the reasons, from fish being rich in healthy fats and quick to cook to the most primal: fish just tastes good. No, better than that: well-prepared fish will knock your dinner guests' socks off.

But face it: for many home cooks, buying a piece of fish raises issues they don't have when they're on the more familiar turf of beef, pork, and poultry. There are understandable fears. "I can't get the fish this recipe calls for; what do I do?" "How do I know if it's fresh?" "What if all I can get is frozen fish?" "I don't have problems when I broil chicken, but when I try to broil fish, it sticks to the pan." "I don't know if it's done."

My aim in this book is to give you the tools and information you need so you can cook fish with the confidence of a pro. Call it fish without fear, or better, fish without a doubt.

Let's start with the most basic reason home cooks balk. I can't tell you how many people tell me they're afraid of their kitchen smelling "fishy." (Why have I never heard anyone say they're afraid of cooking steak because they don't want their kitchen to smell "beefy"?) I've got some advice later in the book about what you can do to combat the aromas that are inevitable when you cook anything, but here's your first big hint: fish shouldn't smell "fishy." If it does, it's not as fresh as it should be — and that smell is just going to get stronger when you cook it.

What should you look for, both in your fish market and in the fish and shellfish you buy? I give you plenty of tips, easily identified cues that I've learned over years of shopping for fish, but one of the best ways to get good fish is find a source you can trust and make friends with the guy behind the counter. Talk to him, ask his advice, and let him know your preferences and uncertainties.

Not all of us are fortunate enough to have a great fish market in our town, though. I certainly don't. My restaurant is in Las Vegas — not exactly a seaport — so I rely on some great suppliers on the East and West Coasts to ship fish and shellfish to me. The Internet opens up a world of possibilities, and you can find similar suppliers of high-quality sustainable seafood online. I've given you a start on page 477. For those of you who wonder about the wisdom of having fish shipped to you, trust me: when you order from a reputable source, your fish arrives in pristine condition.

When it comes to the recipes, I have a couple of things in mind. First, I want you to learn about the cooking processes, so there are a lot of chapters of recipes organized by technique. When you start comparing the recipes, you'll see that you can adapt and use them with a lot of different fish. Second, I've given you things you would really make at home. You'll find both old favorites in these pages and plenty of delicious new dishes. I've distilled years of experience into giving you recipes you really *can* make and impress your friends and family with.

I start with the most forgiving techniques. Poaching may seem old-fashioned, but cooking fish in a moist, flavorful bath protects its delicate flesh. Like poaching, steaming is forgiving. It's not easy to overcook fish when you steam it. The moist heat keeps the fish's own natural juiciness inside it.

When you move on to grilling, you're advancing in technique, but the effort is well worth it. The combination of direct heat and smoke will reward you with flavor that can't be duplicated in the kitchen.

I did a lot of broiling when I worked at Le Cirque and some other very fancy

ACCEPT SUBSTITUTES

There are going to be days when you go shopping for fish and not find what you were expecting to buy. Or you may live in a part of the country where you just don't see turbot—or char or sole—for sale very often. That shouldn't stop you from making many of the recipes in the book.

The "Accept Substitutes" boxes give you two kinds of options. First, they offer some straight-on substitutions, a reminder that you can replace king salmon with sockeye salmon, for example. Often, they offer more than that. Say you're in the mood for "chicken-fried" trout, but you can't find good trout. Check the box and you'll see that you can make this dish with cod, or catfish, or tilapia, or even mahi mahi. Butter-poached lobster is a delicious dish, and you can make it with scallops. Or I may offer possibilities based on the combination of flavors. When you take a look at the recipe for sautéed turbot with leeks and red wine butter sauce, you'll see that I also like this dish made with char, salmon, or flounder.

restaurants in New York. I've adapted some of those dishes, simplifying them for the home kitchen, so you can share, for example, the broiled sole with butter and herbs that the "ladies who lunch" loved. And the sooner you learn that a cast-iron griddle is your friend in the broiler, the easier it will be for you to shine with these dishes.

The oven offers opportunities too. Do me a favor and try the roast tuna. It's an ideal Sunday-dinner kind of dish and simple, simple, simple. And when you love the taste of fish, there may be no better thing to do than roast it in salt. The crust seals in all the ocean flavor, and cooking the fish on the bone means you pull out every bit of gelatin to make the fish lip-smackingly good.

Sautéing may be my technique of choice. It's on the advanced side, since every-thing happens so quickly, but you can see what you're doing—which will take some of the guesswork out of judging when the fish is done—and observe how the fish changes color from the bottom up as it cooks.

I've got hints for making the crispest calamari—which is so much better at home, since you can eat it right out of the fryer—the juiciest fried oysters, the light-est shrimp toast, and "chicken-fried" soft-shell crabs that you can turn into a BLT sandwich that will rock your mouth.

With techniques in hand, I move to chapters that focus on specific kinds of dishes.

What's more fun to eat—or make—than a burger? Fish burgers are classic kitchen-table dishes and a terrific way to introduce kids to fish. Chowders and stews are as friendly and embracing as you can get. But we can always also use something lean and exhilarating like Hot-and-Sour Soup, or a Caribbean-style stew with shrimp and branzino that can be inspiration for a lot of your own variations. Salads run the gamut from a homey American tuna salad to an elegant combination of smoked salmon, potatoes, and frisée. There are tangy and refreshing ceviches and simple gravlax. Pasta and rice are naturals with fish and shellfish. Think paella, shrimp risotto, and linguine with clams. Then get into the kitchen and start cooking.

When you cook fish simply and well, you have a world of options for building flavors on your plate. The sauces and relishes, the vinaigrettes, and the spice mixes in later chapters reinforce the idea that you can—and should—play with combina-tions and make up dishes of your own. And after years of cooking, I've found a handful of recipes that are essential companions to fish on a plate, from my Mom's cucumber salad to the simplest lentils to sweet and easy creamy corn. I've given you these recipes as well.

FISH AND HEALTH

Fish is among the best sources of protein available. Low in calories, low in sodium, almost all fish are carbohydrate-free and lower in cholesterol than most animal protein (even the cholesterol levels in shellfish are relatively low). Fish contains plenty of B vitamins; fatty fish supply vitamins A and D. As for minerals, fish are reliable sources of calcium, iron, copper, and phosphorus. Saltwater fish have a high iodine content. All good stuff.

White-fleshed fish, particularly the flatfish, are low in fat. Fattier fish are rich in omega-3 fatty acids — the "good" fats essential for a healthy diet and cardiovascular health. And when it comes to the "bad" fats, the omega-6 fatty acids, you won't find them in significant amounts.

That's the upside. However, decades of negligence and downright arrogance have damaged our oceans, rivers, and lakes. Discharges from industrial plants and chemical fertilizers used in agriculture are just two of the ways that contaminants such as mercury, PCBs, dioxins, and DDT have found their way into our waters and from there into fish.

THE "BEST" FISH TO EAT

The Environmental Defense Fund's Web site is a very good source of information on healthy fish to eat — the ones high in omega-3 fatty acids and low in environmental contaminants. You can print out the group's "Pocket Seafood Selector" in wallet size and take it with you to the fish market.

www.edf.org/seafood

I'm listing only those fish and shellfish for which I give you recipes in the book.

Anchovies	Sablefish (Alaska)
Arctic char (farmed)	Salmon (wild)
Catfish (farmed in the U.S.)	Sardines
Dungeness crab	Scallops (bay / farmed)
Halibut (Pacific)	Shrimp (farmed in the U.S.)
Mackerel (Atlantic)	Striped bass (farmed)
Mahi mahi (U.S. Atlantic)	Sturgeon (farmed in the U.S.)
Mussels (farmed)	Tilapia (farmed in the U.S.)
Oysters (farmed)	

OUR OVERFISHED OCEANS

The populations of the following fish are compromised. You should avoid them, whether you're shopping for dinner or eating in a restaurant.

Chilean sea bass	Orange roughy
Cod (Atlantic)	Pompano
Conch	Skate
Corvina (Gulf of California)	Snapper (red, ruby)
Dogfish/shark (except from British Columbia)	Sturgeon (imported)
Flounder/sole (Atlantic)	Tilefish (golden, from the Gulf of Mexico and our
Grenadier	southern Atlantic)
Grouper (Atlantic, Gulf of Mexico, and Hawaii)	Totoaba
Halibut (Atlantic)	Tuna (bluefin)
Monkfish	

This isn't to say that you should avoid eating fish. The Environmental Protection Agency says, "A well-balanced diet that includes a variety of fish and shellfish can contribute to heart health and children's proper growth and development," and it also notes that for most people, the risk from mercury by eating fish and shellfish is insignificant. However, higher levels of mercury can have a real impact on the unborn and young children. Women who are pregnant, likely to become pregnant, or nursing should watch the amount and kind of fish they eat, and parents need to take equal care in the fish and shellfish they serve young children.

SUSTAINABLE SEAFOOD

It should come as no surprise that our oceans are in crisis.

Dragging the ocean bottom with tires and chain-mesh nets may be effective ways of catching fish, but some scientists believe that this harms the ocean more than any other activity. Catching fish by longline, hook-and-line, and traps are all much less detrimental to the ocean environment. Look for fish caught by these methods.

Aquaculture, or fish farming, sounds like a good idea, and often it is. Many inland farms, for fish like catfish and tilapia, do little to damage the ecosystem. The same goes for oyster, clam, and mussel farms. In fact, since these shellfish filter seawater for their food—like powerful little vacuum cleaners—farmers raising oysters, clams, and mussels are often in the fore in keeping coastal waters clean.

Net-pen farming, on the other hand, poses major issues for the environment. Here large pens, reminiscent of cattle feedlots, are built in the ocean, and the fish are often raised in crowded conditions. The farming of salmon is a prime example of the problems. These farmed fish generate a large amount of waste, which is released, untreated, into the ocean. The crowding leads to diseases and parasites, which are treated—with varying degrees of success—with antibiotics. And farmed fish can escape from the pens, spreading any disease and interbreeding with wild populations, weakening them. The escaped fish also compete with wild fish for food.

What is called bycatch—unwanted or unmarketable marine life that is accidentally caught in nets and then discarded—damages the ocean population. Fish too small to be sold are thrown back, dead or dying; these young fish would otherwise rebuild depleted species such as snapper or provide food for larger fish. The fish you choose to eat should be those caught with minimal bycatch.

The oceans cannot provide an endless supply of fish. More effective fishing methods have led to fish populations being caught faster than they can reproduce.

Cod have now been depleted—as much because of overfishing as from damage to the ocean floors. So fishermen turned to monkfish, a "trash fish" once discarded as bycatch. Now monkfish is depleted. A savvy marketing campaign renamed the Patagonian toothfish "Chilean sea bass." These are slow-growing fish, living forty years. A fish that takes that long to mature is particularly susceptible to over-fishing—something that is clear when you find out how few of these fish are left in the world.

I kept these issues in mind as I selected the fish for the recipes in this book. You won't find monkfish, skate, red snapper, pompano, and other fish I love and wish I could eat. I'm holding off for the time when I can feel confident that these popula-tions are strong again. I suggest you do, too, and make sustainable choices for both the fish you cook at home and the fish you eat in restaurants.

Have fun, and cook some great fish.

THE *Basics*

IS IT COOKED?

Whenever I teach a class or do a demonstration on cooking fish, I hear two questions: "How do I tell if fish is cooked?" and "What if I overcook it?" These are valid concerns, particularly when you're paying a high price for a great piece of fish. To begin with, let me tell you that my preference for most fish that I'm cooking all the way through — bluefish, say, or sardines or sole or halibut or striped bass — is to undercook it slightly and let the residual heat finish the job. The outside of the fish you're cooking is going to be hot when you remove it from the heat source, and that heat — the residual, or carry-over, heat (more about this later) — will continue working its way to the center of the fish, cooking it perfectly. I like salmon medium-rare and tuna rare. The timing in my recipes should lead you to these results. But while I may tell you to cook a piece of fish on one side for 4 minutes, I know there are a lot of variables in play. The pan you're cooking in may be lighter than the one I use. Your stove may be hotter than mine (most of these recipes were tested on a pretty dinky home stove). The kitchen itself may be hotter, or cooler, and when you take the fish out of the refrigerator, it reacts to the room temperature. So keep these things in mind:

- FISH CHANGES COLOR AS IT COOKS. Fish is a high-moisture protein, and as the protein cooks, it will change from translucent to opaque (think of what happens to egg whites when they cook). That piece of salmon may look bright pink when you take it out of the refrigerator, but as it cooks, the color softens, almost turning pastel. Bluefish and sardines turn grayer. White fish may start translucent, but the white becomes chalkier as you cook.

- WATCH FOR CUES. When you're sautéing a thicker piece of fish, you can see it cooking from the bottom up; when you broil, you can see it cook from top and bottom toward the middle. With thinner fillets, you will notice a definite change around the edges. Fried food will start turning golden and then brown. The eyes on a whole fish turn opaque as it cooks.

- DON'T BE AFRAID TO TOUCH. Remember what the fish felt like when it was raw. As it cooks, it will become firmer and resilient. Use the flat part of the first joint of your index or middle finger to check as the fish cooks (the tip of your finger is really pretty useless for this; it's not sensitive enough). And don't wait until the moment you think the fish should be cooked; check it along the way and track the changes — always in comparison to how it felt raw. Make it a learning experience, and give yourself a set of references that will guide you to becoming a fish cooking expert.

- REMEMBER RESIDUAL HEAT. Just as when you cook a chicken or a roast of beef, that piece of fish will continue to cook when you take it off the stove and even out of the pan. Think of this as temperature momentum — the larger the "vehicle," the longer the coasting.

- PEEK. Who says you can't poke a knife into that salmon fillet so you can see what it looks like inside? And when presentation is important to you, put the piece you checked on your plate so you can still impress your guests. For most fish, other than tuna and salmon, you are looking for a glistening moistness in the center and a color that hasn't changed all the way through. Residual heat will take care of the difference. For fish that you want to serve less well cooked, the center should still look raw.

- ADAPT. I've told you that I like salmon medium-rare. If you like it more cooked, approach my recipes knowing that you will be cooking the fish another minute or so.

- ABOUT FLAKING. I bet someone's told you that if the fish is flaking, it's overcooked. There's some truth in that. If a dense fish like tuna or salmon is flaking, you can be sure it's very well done. But a flaky fish like cod will start to separate into those individual slivers, or flakes, when it's medium-rare. What this means is that you should start by relying on the other cues. Be curious, and taste often.

Overcooking is another issue. I can't lie to you; cooking fish is definitely a case where practice makes perfect. That said, if you follow the tips I've just given you and the cues in the recipes, you won't overcook a piece of fish to the extent you

ABOUT THAT "FISHY" SMELL IN THE KITCHEN

This is a topic that invites endless discussion, and it seems to be one of the new fish cook's biggest fears. It shouldn't be. For the most part, cooking fish shouldn't make your kitchen smell more than cooking most anything else. But here are some things I've learned in my years in the kitchen.

- The best thing you can do is to make sure your fish is fresh. That off, "fishy" odor you smell when the fish is raw will only get stronger when you start cooking.

- If your fish is a bit past its prime, look for recipes that have a good dose of acidity to them (vinegar, lemon juice, tamarind, and tomatoes, for example). Other ingredients that fight the smell of "fishiness" are onions, bay leaf, and ginger.

- Be aware of the technique you're using. Frying and broiling in particular release more odors into the air.

- Empty the garbage right away. It sounds so logical, doesn't it? But you'll be surprised how easy it is to forget, and fish scraps — even the packaging fish came in (since it will have fish juices on it) — will deteriorate and start smelling quickly in the warm environment of a trash bin. If you use a compactor, find another way of discarding fish scraps and packaging.

- Put out a cup of bleach near your work area. You'll be surprised how bleach pulls odors from the air, particularly when you're frying or broiling fish. Just be sure to mark the cup you have the bleach in, maybe by putting a piece of tape across the top, so no one picks it up inadvertently for a taste.

- Cloves and cinnamon also combat fishy odors. You may want to consider simmering these spices in a small pot of water while you cook, or after, while you clean up.

- Use your range hood fan if you have one and it is vented to the outside.

- If you have a sink disposal, save all your lemon and lime rinds and put them through as your last step in cleanup. This does more than just freshen up the sink. As the rinds get ground up, they will release their essential oils and freshen the air. It's almost worth sacrificing a fresh lemon for this. If you don't have a disposal, put some baking soda in the drain and flush it down with white vinegar, followed by cold water.

can't serve it. I wish I didn't have to make the meat comparison again, but I will. What happens when you overcook that roast? It's dry and chewy enough to keep your molars working for much longer than they should. That won't be the case when you overcook fish; it will just be more dry than you want, and it will have lost the taste of the ocean. But you can still eat it without chewing forever.

If you are very concerned about overcooking, let me give you two pieces of advice. Start with steaming or poaching, since these techniques keep fish moist. Or go with a whole fish—steaming it or putting it in the oven or even on the grill. A whole fish gives you a lot of leeway. You have the skin protecting the fish all around when you cook it, sealing in the natural juices. And you have those bones too. Fish bones may vary in size, but they react to heat and release their goodness pretty quickly. Take a look at how long you cook fish fumet and compare it with the hours you should simmer a meat stock, and you will get an idea of what I'm talking about. Cook a fish on the bone, and that flavor and moisture goes into the fish and then happily into your mouth.

THE FISH COOK'S KITCHEN

*T*here's really nothing that different about a kitchen you cook fish in. Sure, you need a couple of pieces of special equipment, but a lot of what I cook with is stuff you probably have anyway. Yes, I work in a state-of-the-art, big-ass kitchen in my restaurant, but I made all these recipes at home, and my kitchen (in New York, when I was living there, and now in Las Vegas) is as basic as they come.

EQUIPMENT AND GADGETS FOR THE FISH COOKING PRO

Your pots and pans should be heavyweight stainless steel. Don't use aluminum for cooking fish. Ever. Well-seasoned cast-iron or black steel skillets belong in any kitchen. I love searing fish in cast iron.

- A well-seasoned cast-iron griddle is essential for broiling fish (don't use that wavy broiler pan that came with your oven for broiling fish: it's designed for meat). Preheated well under the broiler, the griddle sears the bottom of the fish while the broiler cooks from the top down. And since it has a flat surface, it's easy to remove the fish when it's cooked.

  Some griddles are double-sided. The flip side, with ridges, is what you want for stovetop grilling.

- Cast-iron grill pans come in a variety of shapes and sizes. You'll need one for indoor grilling if your griddle pan isn't double-sided.

- Bamboo steamer sets (two steamer racks and a lid) are inexpensive and really the best pieces of equipment when you want to steam fish. If you don't have access to a Chinatown market, you can buy them online from www .pearlriver.com.

- A fish basket makes your life much easier when you're grilling small whole fish or fish steaks. There are a lot of versions available (I got mine in a local grocery store). Find the one that works for you, and just make sure you oil it well before each use.

- My favorite knife for cutting whole fish is a lightweight Swedish carbon steel "petty," with a 15-centimeter blade; it's made in Japan by Misono (available online from www.korin.com). I can feel the bones better with this semi-flexible blade.

- If you plan on shucking oysters, invest in an oyster knife with a nonslip handle and a 3-inch blade (if your kitchenware store doesn't carry it, try an online source like www.amazon.com or www.surlatable.com). I use a small paring knife for shucking clams.

- A flexible fish spatula has a beveled end, a head that's much wider than its base, and ribs, or slots (which allow fat to drain quickly and easily). You want something thin to get under delicate fish fillets. Big ones will come in very handy if you're grilling. You'll find them in most kitchenware stores and online from many sources.

- Yes, you can use needle-nose pliers to pull out pinbones, but fish tweezers work better. They're available in kitchenware stores and online.

- An immersion (or hand) blender, a wand with a blender at the bottom, is an essential tool for making any of my butter sauces. A conventional blender won't work here, because the sauce base will cool down and stop the butter from emulsifying, and a whisk won't puree the solids. And I bet you'll find plenty of other ways to use this handy gadget.

PANTRY STAPLES

SALT. I use coarse kosher salt for my cooking, and I think Diamond Crystal has the most consistent quality. For finishing a dish, it's coarse sea salt. I like both the great flavor of fleur de sel from France and the big, beautiful flakes of Maldon salt from England.

CRACKING PEPPERCORNS (OR SEEDS)

Set a paper towel on the counter and spoon on the peppercorns. Use the bottom of a small heavy pot or skillet to crush the pepper, holding the handle and the opposite rim of the pan and rocking it back and forth. The paper towel helps prevent the peppercorns from flying around as you crack them, and you can use it to pick up the cracked pepper.

PEPPER. White pepper is my pepper of choice when I'm cooking fish, but there are some dishes that call for black. If you can find Penja pepper—white peppercorns from the Penja Valley in Cameroon—try it; this pepper is very fragrant and has a delicate flavor (buy it online from www.vannsspices.com). For black pepper, I prefer Tellicherry peppercorns.

OILS. I stock several kinds of oil in my kitchen.

BULK EXTRA VIRGIN OLIVE OIL: This is what I use for most of my cooking. Find a good, inexpensive oil with a flavor you like (I tested the recipes in the book with Whole Foods' house brand).

FANCY EXTRA VIRGIN OLIVE OIL: Invaluable for finishing a dish. I love the flavor of Terre Bormane Riviera Ligure, which you can find online at www.lepicerie.com.

PORCINI OIL: This extra virgin olive oil is infused with porcini mushrooms and adds terrific depth of flavor to sauces. My favorite is from Urbani, which you can find online.

TRUFFLE OIL: The most exciting of the infused oils on the market. The best versions add a great truffle "punch" when you use them to finish a dish. My favorite is Urbani white truffle oil, which you can find at many online sources.

FRYING OIL: I think peanut oil is best for deep-frying, but I've been known to use canola oil too.

VINEGARS. Every kitchen needs a selection of vinegars. You'll find that I use good-quality red wine vinegar, champagne vinegar (which is lighter and more elegant in flavor than white wine vinegar), sherry vinegar, and basic white vinegar in my recipes.

OTHER ESSENTIALS

ANCHOVIES. I buy imported anchovies in glass jars. Then I can just pull a couple of fillets out of the jar and put it back in the refrigerator instead of finding a little container for the leftovers out of a tin. Add more oil to keep the anchovies covered.

CAPERS. The capers I use are the small "nonpareils." Always drain capers before adding them to a dish or sauce. To do this, I just overfill the measuring spoon and hold it upside down over the sink, with my fingers pressing down on the capers.

CHIPOTLES IN ADOBO. Cans of these chiles braised in a spicy, smoky sauce are available in the Mexican section of many groceries and in Latin markets.

CLAM BROTH OR CLAM JUICE. For most of the recipes in the book, I call for the clam juice you'll capture when you shuck clams, but clam broth or juice should be a staple in the fish pantry. I like St. Ours, which is a dehydrated natural broth from steamed clams, but the stuff in the bottle that you'll find in most grocery stores works fine.

FISH SAUCE. It may not have the most appealing fragrance, but fish sauce adds amazing depth of flavor. It's becoming more and more available in grocery stores. The brand I prefer is Tiparos, from Thailand.

DRIED OREGANO. To me, nothing compares to the flavor of dried oregano from Sicily, which I sometimes find in little Italian markets, still on the stem and packaged in cellophane. Chances are you'll never see it, but please try to use Mediterranean oregano rather than Mexican (which is actually from a different plant) or unidentified (which could be anything).

PANKO. The Japanese bread crumbs called panko are larger than the American versions and give you a much crisper coating on fried foods. Look for it in specialty stores, Asian markets, and some groceries.

TOASTING SEEDS

Put the seeds in a small heavy skillet, either over medium heat or in a preheated 350-degree oven. Cook, shaking the pan often, until the seeds are lightly colored and aromatic. Remove them from the skillet immediately, so they don't burn, and let cool before you grind them.

MAKING TAMARIND PASTE

Cut up a 2-inch hunk of brick tamarind, put it into a heatproof bowl, and cover it with boiling water. When it's cooled, work it through a strainer, water and all. Most of the paste will stick to the outside of the strainer, so be sure to scrape it off, and discard the tough bits.

SOY SAUCE. Using this all-purpose seasoning is a great way of adding salt *and* flavor. Quality varies, though, from brand to brand. If you can find it, buy Tokusen Shoyu (extra fancy soy sauce) from Kikkoman for its depth of flavor. It comes in a 1-liter plastic bottle, with a red cap.

SPICES. I don't think I could cook without having cumin seeds, coriander seeds, and fennel seeds in the cabinet. Toasting the seeds not only deepens the flavor, it also opens up the flavor.

TAMARIND PASTE. Fruity/sour tamarind is often used as a flavoring in Indian cooking. You can find commercial tamarind paste in many Asian and specialty markets, but it's often more sour than fruity. Making your own is better. Both brick tamarind and tamarind paste are available online from www.kalustyans.com.

TANDOORI PASTE. This marinade from India is traditionally used for meat or chicken cooked in a tandoor, a super-hot clay oven. I use it for fish that I cook on the grill or sauté and finish in the oven. There are a lot of commercial tandoori pastes available in better grocery stores and specialty markets, and they vary in quality and flavor. My favorite is Bombay brand, but it's difficult to find. You can get it online from www.bombaybrand.com (it is listed as Tandoori BBQ/Grilling Paste). I've also used Patak's Spicy Ginger and Garlic Marinade and Grill Sauce, which is available from Kalustyan's (www.kalustyans.com) if you can't find it locally.

Check the ingredients on whatever tandoori paste you use. If tamarind is one of the main ingredients, don't marinate for longer than 1 hour, or the acidity will start to cook the fish.

LAPSANG SOUCHONG TEA. Lapsang souchong tea, the fine black tea that is withered over pine or cedar fires and then dried in bamboo baskets set over a pine fire, is my secret weapon when I want to add smoky flavor to a dish. I grind it up in the spice mill and keep the powder on hand for when I want that touch of pure smoke. If you don't find the tea in your grocery store, there are countless online sources.

TOMATO PRODUCTS. I buy tomato paste in tubes. That way, I don't have to try to find a little container to store the leftovers.

When I want the rich flavor of good-quality tomatoes out of season, I use Pomì Chopped Tomatoes. You can find thém (in boxes, packaged by Parmalat) in good groceries.

REFRIGERATED ITEMS

FUMET. Nothing compares with the flavor of fumet (fish stock) you've made yourself. But I know not everyone will make it. If you don't, try to find one made fresh (or sold frozen) by a fish market or specialty store. In a pinch, you can use a commercial fish or seafood stock from the grocery store.

HERBS. I prefer the flavor of flat-leaf parsley, but if it looks limp and tired in the market, I'll use curly parsley instead.

When I measure fresh herbs, I pack them down in the measuring spoon or cup.

LEMONGRASS. Used as an herb in Thai and Vietnamese cooking, lemongrass adds an intriguing layer of flavor, the taste of lemon without the edge of acid. The outer layers of the stalks are too tough to eat, but they are great for stocks that will be strained. Bruising — smashing the stalks with the handle of a heavy knife — before you chop the stalks will release essential oils.

Look for fresh lemongrass in specialty markets, better grocery stores, and farmers' markets. Don't use the dried stuff; it has no flavor.

PEPPERS. The basic hot pepper — the jalapeño — doesn't seem as hot as it used to be when I was learning to cook. Same goes for a lot of other hot peppers. I try to find Thai bird chiles or Indian red chiles or something that has heat *and* flavor. If you don't have access to any of these, just use what you find. The heat will be in the ribs and seeds, so add them.

I think poblano chiles have an interesting flavor, so I often substitute them for plain old green bell peppers.

PREPARING FISH AND SHELLFISH FOR COOKING AND SERVING

Though you can count on your fishmonger to take care of basic preparation for you, knowing how to do things yourself makes you an active participant and a much savvier shopper.

Other jobs—from shucking a clam to pulling the tough bit off a scallop to serving that whole char you've poached so beautifully—are things you'll be doing at home. Read on.

CLEANING A ROUND FISH

Follow these steps when you're planning on steaming, poaching, roasting, baking, or grilling a whole fish like branzino or char.

1: Use a fish scaler to scale the fish, running the teeth of the scaler from the tail to the head. The scales will fly all over, so you should do this in the sink under running water. • 2: Make a shallow incision with the tip of your knife down the belly, taking care that you don't puncture the guts.

3–4: Pull out the guts, snipping them with heavy kitchen scissors if you need to, and discard them. • 5: Use heavy kitchen scissors to cut the gills away from the head. They are attached in two places: under the mouth and near the top of the head. • 6–7: Cut off the fins. Some recipes will also suggest that you cut off the tail (if you can't fit the whole fish into a steamer, for example). Rinse the fish well inside and out.

FILLETING A ROUND FISH

Gut the fish before filleting it (see opposite page). You don't need to remove the gills or fins, but you should scale the fish if you plan on cooking it skin-on.

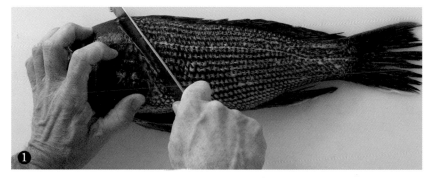

1–3: Cut the head off the fish by slicing through the flesh with a heavy chef's knife, hitting the knife with your palm to cut through the bone when you get to it, and slicing through the remaining flesh. • 4: Use a sharp flexible knife to make an incision down the back of the fish. • 5: Lift the flesh and cut down through the flesh, keeping your knife close to the bones, until you reach the center bone. • 6–7: Hold the fish near the tail to steady it. Rotate your knife and use a gentle sawing motion to remove the bottom half of the fillet from the bones. Keep the blade angled down and in contact with the bones as you cut. Repeat on the other side.

8–9: You will probably have some bones still attached to the belly portion of the fillet. Slip your knife under them and cut up toward the center of the fillet to release them, then cut off the bones. Repeat with the other fillet. You will be left with two neat fillets.

REMOVING PINBONES

Use fish tweezers (or needle-nose pliers) to grip these delicate bones and pull toward the head end. You will see these little bones in some fillets; in others, you'll need to run your finger lightly down the surface, starting at the head end.

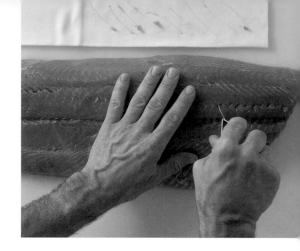

SKINNING A FILLET

Choose a thin-bladed, flexible knife. The length will depend on the size of your fillet. For a side of salmon, for example, I use a 10-inch blade.

1: Hold the tail end of the fillet with your fingertips and make a cut through the flesh down to the skin. • 2–3: Angle your knife so the blade is almost parallel to the work surface, with the cutting edge pointing down slightly. Grab the skin with a kitchen towel (or a piece of paper towel) and pull as you make a sawing motion with the knife. • 4: There may be some fat left on the back of the fillet, which you can trim off.

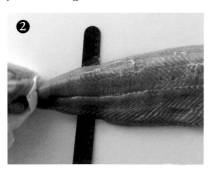

CLEANING UP AFTER YOUR FISHMONGER

There are times when the pieces of fish you've brought home will benefit from some extra attention, both for looks and for flavor.

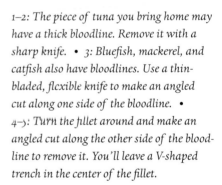

You'll often find a layer of grayish fat on the skinned side of salmon fillets. Use a thin-bladed, flexible knife held parallel to the surface of the fillet and a sawing motion to trim away the fat.

There are times when you get raggedy fillets, usually along the belly edge. For the neatest-looking piece of fish, trim the edge with a sharp knife.

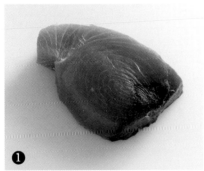

1–2: The piece of tuna you bring home may have a thick bloodline. Remove it with a sharp knife. • 3: Bluefish, mackerel, and catfish also have bloodlines. Use a thin-bladed, flexible knife to make an angled cut along one side of the bloodline. •

❶

❷

4–5: Turn the fillet around and make an angled cut along the other side of the bloodline to remove it. You'll leave a V-shaped trench in the center of the fillet.

❸

❹

❺

CUTTING FISH PAILLARDS

Set the fish fillet on your work surface with a long side facing you. Rest your hand on the tail end of the fish to stabilize it and make a long angled cut, toward the tail, to cut a slice about ¼ inch thick. Repeat until you have sliced all the fish. Don't fret about smaller pieces—they'll cook just fine. Pound any thicker slices gently between pieces of waxed paper, with your palm, so all the paillards will be the same thickness.

TYING FISH STEAKS

Set a steak on your work surface, with the belly facing away from you. Wrap butcher's string around the center of the steak and secure with a single knot made with two twists. Pull snugly, but not so tight that the string cuts into the fish.

PREPPING TORO SALMON

Set the side of salmon on your work surface with the head end facing you. Slice off the belly—which has the lighter, more visible streaks of fat—leaving an evenly shaped fillet. You can make this cut with pieces of salmon fillet of any size.

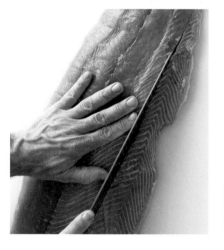

CLEANING A FLATFISH

Use heavy kitchen scissors to cut off the fins and tail from a whole sole or turbot when you plan on baking it in salt (see page 190).

THE DRUGSTORE WRAP

This is the way sandwiches were wrapped back in the days when drugstores had lunch counters, hence the name. The technique of wrapping seafood and other ingredients in a packet before cooking is actually the classic French preparation *en papillote*. In the traditional preparation, parchment is the wrapper of choice. Aluminum foil is much easier to use, and it gives the tight seal that's essential.

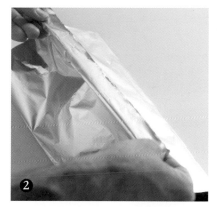

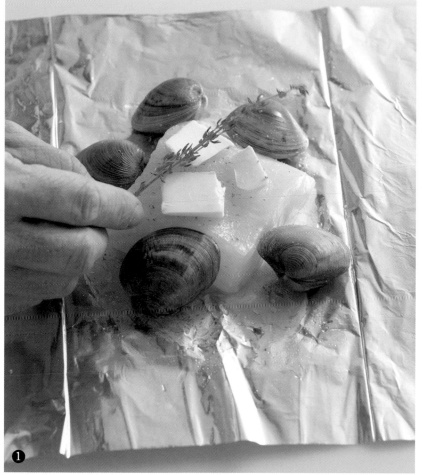

1: Tear off a long rectangle of foil. Fold it in thirds lengthwise, then open it out. Butter the center section of the foil and set your ingredients on top. • *2: Bring the long sides of the foil together and make a fold over the center section.* • *3: Flatten the ends of the packet, pressing down from the edges of the foil to your ingredients.* • *4: Fold in each corner on an angle, pressing down to make a sharp crease.* • *5: Fold the open end over itself, and press down to make a sharp crease. Fold over one more time to guarantee a perfect seal. Repeat for the other end of the packet.*

SERVING A WHOLE FISH

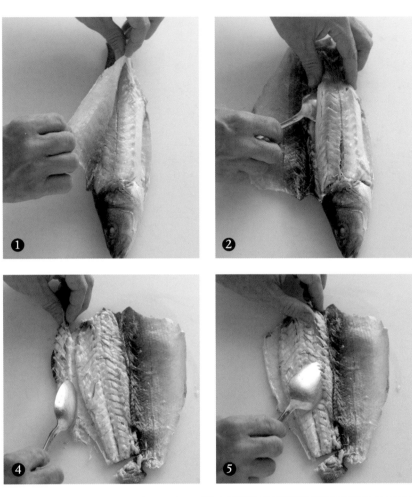

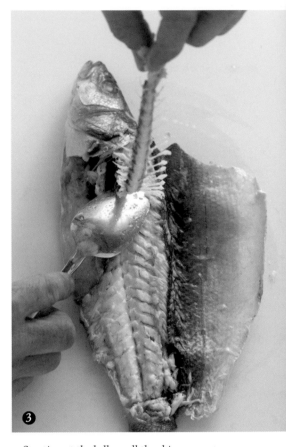

1: Starting at the belly, pull the skin back to expose the top fillet. • 2: Use a large spoon, with the bowl facing down, to release the top fillet from the bones. Work from the head to the tail, pushing the spoon in just past the centerbone. Carefully lift the fillet off the bones and transfer it to a plate. • 3: Starting at the tail, lift up the bones, using the spoon to keep the bottom fillet intact. • 4–5: You'll be left with some bones on the bottom fillet. Cut off the tail, and use the spoon to scrape and lift the bones off the fillet. • 6: Slide the bottom fillet off the skin onto a plate.

SHELLING AND DEVEINING SHRIMP

I like the flavor you get when you leave the tails on shrimp; I like the way they look too. If you don't want that bit of shell, though, keep peeling.

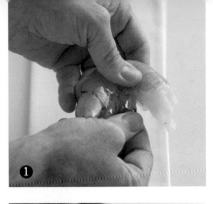

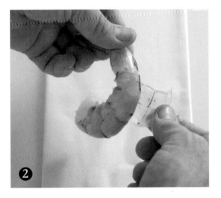

1: Pull off the legs. • *2: Peel off the shell, starting at the head. Pinch down just above the tail to keep that bit of shell intact.* • *3–4: Use a small sharp knife to make a cut down the back and lift out the vein.*

BUTTERFLYING SHRIMP

When I cook shrimp with fish in a packet (see page 220) and want a pretty presentation, I butterfly the shrimp and fold it over itself.

1: Set the shrimp on its side on the work surface. Use a small sharp knife to make a cut —from the center to the tail—almost all the way through the shrimp. • *2: Turn the shrimp onto its back and open it up. Fold the tail over to the head end.*

DEVEINING SHRIMP IN THE SHELL

Pull the legs off the shrimp.

Set the shrimp on the counter, with its back facing your knife hand, and hold it firmly with your fingers. Cut through the back of the shell from the head to the tail. Pull out the vein with the tip of your knife.

CLEANING SOFT-SHELL CRABS

You can have this done at the fish market, but only if you will be going home and cooking the crabs immediately.

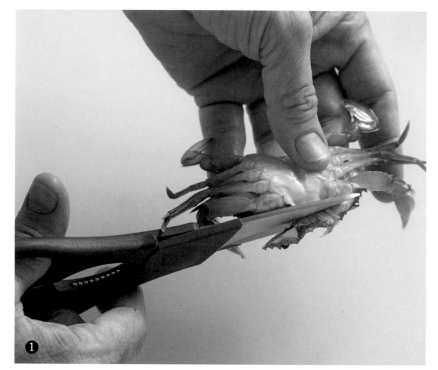

1: Use scissors to snip off the "face" of the crab. • 2: Lift up the sides of the top shell and pull out the feathery gills. • 3: Turn the crab over and pull off the apron, which lifts up like a tab.

PREPPING SCALLOPS

Pull off the fibrous bit on the side of the scallop muscle and discard it.
(It gets very tough when you cook it.)

CLEANING SQUID

Most of the squid you find in the market will have been cleaned already, but you should always check to make sure all these steps have been followed. When you do find fresh uncleaned squid, snap them up. Their flavor is always superior.

1: Grab the head and pull out the innards. Set the head aside. • 2: Pull out the quill from the body and discard. • 3–4: Pull off the "wings," holding onto them to pull off the skin (pull toward the head end). Discard. Rinse the body inside and out and dry it on paper towels. • 5: Cut the tentacles from the head, just in front of the eyes. Discard the head and innards. • 6: Pinch out the "beak" from the center of the tentacles and discard. • 7: Trim the long tentacles. Rinse and dry the tentacles.

SHUCKING CLAMS

Scrub the clams before you shuck them.

1: There are two muscles in a clam, on either side at the widest part of the shell. One side of the shell (under my middle finger here) has a deeper curve than the other. • *2: Hold the clam in your hand, with the side with the deep curve nearest your fingers. Work your knife between the shells and cut through the first muscle. This will release the shells enough for the next steps.* • *3: Run the knife from one side of the clam to the other, with the tip scraping along the top shell, to release the clam from the top.* • *4: When you reach the other side of the clam, push the knife in to cut through the second muscle. Lift up the top shell and twist it. Run your knife under the clam to release it from the bottom shell.*

SHUCKING OYSTERS

Scrub the oysters before you shuck them.

First you need to know where the muscle is in the oyster, so take a look at one. If you place the oyster cup side down, with the hinge end (the narrow one) facing you, the muscle will be on the right, about two thirds down toward the wide, ruffly end.

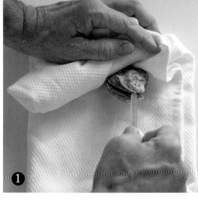

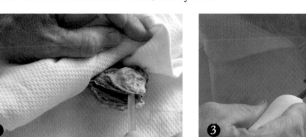

1–2: Set the oyster on a kitchen towel, cup side down, with the hinge end facing your knife hand. Use the towel to hold the wide end of the oyster. Put the tip of an oyster knife—pointed end up—into the hinge, jiggling and twisting the knife to get the hinge to release. Finesse, not force, is what you need. When the hinge releases, pull the knife out and wipe it on the towel (as much as you clean the oysters, chances are there will still be some mud in the hinge, and you want that on the towel, not in the oyster). Then put the knife back into the hinge and twist it to open the shell further. • 3: Use your fingers to hold the shells open as you work the knife down to the muscle. • 4: Sever the muscle and lift off the top shell. • 5: Slide the knife under the muscle to release the oyster from the bottom shell.

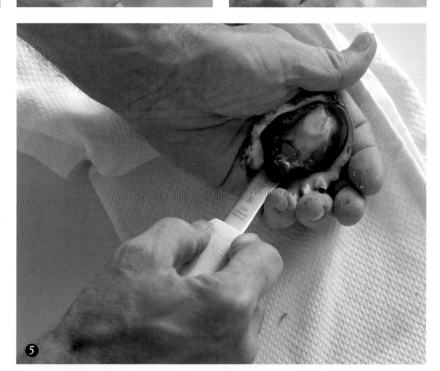

TROUBLESHOOTING

- The hinge end can crumble. Don't worry about it; just wipe your knife and keep jiggling.
- The top shell can crack. Lift the cracked piece off and go for the muscle. Use the tip of the knife to remove any shell fragments.
- The oyster can stick to the top shell. Use the knife to release it, but be gentle so you don't puncture it.

CLEANING MUSSELS

Pull off the "beard" before scrubbing.

DISPATCHING A LOBSTER

Set the lobster on its back on a cutting board (holding it just above the tail if necessary). Push the point of a heavy chef's knife into the center of the body, about 1½ inches from the head, and cut down through the center of the head.

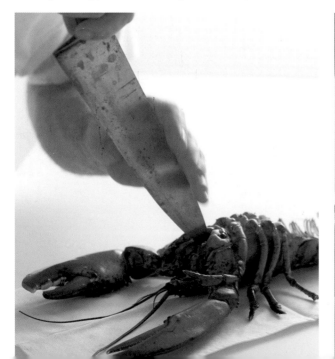

PREPARING LOBSTER FOR BLANCHING OR PAN-ROASTING

Follow these steps when you plan on cooking the claws and tail only, as you will for Lobster Fra Diavolo (page 379) or Citrus Roast Lobster (page 210).

Dispatch the lobster (see opposite page).

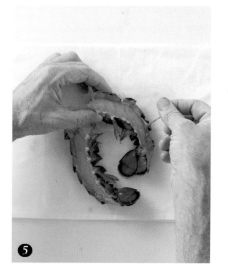

1: Hold the body in one hand and the tail in the other. Pull off the tail, twisting it as you pull. • *2: Twist off the claws at the point where they attach to the body.* • *3: Crack the claws and the knuckles with the back of a heavy chef's knife.* • *4: Cut the tail in half.* • *5: Remove the vein from the tail.*

PREPARING LOBSTER FOR STOCK

Dispatch the lobster (see page 46) and remove the tail and claws.

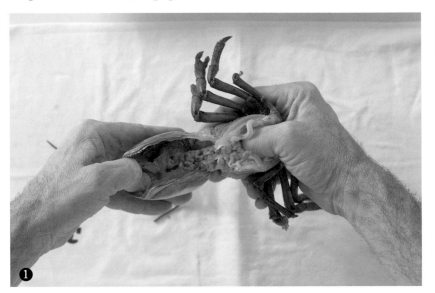

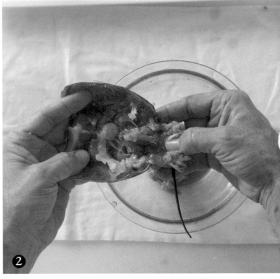

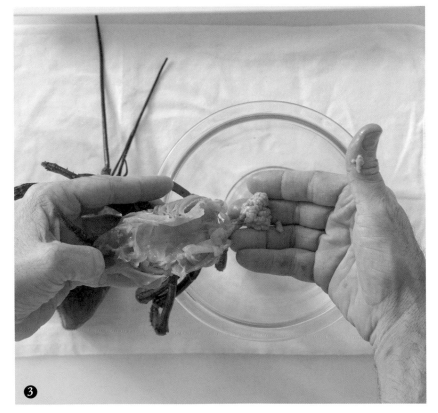

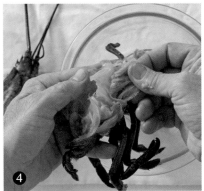

1: Separate the body and small legs from the shell. • 2: Pull out the sand sac, which is just below the head of the lobster. Discard it. • 3: Remove the tomalley (the grayish fat, or "liver") from the body and discard it. While it may be delicious when a lobster is cooked another way, it will just make your stock muddy. If you have a female lobster, remove the egg sacs. If you're making bisque, refrigerate the eggs. If not, discard them. • 4: Remove and discard the feathery gills.

SHOPPING FOR FISH

There's a big, wide world of fish markets out there, and as I was shopping for fish to cook for this book, I saw the good, the bad, and the mediocre.

In New York City, I found a great old-school market called Pisacane, which has been around since 1910. There's a big, heavy butcher block—scarred with age and use—next to a long glass case piled with fillets and steaks and shrimp and scallops. Behind is a stainless steel display heaped with ice and whole fish; oysters and clams are in big burlap bags. Off to the back are worktables with a couple of guys cleaning fish. And, yes, there's sawdust on the floor. But even without looking around, you know you're in a fish market because of that smell in the air. Clean, fresh, like the ocean.

It didn't take more than a visit or two to Pisacane for me to develop a rapport with Mike Cioffi, one of the guys behind the counter. When I wanted tuna, Mike would cut what I needed. (That's my dream for all fish markets, that they'd be more like delis and cut everything to order.) If I wanted dorade and there wasn't any in the shop, Mike would suggest a substitute. He also let me know what would be coming in later in the week or offer to bring a particular fish in for me. And while I shopped, I saw all the other customers getting the same treatment.

I found fine fish departments in supermarkets too. In the good ones, whole fish and shellfish are segregated from one another in separate containers set into ice. Steaks and fillets are labeled with shopping cards identifying the fish and its origin. Anything that has been cooked (like shrimp or crabs) or prepared in some way (like marinated fillets or even crab cakes) is in a different case to prevent cross-contamination. A fishmonger behind the counter is ready to answer questions and clean or fillet a whole fish.

In some stores, I found fish already packaged, wrapped in plastic on Styrofoam trays. Often this fish was in great shape; other times it wasn't.

It was easy enough to tell if the store cared about fish. Fillets or steaks set directly on ice and pushed tight against marinated fish are signs of problems (direct exposure to ice speeds deterioration). Sides of salmon with big gaps in the flesh indicate that the fish has been handled badly or is past its prime.

Regardless of the store, I could usually find a good piece of fish to bring home to cook. Here are some tips and guidelines so you can do the same.

- Make friends with the person behind the counter. There's no better way of getting good fish and of learning about fish too. Your fishmonger should be able to tell you when the fish came in and where it came from. And those are good questions for you to ask. Ask, too, about how long you can keep the fish. If the fishmonger tells you to cook it today, it's probably older than you'd like.

   Good fishmongers will have tasted all the fish they're selling. They are great sources of information on new fish for you to try and how to cook it. The best ones can tell you about the flavor and texture of the fish.

   While regulations make it difficult for a shopper to really examine a fish in the market, it's not impossible when you're friendly. You can ask to have specific things shown to you (are those gills really red?), or you can ask for a latex glove (there will be boxes of them) so you can poke and prod the fish yourself.

- Know what you're looking for. There is information on buying specific fish and shellfish on pages 55–74, but here are some rules of thumb — common sense, really — to guide you.

WHOLE FISH

The best whole fish will look as if they're almost alive.

- The skin should be intact and glistening or shimmering. Coloring should be bright. Avoid fish if the skin looks faded.

- The scales on scaly fish should be intact and even. The scales continue to act as a kind of preservative. You can ask to have the fish scaled when you buy it (or do it yourself when you are ready to cook it), but a fish that has scales should not be displayed without its scales.

- Fish eyes can be damaged in the process of getting the fish out of the ocean and into the market, so they are not always an indicator of freshness. If the eyes are intact, they should be shiny and bright and unsunken. Dull, very opaque, and dry eyes are a sign of age. As the fish sits around even longer, the eyes will no longer look rounded; they flatten, then sink into the head and become concave.

- A whole fish will sometimes be gutted before it's presented for sale. This shouldn't be a problem, but look at the cut in the belly. It should look fresh and straight, not dried out.

- Gills should be clear and red. You will find different shades of red, of course, but you are looking for that clear color. Dull, flat colors here are another sign of age, as is brown slime.

- By and large, the fish should feel firm and resilient. Avoid mushy fish.

- Trust your nose. That "fishy" smell means the fish has been sitting around too long for anyone's liking. The aroma should remind you of fresh breezes on the beach, whatever other characteristics the fish may have. Some will have an earthiness behind that sea breeze; others may be reminiscent of grass or cucumbers. Still others will smell deeply of the ocean, and that will be good. "Fishy," on the other hand, is a distinctive off smell.

FILLETS AND STEAKS

There are a lot of similarities here to buying fresh cuts of meat and chicken.

- The fillets or steaks should be evenly colored, whatever the color—pearly white, creamy, soft gray, pink, or red. Fading and the kind of yellowing you see in gray hair is a sign of age.

- Check the edges. They should match the rest of the fillet and show no signs of dullness and browning.

- Mind the gap. That sign in the subways in England is pretty funny, and it's also a good rule of thumb when you're looking at a fish fillet. If the fillet looks as if it's starting to come apart, with gaps where the flakes should be hugging each other tight, pass it by. An exception is soft, tender fish like king salmon. Often these fish are yanked by the tail in their journey from the ocean to the fish counter, and that results in a visible separation or two. Someone wasn't gentle to the fish, but it doesn't mean it's not fresh.

- The flesh on steaks should not be pulling away from the bone.

- You will find a big range in texture with fillets, running from very firm (tuna, say) to soft (like bluefish). Soft is fine, but fillets should never be mushy.

- Again, trust your nose. All the cues for a whole fish apply here.

- Fillets should never be swimming in liquid. This applies equally to fish in a plastic tub and fish packaged on Styrofoam.

- Check expiration dates. Fish has a very short shelf life. I would avoid any fish that is supposed to be sold by the day you're shopping.

- Check the display. Fish needs to be kept very cold, but unless it's a whole fish, it shouldn't be stored directly on ice. Its scales and skin protect the whole fish from melting ice.

  Ideally, each type of fillet and steak and each kind of shrimp and scallop should be displayed in separate plastic tubs set into ice or on paper resting on ice. You can check for lots of liquid in the bottom of the tub, which is a sign that the fish has been around for a while and is losing moisture. It will be dry when you cook it. Since fillets and steaks are usually set over chipped ice, look at the ice under the fish. Discoloration, the kind that would result from juices dripping into the ice and not simple melting, isn't a good sign.

- When frozen is your only option: a lot of fish in the market were frozen when caught and then defrosted. Many of these have been well treated and will be fine. I'm not a big fan of frozen fish (though I purchase vast quantities of frozen shrimp for my restaurant). That said, there are some acceptable products out there. Look for IQF (individually quick frozen) fish and shellfish. As with any frozen food, there should be no sign of freezer burn (spots or areas that are desiccated) and no frost buildup. Cryovac seems to provide the best protection, and it allows you to defrost the fish or shellfish quickly in a bowl of cold water set under the faucet, so you can run the water slowly over it. Otherwise, defrost overnight in the refrigerator.

ABOUT REJECTING OR RETURNING FISH

If you've formed a relationship with the person selling you your fish and you've followed my cues for what to look for and the questions to ask, you shouldn't have any problem with the fish you buy. But let's face it: it takes time to form that relationship, and some of the people behind the counter are more knowledgeable than others about what they're selling. And fish can be expensive. So there's no reason for you to take something home that doesn't satisfy you.

Here's my advice if you have doubts about the piece of fish you're buying and you don't know your fishmonger and you haven't had the chance to really examine the fish: don't leave the counter. Once the fish is in your hands, inspect it more closely. Even from in front of the counter, you should have been able to check the visual cues, but this is your chance to smell the fish. If it's off, hand it back and tell your fishmonger, nicely, about your concern. Not only is this a way to make sure you don't bring home inferior fish, it can be a way of forging a good relationship with the person behind the counter.

If buying prepackaged fish is your only option and you have doubts, I suggest opening the package and giving the fish a whiff before you leave the store. For those who find that too radical, check the fish as soon as you get home, and return it immediately if it's bad.

WHAT YOU CAN ASK FOR

A good fish market should be able to provide the following services:

- Cleaning a whole fish, which includes scaling, removing gills, gutting, and trimming fins. You can ask for any or all of these.

- Filleting a whole fish. There's a list of fish that are good for making fumet on page 297. If you're buying one of these and having it filleted, take the head and bones. You can freeze them or make fumet right away.

- Skinning fillets and removing pinbones.

STORING FISH AND SHELLFISH

There's no doubt about it: fish has a short shelf life. At best, finfish will last a week, but that time shortens for fattier fish like bluefish, mackerel, and sardines. Yes, you'll be asking your fishmonger when the fish came in, but remember that isn't always a guarantee of freshness. Sometimes fish may sit on the deck of a boat for a while instead of being stored on ice. This is something your fish market has no control over, but it does have an effect on the shelf life of the fish. So trust all the other cues for buying.

Exposure to warm air comes into play when you buy fish too. Here are some tips that will help keep your fish fresh on the way home.

- Save fish for your last stop when you're shopping. Don't put the fish in your cart and then start walking the aisles. Alternatively, you can select your fish and ask the fish guy to keep it on ice for you until you're ready to check out.

- Ask to have a bag of ice packed with your fish. Or bring a couple of freezer packs with you to keep the fish cold.

- If you're driving, have a cooler in the trunk and put the fish in it for the ride home.

When you get the fish home, follow these simple steps: ideally, you'll be cooking the fish the same day, but if you're not, this will help extend its shelf life.

- Unpack the fish as soon as you get home.

- Remove the fish from the store packaging.

- For whole fish, set a rack in a plastic container, put the fish on the rack, and cover it completely with ice (preferably chipped ice). The rack will keep the fish out of the water that will accumulate from the melting ice.

- For fillets, blot dry and pair them up, skin sides out, as if you were reconstructing a whole fish. Pack, resting on a paper towel, in sealable plastic bags. Fill a plastic container with ice and set the fish on top.

- For scallops, transfer to a sealable plastic bag. Fill a plastic container with ice and set the scallops on top.

- For clams and mussels, line a bowl with a damp kitchen towel or wet newspaper. Fill with the clams or mussels and fold the towel over the top.

- For lobsters and crabs, wrap in wet newspaper and set in a box or deep plastic container.

- Store all fish and shellfish in the coldest part of the refrigerator.

NOTES ON THE FISH
IN THIS BOOK

ANCHOVY

This small schooling fish is important in the diets of larger fish like halibut and coho salmon. Anchovies are a great source of protein, omega-3 fatty acids, iron, and calcium. They are most commonly found canned in oil or salted. The fresh fish have very soft flesh and are easily bruised.

FLAVOR. Fresh anchovies are rich, with an assertive ocean flavor. They have a slightly metallic edge, almost like zinc. Even when cooked, their texture is soft.

BUYING TIPS. Fresh anchovies should look almost alive, as if they've just been pulled from the ocean. The skin should be smooth, shiny, and bright; the eyes should be clear and unsunken. It's easy to tell when they aren't fresh, because anchovies deteriorate visibly.

Anchovies are very delicate fish. You want to buy them as fresh as possible, so they are relatively firm, and they are best prepared as soon as you bring them home. You can extend their refrigerator life by salting them lightly on both sides and packing them snugly, in a single layer, in a plastic bag; refrigerate them for no more than a day.

HOW TO COOK. Broil or grill whole anchovies. Or cure them (see page 351).

ARCTIC CHAR

I like to describe char as "salmon lite," as the fish is related to salmon but possesses a troutlike mildness.

Two thirds of the world's supply of char is now farmed, making it an environmentally sustainable "Best Choice" for Monterey Bay Aquarium's Seafood Watch program. The color will range from pale orange-pink to bright red, depending on where it was farmed and the amount of pigment in the feed. Farmed char are smaller than most salmon.

FLAVOR. If you like salmon, you'll love char. It has a high fat content, and it's a great source of omega-3 fatty acids. The aroma is sweet and less intense than that of salmon, and the fish tastes buttery and rich, with a slight hint of vanilla and salt. The texture is silky to soft, with a small flake when cooked medium.

BUYING TIPS. Look for clear pink markings along the sides of the fish; dulling is a sign of age. The eyes of whole fish should be bright, clear, and unsunken.

Fillets should be firm, with even coloring and no gaps.

HOW TO COOK. Poach or roast whole fish for a real treat. Skin-on fillets should be broiled, sautéed, or grilled.

BARRAMUNDI

The name of this Australian farmed fish is Aboriginal for "large-scaled silver fish." The fish are "chill-killed" in an ice slurry in Australia and arrive in the United States within 24 hours. Very sustainable fish farms in the United States are also now producing barramundi. The fish are hatched in Australia and flown to farms here, where they are fed and raised with consideration for the environment.

FLAVOR. Barramundi is buttery and sweet. It may be closest in flavor to wild sea bass. The texture of the flesh is delicate.

BUYING TIPS. Follow the guidelines for buying any whole fish: firm flesh, bright gills, unsunken eyes. The skin should be shimmering, with a soft yellow stripe along its length.

HOW TO COOK. Barramundi is an incredibly versatile fish. It can be broiled, fried, sautéed, poached, or grilled.

BLACK SEA BASS

An important recreational fish, black sea bass is part of the grouper family. I think it's a very beautiful fish, the skin a deep dark brown or black marked with a white diamond pattern.

FLAVOR. There's a slightly nutty taste to this delicate, sweet white fish. Look for fine flakes.

BUYING TIPS. High season for black sea bass is October through April, but you will find the fish whole in the market year-round. The fish should be firm and resilient to the touch; the eyes should be bright and clear. Have the fishmonger fillet it (or do it yourself) if you're not cooking it whole.

HOW TO COOK. I love steaming whole black sea bass. Fillets are great candidates for sautéing. The head and bones are highly recommended for fumet.

BLUEFISH

This flavorful, migratory fish is an excellent source of omega-3 fatty acids. Some problems exist with overfishing, though, and you should look for bluefish caught by hook-and-line.

Note: There is currently a health alert due to high levels of PCBs and mercury.

FLAVOR. The meat cooks to an opaque grayish white and is really tasty when fresh; it's briny, with a sweet finish—oily, grassy in a way that's almost like pork. The flesh has a tender chewiness when cooked, with moist, soft flakes.

BUYING TIPS. Bluefish deteriorates quickly (given its oiliness). Pristine fillets will have a heavy aroma of ocean and grass. Avoid fillets that are mushy looking or that have big gaps.

HOW TO COOK. There's a line of very dark, oily meat that runs the length of the fillet; this bloodline should be cut out and discarded before cooking.

Strong flavors—mustard, garlic, and tomatoes, for example—work well with bluefish. Bake it, grill it, broil it, sauté it. Bluefish also smokes very well, and commercial smoked bluefish is often used as the base of a fish pâté.

BRANZINO (LOUP DE MER)

This meaty white fish is farmed using methods similar to those for salmon. There are some concerns about the effects of this farming on the ocean, but the branzino business is a relatively small one.

FLAVOR. Branzino has an earthiness to it, an almost mushroomy taste of autumn leaves. It's pleasantly mild, with a texture that's tender but firm.

BUYING TIPS. You will usually see branzino sold whole. Look for eyes that are clear and not sunken. The body should be firm, the skin shiny and silvery, and the scales intact.

HOW TO COOK. Given its high gelatin content, branzino is ideal cooked on the bone. Try it baked in a salt crust (see page 190).

CATFISH

Monterey Bay Aquarium's Seafood Watch calls American catfish "one of the most sustainable seafoods available." Farming in controlled environments has led to a consistently fine product.

FLAVOR. Farmed catfish is sweet and mild, with a freshwater earthiness. The fine-grained fillets are tender, with soft flakes.

BUYING TIPS. Look for firm, moist fillets with no gaps, no yellowing or browning, and no signs of freezer burn. There should be a translucent iridescence on the surface.

I don't recommend buying wild catfish; the quality is too inconsistent. I also don't recommend catfish imported from China, both because of the quality of the fish and because of the damaging effects of China's farming techniques.

Go for catfish farmed in the United States. Most American processors test their catfish before they harvest it to make sure it doesn't have a muddy flavor.

HOW TO COOK. Catfish is a very versatile fish. Broil it, bake it, fry it, sauté it.

CLAMS

Of the three basic types of clams—hard-shell (your basic clam on the half-shell), soft-shell (your basic steamed clam), and razor (a long, narrow Pacific soft-shell clam)—hard-shell are my favorites and the ones I've included recipes for.

FLAVOR. Clams taste like the ocean to me: salty, minerally.

BUYING TIPS. Hard-shell clams should be tightly shut, without cracked shells.

Soft-shell clams will always gape open around that chubby siphon. You can tell they're still alive by touching the siphon; it should react a little. Razor clams will also gape open.

Clams need to breathe, so make sure the bag they're packed in remains open until you get them home. Store clams wrapped in a damp kitchen towel or damp newspaper.

HARD-SHELL CLAM SIZES

Manila clams	about 20 per pound
Littlenecks	10 to 12 per pound
Topnecks	6 to 8 per pound
Cherrystones	3 to 5 per pound
Chowders/quahogs	1 to 2 per pound

HOW TO COOK. I love littlenecks on the half-shell, but clams can also go into chowders and stews. Bake them, make a fritter batter and fry them, or throw them on the grill.

COD/HADDOCK/POLLACK/SCROD

The Atlantic cod fishery dates well back before the first English settlements in the New World, and it's likely that cod was consumed at the first Thanksgiving. The lean white flesh was easily preserved by salting and drying, and it became an important trade staple in New England. However, Atlantic cod has been so overfished that the industry is considered to have collapsed. Cod is a prime example of the results of careless management: the fish were once so plentiful that it was said you could walk across the water on their backs. No longer. The catch is now highly regulated.

Pacific cod is smaller than Atlantic, with a higher moisture content and a less firm texture. But it's more abundant (in the last decade, Alaska catches have been stable) and a great substitute for its Atlantic cousin.

Haddock and pollack are members of the cod family, as are whiting and hake. Pollack is used mostly for frozen fish products (like prepared fish fingers) and for surimi (that pulverized fish paste used to make imitation crab and lobster).

There is no such fish as scrod. The term refers to juvenile members of the cod family.

The only environmentally friendly way of catching cod is true hook-and-line fishing.

FLAVOR. Fresh cod has a mild, faint, sweet aroma. The flavor is delicate and sweet, slightly nutty, and the texture is smooth, with large flakes.

Fresh haddock has a slightly grassy aroma with some vegetal overtones. It cooks to a softer texture than cod.

BUYING TIPS. Fresh fillets should be moist and firm—not mushy and broken looking. They should be translucent and white to pinkish white, with no bruising. The fillets should have a mild, slightly briny smell. Sometimes cod will have a sweet aroma similar to shellfish, but it should never have the smell of ammonia.

Frozen fillets should not show any sign of freezer burn or discoloration.

HOW TO COOK. All the members of this family can be deep-fried, sautéed, broiled, poached, steamed, or baked. Keep them off the grill, though; they will fall apart.

CRABS

Other than jumbo lump crabmeat, the crabs I cook with in this book are Dungeness and soft-shell, so that's what I'm addressing here.

The most popular crab on the West Coast, Dungeness are big guys—the average weight is 2 pounds, but they can go up to 4—with a very high yield of crabmeat.

Soft-shell crabs are blue crabs in the molting stage; the entire crab is eaten. They're a seasonal product, with the season beginning in early May and lasting as long as into September.

FLAVOR. Dungeness crabs are packed with sweet, moist, delicately textured meat.

Soft-shell crabs have a distinct sweetness with a rich mineral accent; cooked, the texture is not unlike creamy scrambled eggs with a crunchy coating.

BUYING TIPS. As with lobsters, look for a fishmonger who has a high turnover, and ask how long the Dungeness crabs have been in the tank. The crabs may look sluggish in the tank, but they should show some movement.

Take particular care when handling Dungeness crabs. Their claws are very strong, and you could end up with a nasty pinch. Store wrapped in wet newspaper in a box in the refrigerator.

Soft-shell crabs should be purchased the day you plan to cook and eat them. You should see some movement in the flippers, a sign that they're still alive. Ask your fishmonger to pick out the softest crabs of the bunch (the shells begin to harden and become leathery about 4 days after molting).

SOFT-SHELL CRAB SIZES

Mediums	3½ to 4 inches
Hotels	4 to 4½ inches
Primes	4½ to 5 inches
Jumbos	5 to 5½ inches
Whales	over 5½ inches

HOW TO COOK. I love Dungeness best boiled in a spicy court bouillon (see page 116) and served cold. Soft-shells are best marinated in some kind of dairy product (see page 273), coated with flour or cornmeal, and fried.

DORADE ROYALE (ORATA)

This sea bream is found wild in the Mediterranean, but most in the market is farmed. Substitute it for such compromised fish as pompano and red snapper.

The fish has many different names throughout Europe. In France, where it is often an ingredient in bouillabaisse, it is called *dorade gris;* in Spain it is called *dorado;* in Italy, it is *orata.* According to Pliny, this last name comes from an ancient fish farmer, one Sergius Orata, who fed oysters to the fish he was raising.

FLAVOR. Dorade is rich and succulent, with an almost meaty flavor. Because of its layer of fat, the flesh stays moist when cooked.

BUYING TIPS. Whole fish should have shimmering silver skin and bright, unsunken eyes.

HOW TO COOK. Dorade is particularly good grilled or sautéed.

GROUPER

Groupers are part of a very large family of sea bass; red and black groupers are the most common domestic varieties. They are caught in southern waters along the East Coast and are not as plentiful as they once were due to overfishing and a slow maturation cycle. A quota was placed on grouper in 1990; look for line-caught grouper from the northwest Hawaiian Islands.

Note: There's currently a health alert for grouper due to high levels of mercury.

FLAVOR. Grouper has dense, very flaky flesh. It is sweet and slightly meaty, with hints of vanilla and lemon.

BUYING TIPS. Fillets are often sold skinless. They should have a firm texture, with a healthy reddish-pink layer where the skin was removed.

HOW TO COOK. The pinbones are substantial and difficult to remove by yanking; an easier method is to cut around them. The flakiness of grouper makes it an ideal candidate for deep-frying as fish fingers. I also like it in ceviche.

HALIBUT

There are two species that can be labeled halibut: Eastern, or Atlantic, and Western, or Pacific, halibut. Pacific halibut is closely regulated and is the fish you're most likely to see in the market. Atlantic was once common, but it is now rare due to overfishing. The largest of the flatfish, halibut can grow to as big as 500 pounds, but 100 pounds is the average size seen in the market.

FLAVOR. The fine-grained, snow-white flesh of halibut is very mild and sweet, with a distinct milklike quality. The aroma is very faint, and I think of this fish as a perfect blank canvas, ideal for pairing with flavorful sauces and butters.

BUYING TIPS. Fresh halibut should appear translucent and glossy. The flesh should look and feel firm.

A large amount of halibut has been frozen and then thawed for the market. Previously frozen halibut loses moisture and cooks about 30 percent more quickly than fresh. Avoid fish that appears chalky white, with no translucence; it will definitely dry out quickly.

HOW TO COOK. Halibut can be grilled (as brochettes), baked, broiled, sautéed, or poached. It is a very lean fish, which means it will dry out when overcooked.

LOBSTER

Lobster falls into two categories: the true American lobster (usually called Maine lobster) and the spiny lobster, which lives in warm waters. Maine lobsters are distinguished by their two large claws. They mature fairly slowly; it takes seven years for them to reach a weight of 1 pound. Spiny lobsters are clawless and have sharp, short spines along the length of their bodies and tails.

FLAVOR. Maine lobster has a distinctive flavor reminiscent of sweet summer corn (a natural companion ingredient in many dishes) and an earthiness that lends itself to being combined with butter. Spiny lobster is sweeter still and to me has less of a "lobster" flavor.

BUYING TIPS. Nothing will be better than a lobster that has just been pulled from the sea, but that's not always possible. Buy from a fishmonger who sells a lot of lobster and so has rapid turnover for these crustaceans. Lobsters can be held for extended periods in saltwater tanks, and this can have an effect on their delicate flavor. They can look sluggish in the tanks, but they should show some movement. When they are picked up, the tail should curl in on itself.

Lobsters molt as they grow, and a large proportion of the catch in summer months is "soft shell," or "new shell." These lobsters have less meat than hard-shell lobsters of the same size, but there are many folks who consider the meat sweeter.

HOW TO COOK. Maine lobsters can be boiled or roasted, and they are delectable poached in butter.

Spiny lobsters can be substituted in many of the lobster recipes in the book, but I recommend cooking them like Dungeness crabs (see page 116) and serving them cold.

MACKEREL (SPANISH, BOSTON, KING)

These small fish from the tuna family have a very high oil content, which is highest in the summer.

Note: There is currently a health advisory for Spanish and king mackerel due to high levels of mercury.

FLAVOR. Mackerel has a slightly metallic, almost silvery taste. It's reminiscent of tuna, but not as meaty, with an earthiness to the flavor as well. The fillets are soft and moist, and unlike many other fish, they don't really firm up when cooked.

BUYING TIPS. With its high oil content, mackerel deteriorates quickly, so freshness is very important.

When buying whole fish, check for a clean, fresh ocean aroma. The skin should be bright, shiny, and glistening. If the mackerel has already been gutted, look for a clean cut along the belly.

Fillets should also have bright, glistening skin. There shouldn't be any discoloration along the edges of the fillets. You can find frozen fillets, but fresh will be best.

HOW TO COOK. Mackerel stands up to strong, assertive flavors. Bake it, or grill it whole.

MAHI MAHI

Mahi mahi is Hawaiian for "strong strong," referring to the fact that this fish is such a strong swimmer. Also marketed as dolphinfish (don't confuse it with the mammal) or dorado, mahi is considered a good choice because the population is abundant (this fast-growing fish reaches sexual maturity in six months). Look for mahi mahi that has been trolled or pole-caught; these methods have the least environmental impact.

If you're a sport fisherman, hooking a mahi is a great experience. It will give a terrific fight and will almost always leap from the water, showing off an amazing spectrum of colors from neon green to gold to blue.

FLAVOR. The meat is lean and firm, dense and silky when cooked. The flavor is almost lemony, with a rich sweet balance.

BUYING TIPS. Look for brightly colored skin. Colors that have dulled or turned an ugly gray are signs of mahi that's past its prime.

If you are purchasing skinless fillets, the best quality will exhibit a pinkish hue.

In either case, the flesh should be firm, with a delicate, almost creamy aroma.

HOW TO COOK. This lean fish is best cooked medium-rare. Mahi can be sautéed, fried, grilled, steamed, broiled, baked, or poached. The flesh will turn from pink to white when cooked.

MUSSELS

These mollusks may be the best value in the fish market.

The most commonly available American mussels are farmed and seasonal. Mediterranean mussels (Prince Edward Island mussels fall into this category) predominate in the summer and fall; the smaller blue mussels are available in winter and spring. The vibrant green-shelled mussels are from New Zealand.

FLAVOR. Sweet, fatty Mediterranean mussels are usually large and can stand up to spicy preparations (like the black bean sauce on page 287). Given their fat content, they can take longer cooking.

Blue mussels are smaller and leaner, with more ocean flavor. They match well with the flavors of white wine, garlic, and parsley. Blues tend to become tough and stringy when overcooked.

Large New Zealand mussels have the most assertive flavor of the bunch, almost reminiscent of cured anchovies.

BUYING TIPS. More markets are selling mussels packaged in string bags—which is good, because mussels need to breathe. If you buy loose mussels, make sure the bag remains open, and transfer them to a bowl when you get home.

Conventional wisdom says mussels should be tightly closed, but let's face it: some mussels will be gaping open for any number of reasons. Give the mussel a pinch; it should react by closing. If it doesn't, discard it.

HOW TO COOK. Steam, steam, steam. Fattier Mediterranean mussels can be baked.

OYSTERS

These bivalves are great sources of zinc, iron, and vitamin A.

FLAVOR. The environment—which includes the kind of oyster bed (mud, sand, or rock), the water temperature, the salinity of the water, and the available food—an oyster grows up in determines its flavor. In general, oysters from colder water have a brighter taste and are great on the half-shell. Warm-water oysters are blander (there's often less salt in those waters) and are the better cooking oyster.

Flat European oysters are mild, with a metallic edge. Eastern oysters have an ocean brininess, and here the edge is of minerals. Western oysters are blander, with a mild ocean flavor and overtones of cucumber and melon. River oysters are generally bland but acceptable for cooking.

BUYING TIPS. Oysters should always be tightly closed. They should feel heavy for their size and shouldn't sound hollow. If you can select them yourself, knock them together gently to check; if your fishmonger is picking them (which is likely), make sure he does that as well, and listen. Avoid oysters that look as if they have pinholes in the shells; they're prone to crumbling when you open them. Oysters should be stored cup side down (both in the store and when you bring them home).

Oysters need to breathe, so make sure the bag they're packed in remains open until you get them home. Transfer them to a tray, cup side down, and refrigerate right away.

Check the date on shucked oysters, which are usually sold in glass jars. The liquid in the jar should be relatively clear, not murky.

HOW TO COOK. I love oysters best on the half-shell or in oyster shooters (see page 279). But you can fry them or steam them or grill them.

ROUGET (RED MULLET)

You won't find this fish in the market very often, but if you do, snap it up, because it's a real treat, and it's rich in protein, iron, iodine, and phosphorus too. These small fish are notable for their "beards," which are fleshy extensions hanging below their mouths, and for being spiny and bony.

FLAVOR. Rouget has a deep, nutty-earthy flavor, rich fat content, and firm texture. Look for a slight grassy, piney aroma.

BUYING TIPS. When you do see this fish in the market, it will be whole. The skin should be a striking bright pink with streaks of gold. Avoid fish that have sunken eyes or feel flabby. Prime season is October through May.

HOW TO COOK. These are bony little fish, so filleting takes time and patience. You might ask your fishmonger to do it. But do take the head and bones home with you, because they make an amazing sauce (see page 242), and they're great in a fumet. Sauté or broil the fillets.

SABLEFISH (BLACK COD)

Also known as black cod or butterfish, sablefish isn't a cod at all. It belongs, with skilfish, to a family all its own. Sablefish is a fine alternative to Chilean sea bass, given its creamy fat content and the sustainable fishing practices that keep sablefish in the green.

FLAVOR. A sweet fish, like cod, sablefish has soft, velvety flesh with large white flakes.

BUYING TIPS. Most of the catch (mainly from Alaska) goes to Japan, and much of what is seen here is smoked. Given its high fat content, sablefish has a fairly short shelf life and so is often flash-frozen; but this usually does not have an effect on quality.

Sable doesn't have a specific aroma, just a mild, sweet ocean scent. Avoid fillets that smell fishy.

HOW TO COOK. Sablefish is forgiving; the high fat content makes it less prone to drying out when overcooked. It's also versatile: smoke it, grill it, sauté it. Many chefs marinate sable in miso and broil it until crisp and brown on the outside.

SALMON

One of the most interesting species in the ocean, salmon begin their life in freshwater. Once nature sends its signal, salmon swim down the river in which they were born to the open ocean. The color of their skin changes, the better to blend in with the new environment, and in the ocean, the fish find a diet of tiny shrimplike creatures (krill), whose pigments dye the salmon flesh a shade of red. After a few years of life in the open ocean, the salmon again hear nature's call and return to the river, swimming against the current and up waterfalls to the spot where they were born, there to lay their eggs and die. This is the natural cycle of most wild salmon populations.

In order for salmon to fuel that trip back upriver—they stop feeding once they return to freshwater—they must store a tremendous amount of fat in their system. The salmon that must make the hardest journeys have the highest amounts of natural fats and are most highly prized as food fish.

Due to overfishing, environmental destruction, and pollution, there are virtually no wild Atlantic salmon left in North America. Reduced populations of healthy wild Atlantic salmon can be found, according to the World Wildlife Fund, in Norway, Iceland, Scotland, and Ireland. Almost all the Atlantic salmon that is consumed is farmed, and this is a huge business. Again according to a WWF report, production of farmed salmon is 300 times greater than the catch of wild salmon.

There is a price to be paid for farmed salmon. The high concentration of fish in open-water pens can have detrimental impacts on the ocean environment. Diseases and parasites are a constant battle, and many of these are combated with chemicals and antibiotics. There is also concern about the impact these fish have on the remaining wild populations living near the farms. Efforts are being made to farm salmon in a more responsible manner, but the challenges are tough.

There are still five species of wild Pacific salmon available in the American market: chinook (king), sockeye, coho, chum, and pink. Chinook and sockeye are the most widely available, and I'm focusing my discussion on them.

FLAVOR. Chinook, or king, salmon is the largest of the Pacific species and generally has the highest fat content. This fat content means that it is softer than other salmon, but the flesh is rich and slightly smoky or toasty, sometimes with a faint taste of oyster to it. Even with the high fat content, king salmon isn't oily on the palate; it has a clean earthiness and a nice ocean finish. The flesh ranges in color from a pleasant standard "salmon red" to almost pure white.

Sockeye is smaller than king and has a dark, almost brick-red color, so rich looking that it is stunning. The flesh has a mild woody aroma and delivers a wild mushroom–spruce needle–buttery experience to the palate. To my mind, sockeye is the best value in wild salmon. It has the richness and full flavor you look for in salmon, but it is less expensive than king.

Farmed Atlantic salmon has firm, pink-red flesh streaked with white fat lines, almost like a prime steak. It has a clean cucumber aroma combined with a grassy, almost herbaceous flavor.

BUYING TIPS. I recommend that you seek out wild Pacific salmon.

King salmon is found from central California up to the Yukon River in Alaska. When shopping for king, ask what river the fish was caught in. Fish from the Colorado River, Copper River, and Yukon River are the most prized and can be a special feast.

Much of the sockeye catch is exported to Japan, but it is becoming more and more available in American markets.

Look for even coloring, whatever the color of the flesh. In general, avoid fillets with gaps, but some gaps will be inevitable in king salmon because the fish is so soft. There should be a distinct scent of fresh seaweed, with an almost cucumber overtone.

HOW TO COOK. Salmon, particularly king, is suitable for all cooking methods. It's an excellent fish to serve with wild mushrooms or spring asparagus.

Sockeye cooks more firmly than other salmon and has a tendency to dry out if overcooked. Serve it medium-rare.

SARDINES

Rich in protein, calcium, iron, phosphorus, potassium, and omega-3 fatty acids, sardines are almost the perfect ocean protein for your health. Beyond that, this member of the herring family is damn tasty! And the populations of both coasts are abundant and healthy.

FLAVOR. Sardines have mild to strong ocean flavors, and they're slightly metallic.

BUYING TIPS. You'll be buying sardines whole. Look for them to be shiny and bright—almost alive looking. Sardines deteriorate quickly, so avoid any with sunken red eyes or exploded bellies.

You want to buy sardines as fresh as possible, when they are firm, and they are best prepared as soon as you bring them home. You can extend their refrigerator life by salting them lightly on both sides and packing them snugly, in a single layer, in a plastic bag; refrigerate them for no more than a day.

HOW TO COOK. The oil content of sardines is highest in the summer, and that's the time to grill them over hot coals and serve with a drizzle of extra virgin olive oil, a squirt of lemon, and good sea salt. They're great broiled too. Don't forget the crusty bread.

CANNED SARDINES

These beauties have a softer texture than fresh. Serve them with crunchy French bread or as part of that classic combo: Triscuits, mustard, cornichons, and sardines in front of the television.

SCALLOPS

Sea scallops, the larger ones, are usually caught wild by boats that dredge the ocean bottom, but there is a small percentage of scallops that are harvested by hand by divers and command the highest price on the market.

Smaller and sweeter, bay scallops are one of the true treasures of the sea. Premium bay scallops are dredged in North Atlantic waters, with the best coming from Nantucket and Peconic Bays. A large percentage of the bay scallops on the market these days are imported from China, where they are farm-raised on suspension nets.

Because they are so tiny, calico scallops are steamed open rather than being shucked, and they possess none of the ocean flavor of sea and bay scallops. I consider them useless.

FLAVOR. Sea scallops are meaty, almost elastic, and should have a sweet, fresh-almond nuttiness. They have a clean, sweet, buttery aroma.

Good-quality bay scallops are rich and sweet like summer corn and possess no apparent fishy aroma.

BUYING TIPS. Many scallops on the market have been "dipped" in a solution of sodium tripolyphosphate. This is partly an attempt to extend shelf life, but it also allows the scallop to absorb up to 20 percent of its weight in water—so you will be paying a very high price for water, and that water is just going to weep out of the scallop when you cook it. The moral is to make sure the scallops you buy are "dry" or "dry-packed," meaning that they haven't been dipped.

Sea scallops should appear whole and firm, and they should feel slightly sticky. Their color will range from a translucent white to almost light orange. Scallops that look like opaque marshmallows are almost certainly dipped.

Bay scallops will have the same range of colors as sea scallops. They, too, should look firm and feel slightly sticky. Bay scallops from Nantucket and Peconic Bays are never dipped.

"Diver scallops" usually refers to scallops that have been harvested by hand (rather than dredged), but some markets use the term to refer to scallops that haven't been dipped. When you find them in retail markets (which is rare), expect them to be much more expensive than dredged.

HOW TO COOK. To my mind (and mouth), sea scallops are best seared in a hot pan to caramelize the surface and cooked just to medium. But they are also wonderful on the grill (that caramelization thing again).

Bay scallops are delicious poached in butter, and they can also stand up to frying (see pages 260 and 263). Or slice raw Nantucket scallops and serve them drizzled with your best extra virgin olive oil and a sprinkle of sea salt.

SHRIMP

Shrimp is, by far, the world's most popular seafood. Millions of pounds of these crustaceans are caught or farmed annually. Varieties include white shrimp, pink shrimp, brown shrimp, tiger shrimp, prawns, and rock shrimp, to name just some of them, and they come from both freshwater and salt, warm water and cold.

Trawling for shrimp and shrimp farming both pose environmental problems. Imported black tiger shrimp and white shrimp are the most problematic. Take the time to find out where the shrimp you are buying come from, and seek out American wild-caught shrimp. Avoid those from foreign sources. Note, too, that the names "prawn" and "shrimp" are often used interchangeably.

FLAVOR. My favorite shrimp is the Gulf white shrimp. It smells and tastes like buttered popcorn, with a nice sweet bite and little of the iodine finish that plagues most other shrimp. The smaller pink shrimp are much more tender than larger ones. Rock shrimp have the softest texture and are very sweet.

BUYING TIPS. Chances are the shrimp you find piled up at the seafood counter were frozen as soon as they came out of the water, for shipping. Shrimp should look and feel firm. A good test is pinching; if the shrimp shoots out from your fingers, it's in good shape. Avoid shrimp that have broken shells, missing legs, or other signs of rough handling.

Because of their very hard shells, rock shrimp are usually sold shelled.

SHRIMP SIZES

Colossal	10 shrimp per pound
Jumbo	11 to 15
Extra-Large	16 to 20
Large	21 to 30

Medium	31 to 35
Small	36 to 45
Miniature	about 100

HOW TO COOK. What can't you do with shrimp? I don't know. I boil them, steam them, fry them, grill them, poach them, sauté them, add them to soups and stews. The list can go on and on.

You can use just about any shrimp for the recipes you'll find in the book. Rock shrimp, however, should be saved for popcorn shrimp (see page 262) or for stirring into a chowder.

SOLE/FLOUNDER/FLUKE

This category of flatfish can be very confusing for the consumer because there are so many different types and names. The term "flounder" is often used interchangeably with "sole," sole having the higher perceived market value. Summer flounder, an Atlantic fish, is also known as fluke. Blackback and witch flounders, also from the Atlantic, are often marketed as lemon or gray sole. The Atlantic populations are overfished. Pacific flounders and soles are good alternatives (petrale is my favorite).

Dover sole is probably the firmest of the soles, with the densest flesh — in a great way. It is a very elegant fish and by far my first choice in this category.

FLAVOR. Sweet and mild.

BUYING TIPS. When you find whole fish, look for uniform color with no bruising. The fish should have a sticky coating, almost like egg white. The aroma should be clean, the smell of the ocean.

Individually quick frozen (IQF) fillets are usually of decent quality, but try to find fresh fillets.

Fillets are generally translucent and pearly to pinkish white. There should be no bruising, no yellowish drying on the edges. The fillets should smell buttery and ocean fresh; avoid any with off odors.

HOW TO COOK. This is a versatile fish. It benefits greatly from cooking on the bone (try the salt crust on page 190), but you can sauté, broil, bake, or poach Dover sole. The fillets have a tendency to curl, so pound them lightly before cooking.

SQUID (CALAMARI)

A relative of mollusks, squid have long, tubular bodies (known as mantles), wings (or fins) on either side, and ten tentacles. They're a great bargain, because close to 80 percent of the squid is edible, and they're inexpensive.

FLAVOR. The flavor of squid is sweet. Properly cooked, squid will be tender and toothy at the same time.

BUYING TIPS. Squid is usually sold cleaned, and it's often found frozen—which doesn't have an effect on quality. There should never be a fishy odor, and the body should be a clean, bright white.

If you find squid that hasn't been cleaned, the membrane covering the body should look almost like mahogany lace; the color will fade to gray with age. See page 43 for information on cleaning squid (and some things you should check even if the squid you buy has been cleaned).

HOW TO COOK. I usually prefer a short cooking time to maintain the tenderness and integrity of this sweet ocean treasure. Fry it or grill it quickly. You can also stuff squid and braise it gently for a long time.

STRIPED BASS

Sometimes called rockfish, stripers are a fish lover's fish.

The recent history of wild bass is often cited as a success story. Bass were severely overfished, and the population was decimated. But restrictions were put into place in order to rebuild the population, and wild striped bass is now on the rebound; however, there are health alerts for PCBs.

Farmed striped bass is a hybrid of wild and white bass. It is considered an "Eco Best" choice by Monterey Bay Aquarium's Seafood Watch.

FLAVOR. Striped bass isn't an assertive fish. The flavors of the wild are mushroomy and meaty. The farmed hybrid is grassier in taste, slightly muddier; it's got a good but not great flavor to my taste, but since it's much more readily available than wild, I consider it a fine substitute.

Wild striped bass is firm, with a dense flake; the flesh of the hybrid is more tender.

BUYING TIPS. Whole striped bass should be sparkling in appearance. Look for a firm body—no indentations anywhere—and bright, unsunken eyes. The colors should be well defined: a black back, clear stripes (for the wild), and a white belly. Don't expect continuous stripes on the hybrids; the lines will be broken.

Fillets shouldn't have a strong aroma. Avoid any that are yellowing or browning; look for moist, firm fillets.

Peak season for wild is March through June and July, and for hybrids, year-round.

HOW TO COOK. Striped bass is easy to handle and suitable for most techniques. Steam it, bake, broil, sauté, grill, poach it.

STURGEON

This prehistoric survivor (it was swimming around when dinosaurs roamed) is the fish caviar comes from. Wild populations have been severely overfished (the Caspian sturgeon is near extinction); farmed sturgeon is a responsible alternative.

FLAVOR. Like catfish, sturgeon has an earthy sweetness, but its texture is unique: smooth, firm, meaty, and toothy.

BUYING TIPS. It's unlikely you'll ever see a whole sturgeon in the market. Fillets will vary in color from light pinkish to almost snowy white. They should be firm and moist, with no yellowing or browning and no signs of freezer burn.

HOW TO COOK. Sturgeon is great poached, smoked, grilled, or butter-basted.

SWORDFISH

A meaty white fish, swordfish varies greatly in fat content. The fattier the fish, the more flavorful and the less it will dry out. The easiest way to gauge fattiness is to check the knife when your fishmonger cuts the steaks: it will look almost as if it's been slicing vegetable shortening. Note: There is a health alert for swordfish because of mercury.

FLAVOR. Swordfish is delicate and mild, almost sweet, and at the same time, it's a rich fish (given the fat content). Like tuna, it has a meaty texture, and it dries out when overcooked.

BUYING TIPS. Swordfish steaks should be bright and glistening, with firm, resilient flesh. Fattier steaks will look almost marbled (yes, another cue). Depending on the fish's diet, the flesh will run from off-white to pink; browning and discolorations are signs of age or poor handling. Avoid steaks with very dark bloodlines or that smell fishy. Good swordfish has a mild, subtle aroma.

HOW TO COOK. I prefer swordfish broiled or grilled, but you can certainly fry or sauté it. Unlike tuna, swordfish shouldn't be served rare—but don't overcook it. Remember my advice about residual heat (page 24).

TILAPIA

When I started developing recipes for this book, I considered tilapia not really worthy of culinary consideration. Boy, did my opinion change. Experiment after experiment in the kitchen led to surprisingly tasty results.

The quality of this farmed fish continues to improve, and according to the American Tilapia Association, tilapia is now the fifth most popular seafood in the United States. But China and Taiwan employ net-pen farming methods, and there is serious ecological impact from escaped fish. Avoid tilapia from these sources.

FLAVOR. Tilapia is mild and sweet, with the slight muddiness characteristic of freshwater fish. It's firm and tender—tilapia's not what you would call a flaky fish—with a high moisture content.

BUYING TIPS. Tilapia is most often sold as skinless fillets. The fillets should be slightly glistening; avoid any that are dull or gray. As always, browning along the edges is a sign of age.

HOW TO COOK. One of my biggest surprises was how good tilapia tastes broiled. I really like the flavor in burgers and Sloppy Joes (see pages 360 and 373).

TROUT

Most of the rainbow trout available in American stores is responsibly farmed in Idaho, but many smaller trout farmers also sell their fish in local markets. Monterey Bay Aquarium's Seafood Watch calls American rainbow trout a "Best Choice."

FLAVOR. Rainbow trout has a mild, almost nutty flavor. Ruby red rainbow trout has a hint of citrus.

BUYING TIPS. You will find fresh trout sold whole and gutted, whole with the backbone removed, and filleted.

Whole fish should be brightly colored. The flesh may be cream, pink, orange, or, in the case of ruby red rainbow trout, which is fed on a diet rich in carotene, salmon red.

HOW TO COOK. Sautéing is a natural, and I love smoking this fish too.

TUNA

I think of tuna as the steak of the ocean. Its flesh, which ranges from pale rose to deep red, gets its color from myoglobin—a molecule that captures and binds oxygen. For testing the recipes in this book, I used mostly yellowfin, followed by albacore.

Note: Given its high place in the food chain, tuna often contains high levels of mercury.

FLAVOR. Full-flavored yellowfin is meaty, steaklike, beefy. When cooked rare, the flesh is silky and moist; when well-done, yellowfin will be flaky and dry.

Albacore is a smaller fish than yellowfin, much lighter in flavor and in color. It's also less expensive. It has a slightly finer, firmer texture.

BUYING TIPS. Look for tuna that has been trolled or pole-caught; if you're not sure, ask your fishmonger. Try to have the tuna cut to order. Tuna should be stored over ice, but not touching it.

The price of tuna steaks and loins will depend on how the fish has been graded, a determination based on fat content, color, and freshness. Sashimi grade (#1 grade) is the highest quality and the grade to choose when it is to be served raw. The fry or grill grades (#2 and #3) will have lower fat content and a less vibrant color. They are, however, perfectly acceptable for cooking.

As with any fish, avoid off odors. The steaks or loins should be uniformly colored, with no gaps. Tuna that is washed out or browning is old and not worth buying. The flesh should be firm, with no softness or sagging on the sides.

Vacuum-packed tuna steaks are available in many markets, and many are acceptable. The color is often very red, a sign that the fish has been treated with carbon monoxide (called "flavorless smoke") before packing.

HOW TO COOK. Yellowfin is best served rare. Grill it, sear it, flash-cook it under the broiler, or roast it. Albacore also responds well to these techniques and it's the kind I choose for water poaching.

TURBOT

This big flatfish is part of the flounder/sole family. Now primarily farmed, it has a good shelf life.

FLAVOR. Turbot is often treated like halibut, but to my mind, it's superior: firmer and not flaky, with buttery, sweet, tender flesh. Turbot has the most assertive flavor of the sole family, with a rich mouthfeel, like that of a poached egg.

BUYING TIPS. For whole fish, the skin should be dark, with a bumpy texture and an aroma of freshly crushed green leaves. Avoid fillets that are browning or exhibiting gaps or with off odors.

HOW TO COOK. Turbot doesn't dry out readily: I like sautéing and poaching it (particularly in milk).

LET'S Cook

POACHING

CLASSIC COURT BOUILLON

This poaching medium has it all: aromatics, acidity, and salt, concentrated to infuse fish with flavor. Salt's important here. Think of ocean water when you taste it.

Makes about 6 cups

1 large onion, cut into very thin slices
1 celery rib, cut into very thin slices
An herb bouquet (a bay leaf, a few sprigs of thyme, and some parsley stems, tied together with kitchen string)

5 cups water
¾ cup white vinegar
¼ cup coarse salt
1 teaspoon white peppercorns
6 sprigs tarragon (or another soft herb)

Combine the onion, celery, herb bouquet, water, vinegar, salt, and peppercorns in a saucepan. Bring to a simmer over medium heat and cook at an active simmer for 15 minutes. Add the tarragon and simmer for another 5 minutes, then turn off the heat and let the court bouillon infuse for 30 minutes.

It's ready to use.

ABOUT POACHING

You won't find me calling poaching a cutting-edge technique. It's old school, something that's fallen out of favor in most restaurants. But at home, it can yield very favorable results.

Like steaming, poaching envelops fish in moist heat, but it's a more gentle process than steaming because you control the temperature. With all the poaching mediums you'll find in this chapter—classic court bouillon, red wine court bouillon, milk, butter, and oil—you're using liquid to keep the fish moist. You're not adding moisture to the

fish, but the moisture in the fish stays in the fish. The flavors in the poaching medium also transfer to the fish.

When you make court bouillon, remember that it won't cook for a long time, so be sure to slice the aromatics as thin as you can to get the most flavor out of them. Then, when you poach your fish, that higher concentration of flavor will suffuse the fish. The result? Fish that's succulent, tender, seasoned, and moist.

POACHED WHOLE BRANZINO

Cold poached fish was a staple "businessman's lunch" in the 1970s and '80s, and it's the kind of lost treasure that needs to be rediscovered. High-quality responsibly farmed branzino is excellent in this classic dish. Make it in advance for a beautiful summer lunch.   Serves 4

ACCEPT SUBSTITUTES

Striped bass

Black sea bass

1 whole branzino (about 2¼ pounds), scaled and gutted, gills and fins removed

Classic Court Bouillon (page 78)

FOR SERVING

Fresh dill, parsley, or greens for garnish (optional)

Cucumber salad (page 458 or 459)

Spicy Mayonnaise (page 415) or Green Tartar Sauce (page 417)

Heat the oven to 200 degrees.

Rinse the branzino and wrap it snugly in a couple of layers of cheesecloth, with 6 inches of overhang at each end. Tie off the ends with kitchen string. The cloth helps the fish keep its shape and you can use it to lift the fish out of the poaching liquid. Place the fish in a fish poacher or small roasting pan, with the extra cheesecloth hanging over the edges of the pan. Let it sit on the counter while the oven heats.

Bring the court bouillon to a full boil. Pour it over the fish, making sure the fish is completely covered, and slide the pan into the oven. Bake for 25 minutes.

Fill the sink with a few trays of ice cubes and about an inch of water. Set the pan in the ice bath and allow the fish to cool completely in the liquid.

Lift the fish from the pan and unwrap it. Make a shallow cut through the skin down the center of the back and another cut at the base of the tail. Peel back the skin from tail to head. Carefully turn the fish over, make a cut at the base of the tail, and skin the other side. Very carefully—the fish is delicate—transfer the fish to a platter. Tidy up any messy bits, and refrigerate for at least an hour.

Garnish the platter with greenery if you want. Serve the fish cold, with one of the cucumber salads (crunch is good) and a mayonnaisey sauce.

A BIG POACHED CHAR

This is definitely a company dish, something to go out on a buffet table. Serve it with creamy things and crisp things and pickled things, like Green Tartar Sauce (page 417), a cucumber salad (pages 458 and 459), and cabbage slaw (pages 452 and 453), and maybe some Mixed Pickled Vegetables (page 401). A potato salad would be nice too. Maybe a French one, maybe a German one.

Making this dish is fun, but it's also a project, so plan on taking some time. You can easily make this the day before you plan on serving it. Serves 6 to 8

ACCEPT SUBSTITUTES
You could use a salmon, if you can find one this small.

1 whole char (about 3⅓ pounds),
   scaled and gutted, gills removed
1 large onion, cut into thin slices
3 celery ribs, cut into thin slices
2 carrots, cut into thin slices
1 bay leaf
1 teaspoon white peppercorns

Stems from 1 bunch dill
Stems from 1 bunch parsley
3 large sprigs thyme
6 tablespoons coarse salt
5½ quarts water
2 cups white vinegar, or as needed
Fresh herbs for garnish (optional)

Rinse the char and wrap it snugly in a couple of layers of cheesecloth, with 6 inches of overhang at each end. Tie off the ends with kitchen string. The cloth not only helps the fish keep its shape, it gives you something to use to lift the fish out of the poaching liquid.

Layer the onion, celery, carrots, bay leaf, peppercorns, dill and parsley stems, and thyme in a fish poacher or a large deep roasting pan (see the box). Sprinkle in the salt. Set the fish on top of the vegetables and pour in the water and vinegar. The fish should be covered by the liquid. If it's not, add more water and vinegar as necessary, with the ratio of ⅓ cup vinegar to each cup of water.

Bring to a slow simmer over medium-high heat. This will take close to 30 minutes, but start checking at 20 minutes. You should see steam rising from the poaching liquid, and it will shimmer across the surface, with an occasional bubble rising. If you have an instant-read thermometer, you're looking for 160 degrees. Then poach the char—monitoring the heat so you keep the liquid at that very slow simmer—for 15 minutes.

POACHING A BIG FISH

Ideally, you would have a big fish poacher for this recipe, but that's a pretty specialized piece of equipment. I've made this successfully in a big (17-X-14-X-3-inch) regular roasting pan, but one of those inexpensive deep roasting pans with a lid would work even better.

The ice bath can be another issue. If you find that you can't spare your sink for a couple of hours, you can improvise an ice bath in the bathtub. Get 3 bags of ice and put them in the tub with about 3 inches of water. Set the pan on top of the ice.

Move the pan to an ice bath (see the box) and cool completely.

Lift the fish out of the pan and place it on a cutting board lined with a couple of kitchen towels. Refrigerate for about 1 hour. This gives the fish time to drain, and chilling makes cleaning the poached fish much easier.

Carefully take the cheesecloth off the fish. Blot the fish dry—including the cavity. Slowly pull out the fins so the bones they are attached to come out as well.

Use a small sharp knife to score the skin down the center of the back, just behind the head, and along the base of the tail. Gently, patiently, lift off the skin, starting at the head end and working down to the tail. Again working from the head to the tail, use the back of your knife to scrape off the layer of grayish fat.

Carefully roll the fish onto a serving platter. Repeat the process of skinning the fish and scraping off the fat. Check for fat in the center of the back too. Clean up the platter. If any part of the fish looks ragged, pat it down and smooth it out with your fingers.

Cover with plastic and chill the fish for 2 hours, or overnight.

You might want to garnish the platter, piling herbs around the fish before you serve it. To serve, lift off portions of fish with a serving spoon (see page 40). When all the presentation side has been served, lift up the tail, taking the bones with it, cut the bones off at the head end, and discard them. Check the fish for bones, particularly along the edges, then serve the "bottom" side of the fish.

POACHED SALMON WITH SCALLOP MOUSSE

This is the kind of dish you dress up for. It's French, of course, and I used to make it when I cooked at La Côte Basque in New York City. The fish was always served with a rich butter sauce. It's a great interplay of textures.

Keep sides very simple. Maybe boiled potatoes and sautéed spinach.   Serves 6

ACCEPT SUBSTITUTES

Char

FOR THE MOUSSE

6 ounces sea scallops, tough bits
    removed, chilled in the freezer for
    30 minutes
⅛ teaspoon freshly grated nutmeg
Coarse salt and freshly ground white
    pepper
Cayenne
½ cup heavy cream (very cold)
2 tablespoons unsalted butter,
    softened

FOR THE SALMON

1 (2-pound) piece skinless wild salmon
    fillet (from the head end)
1½ cups Fumet (page 296), heated
1 cup dry white wine
½ cup thinly sliced shallots
1 tablespoon chopped fresh dill
1 tablespoon chopped fresh parsley
1 teaspoon chopped fresh tarragon
8 tablespoons (1 stick) unsalted butter,
    cut into pieces
Coarse salt
Half a lemon

FOR THE MOUSSE: Have ready a bowl set in a larger bowl of ice water.

Put the scallops in a food processor. Add the nutmeg and season with salt, white pepper, and a pinch of cayenne. Pulse until you have a fairly smooth paste, scraping down the sides when you need to. With the motor running, pour in the cream in a steady stream. Then add the butter and pulse to incorporate.

Scrape the mousse out into the bowl in the ice bath and spread it out so it chills quickly.

FOR THE SALMON: Trim the fat from the skinned side of the salmon. Cut the salmon into 12 slices, each about ¼ inch thick, at a sharp angle (see Cutting Fish Paillards, page 38). Spread half the slices with the mousse, using about 2 tablespoons mousse for each slice, then top with the remaining slices, making sandwiches. Press down gently on the edges to seal.

Butter a large (12-inch) skillet. Cut a piece of parchment to fit the skillet and butter it.

Set the fish in the skillet and pour in the fumet and wine. Scatter the shallots into the liquid around and between the fish. Cover with the parchment, buttered side down, and set over medium heat. When the liquid starts to ripple, after about 8 minutes, turn the heat to low. When the tops of the salmon slices are just about opaque, after about 7 minutes, using a spatula, carefully remove the fish (leave all the shallots in the skillet) to a platter, flipping each one over so the bottom side is now the top. Cover with the parchment and keep warm on the back of the stove.

Turn the heat up to high and reduce the poaching liquid to about ¾ cup. Transfer the liquid and shallots to a small saucepan and set over low heat. Add the dill, parsley, and tarragon. Use an immersion blender to start pureeing the shallots, then add a piece of butter and continue to puree with the blender, emulsifying the liquid and butter. Continue adding butter, piece by piece, incorporating each bit of butter before adding another. Tilt the pan as you work—so the liquid will be deep enough for the immersion blender to work effectively—and keep the pot over the heat. The sauce will become light and very pale yellow.

Strain the sauce through a fine sieve, pushing down on the solids—start by using the immersion blender, then switch over to a wooden spoon. Season with salt and a squirt of lemon juice.

Serve the fish bathed in the sauce, like we did in the good old days.

ABOUT FISH POACHERS

Don't pass this section by just because you don't have a fish poacher, though it does make poaching whole fish very easy. All the recipes here were developed and tested with standard equipment: deep skillets or roasting pans.

For poaching, you need a pan deep enough for both the fish and enough court bouillon to cover it. If you don't have a rack with handles—standard in a fish poacher—just wrap a whole fish snugly in cheesecloth, with a lot of extra at both ends so you can lift the fish out of the pan. A fish spatula is all you need to remove steaks and fillets from their bath.

Of course, if you've got the room and the inclination, buy a poacher. You'll find basic ones for about $40 and fancy copper pans for well over $500.

SHRIMP COCKTAIL

Shrimp cocktail is a classic, but so often it just isn't made well. Do me a favor: try my recipe, and make it as close to serving time as possible. The results — crisp, flavorful shrimp — are very much worth the effort.   Serves 4 as an appetizer

Classic Court Bouillon (page 78)   Cocktail Sauce (page 421)
1 pound extra-large (16–20) shrimp in
  the shell

Have a bowl of ice water ready for the shrimp.

Bring the court bouillon to a full boil. Add the shrimp, stir, and bring back to a boil. Turn off the heat and let the shrimp steep for 8 to 10 minutes, until just cooked through. Pull one of the shrimp out at 8 minutes to check.

Drain the shrimp in a strainer and run some cold water over them to cool them down enough for you to handle them. Pick the shrimp out from the vegetables; the shrimp go into the ice water and the vegetables go into the trash. Let the shrimp chill thoroughly.

Divide the cocktail sauce among four cocktail glasses.

Shell the shrimp and hang them from the rims of the glasses. Serve as soon as possible.

ABOUT RED WINE COURT BOUILLON

Red wine is a terrific cooking medium for fish, but unlike other court bouillons — which are designed just to impart their flavor to the fish — a court bouillon made with red wine is meant to be served with the fish.

    This has a few implications for the cook. First is the usual advice about using a decent bottle of wine — something you'd enjoy drinking. Second,

take some care when you're prepping the vegetables. You'll want to slice them thin so they cook quickly, but I like to slice vegetables like celery and carrots on an angle so they'll look nice too. You can adjust the vegetables to the season or to your mood. Try thin wedges of fennel (leave the core so the wedges will stay intact), julienne of celery root, or rounds of leek (white part only).

SALMON STEAKS POACHED IN RED WINE COURT BOUILLON

The flavor of this red wine court bouillon has the added layers of ginger, herbs, and citrus. I poach salmon steaks rather than fillets so the bones will further enrich the broth.

Think of this as a winter dish.   Serves 4

ACCEPT SUBSTITUTES
Char

FOR THE COURT BOUILLON

2 carrots, cut into thin slices (on an angle, so they are pretty)

1 celery rib, cut into thin slices (on an angle)

1 onion, cut into thin slices

1 (750-ml) bottle dry red wine

1 cup water

¼ cup red wine vinegar

2 tablespoons sugar

1 (2-inch) knob fresh ginger, peeled and sliced

An herb bouquet (a bay leaf, a few sprigs of thyme and rosemary, and a handful of parsley stems tied together with kitchen string)

1 lemon (preferably a Meyer lemon), scrubbed and sliced

1 blood (or navel) orange, scrubbed and sliced

4 (12-ounce) salmon steaks, tied (see page 38)

Coarse salt and freshly ground white pepper

FOR THE COURT BOUILLON: Combine the carrots, celery, onion, wine, water, vinegar, sugar, and ginger in an enameled Dutch oven or a large saucepan wide enough to hold the fish in one layer. Bring to a boil over medium heat, then cover, reduce the heat, and cook at an active simmer for 20 minutes. Remove the lid and simmer for another 15 minutes.

Add the herb bouquet, lemon, and orange, cover, turn off the heat, and let the court bouillon infuse for 1½ hours.

Season the salmon with salt and white pepper.

Immerse the salmon in the court bouillon and turn the heat to medium-low. When the surface starts to ripple and the court bouillon starts to steam (at about 160 degrees), turn off the heat, cover, and leave for 30 minutes.

Remove the salmon from the pot and pull off the string and the skin. Cut out the bit of fat in the center of the back of each steak and pull out the bones. Tidy up the steaks and place in soup dishes. Use a slotted spoon to divide the vegetables among the dishes, then spoon in a pool of the court bouillon and serve.

MILK COURT BOUILLON

I'm paying homage to earlier days with this recipe. Poaching in milk is very old-style cooking, but I love what it does to fish. This is the technique to choose for a soft, silky presentation of flatfish like turbot, halibut, and even Dover sole on the bone.   Makes 2 quarts

6 cups water   2 tablespoons coarse salt
2 cups whole milk

Pour the water and milk into a large skillet. Bring to an active simmer over medium heat. Add the salt.

The court bouillon is ready to use.

TURBOT POACHED IN MILK, WITH NOODLES AND MUSTARD BUTTER SAUCE

Just a few simple components on the plate here, but the results are elegant and truly delicious. (The photo is on page 150.)   Serves 4

ACCEPT SUBSTITUTES

Dover sole, flounder, cod, scrod, and fluke will all be fine here.

Coarse salt

1 (10-ounce) package frozen petite peas

½ pound egg noodles

Mustard Butter Sauce (page 406)

4 (6- to 7-ounce) pieces turbot fillet

Freshly ground white pepper

Milk Court Bouillon (page 87)

Bring a large saucepan of salted water to a boil. Put the peas in the colander you'll be using for the noodles and run under hot water to defrost them.

Cook the noodles until al dente. Drain in the colander and transfer the noodles and peas to a bowl. Toss with about 2 tablespoons of the butter sauce.

While the noodles cook, season the fish with salt and white pepper on both sides. Fold the fillets into thirds.

Bring the court bouillon to an active simmer. Slip in the fish and reduce the heat to low. Poach the fish for 5 minutes, then turn the fillets over with a fish spatula and turn off the heat. Let the fish sit for about a minute to finish cooking.

Spoon the noodles and peas into the centers of four dinner plates. Top with the fish and spoon a ring of the butter sauce around each one. Serve right away.

VARIATIONS

This combination of flavors—noodles, peas, and mustard sauce—works equally well with sautéed turbot or any of the substitutes.

For a very fancy presentation, drizzle each fish with a bit of mustard oil and top with a big pinch of micro greens.

HALIBUT POACHED IN MILK, WITH BOK CHOY AND COCONUT GREEN CURRY SAUCE

This is comfort food with a kick: soft fish, tender greens, and a bang from the sauce. Halibut shines when it's poached in milk, which keeps the fish snowy white.

Serves 4

ACCEPT SUBSTITUTES

Try this with mahi mahi or with Dover sole. If you're using sole, fold the fillets into thirds before poaching.

4 (6- to 7-ounce) pieces halibut fillet
Coarse salt and freshly ground white
  pepper

Milk Court Bouillon (page 87)
Basic Bok Choy (page 451)
Coconut and Green Curry Sauce
  (page 431)

Season the fish with salt and white pepper on both sides. Let it sit on the counter while you make the court bouillon.

When the court bouillon is at an active simmer (and you've seasoned it), slip in the fish and reduce the heat to low. Poach the fish for 3½ minutes, then turn the halibut over with a fish spatula and poach for another 2 minutes.

Remove the halibut with the spatula and blot it dry with paper towels. Set each piece of fish on a bed of bok choy and surround with a ring of the sauce. Pass the remaining sauce at the table.

STURGEON POACHED IN MILK, WITH CABBAGE AND WASABI BUTTER SAUCE

Poaching sturgeon in milk gives it a pleasantly resilient texture, like perfectly cooked lobster.

Serves 4

4 (6- to 7-ounce) pieces sturgeon fillet
Coarse salt and freshly ground white
  pepper

Milk Court Bouillon (page 87)
Basic Cabbage (page 451)
Wasabi Butter Sauce (page 406)

Season the fish with salt and white pepper on both sides. Let it sit on the counter while you make the court bouillon.

When the court bouillon is at an active simmer (and you've seasoned it), slip in the fish and reduce the heat to low. Poach the fish for 6 minutes, then turn it over with a fish spatula and poach for another 6 minutes.

Remove the sturgeon with the spatula and blot it dry with paper towels. Set each piece of fish on a wedge of cabbage and surround with a ring of the butter sauce. Pass the remaining sauce at the table.

ABOUT POACHING IN BUTTER

Butter is the best poaching medium for lobster and scallops, which might dry out in a court bouillon. The tender flesh is protected through the (very brief) cooking process by the fat. And as for the fla- vor transfer, well, the combination of butter and lobster is a natural. As with red wine court bouil- lon, the butter sauce you poach with is served as part of the finished dish.

BUTTER-POACHED BAY SCALLOPS
WITH RICE AND PEAS

Rich and intense, this dish plays the bite of garlic off the sweetness of bay scallops. Rice prepared this way gives you the appearance and creaminess of risotto without the elaborate cooking process.   Serves 4

Coarse salt

1 cup Arborio rice

1 (10-ounce) package frozen petite
  peas

1 large egg

Juice of ½ lemon

Garlic Butter Sauce (page 405)

1 pound bay scallops, tough bits
  removed

Chopped fresh parsley, chives, or
  scallion

Bring a large saucepan of salted water to a boil. Add the rice and stir. Bring back to a boil and cook the rice until al dente, 15 to 17 minutes.

Meanwhile, put the peas into a strainer and run them under hot water for a minute or so to defrost them. Set aside in the strainer. Beat the egg and lemon juice together in a small bowl until frothy.

About 4 minutes before the rice is done, bring the butter sauce to an active simmer, whisking as you do so. Add the scallops, stir, and turn the heat down to the lowest possible. Let the scallops poach for 3 minutes.

Scoop out about a cup of the cooking water, then drain the rice over the peas in the strainer, leaving it wet. Immediately return the rice, with the peas, to the pan and stir in the egg mixture. Stir in enough of the reserved cooking water to make the rice loose, then stir in ¼ cup of the butter sauce.

Divide the rice among four soup plates. Remove the scallops from the butter with a slotted spoon and serve on top of the rice. Garnish with your herb of choice.

BUTTER-POACHED LOBSTER
WITH CAULIFLOWER PUREE

With its interplay of textures and contrasts of sensation and flavor, this dish is almost like Japanese food. It's elegant, subtle, and rich.

For the best results, use a thermometer to monitor the temperature of the sauce. If it's too hot, the lobster will be tough.

Serves 4

ACCEPT SUBSTITUTES
Try this with scallops (poach for 3 minutes).

Basic Butter Sauce (page 404)
2 lobsters (each 1½–2 pounds),
    blanched and meat removed
    (see box)

Cauliflower Puree (page 455)
2 Granny Smith apples, shredded on a
    mandoline or a box grater (no need
    to peel)

Pour the butter sauce into a small (1½-quart) deep saucepan, set it over low heat, and warm it to 130 degrees. Add the lobster meat and poach for 8 minutes, until the lobster is just cooked through. Monitor the heat as you poach the lobster, keeping the temperature of the sauce as close to 130 degrees as possible; don't be afraid to turn off the heat at some point if you need to.

To serve, make a bed of cauliflower puree on each of four dinner plates. Top with the lobster, dividing it evenly. Top each portion of lobster with a mound of shredded apple, and spoon a little butter sauce over the apple and more around the cauliflower.

VARIATIONS

Substitute Celery Root and Potato Puree (page 456) for the cauliflower.

In the summer, you might want to serve the lobster on slabs of beefsteak tomato. Throw a handful of chopped herbs into the sauce before you spoon it on.

ABOUT BLANCHING LOBSTER

For those times when you will finish cooking lobster by another method—say, by poaching it in butter—blanching sets the meat, making it easier to remove it from the shell. Your goal is not to overcook the lobster when you blanch it.

Vinegar helps here by coagulating the protein, so you don't need to cook the lobster very long. And while it may sound like a lot of salt, you want the saltiness of the ocean. Remember, those lobsters have pretty hard shells.

See Dispatching a Lobster (page 46) and Preparing Lobster for Blanching or Pan-Roasting (page 47) for instructions on preparing the claws and tails.

3 quarts water
½ cup white vinegar
¾ cup coarse salt
Lobster claws
Lobster tails

Set up a large ice bath. Bring the water and vinegar to a boil in a stockpot. Add the salt and stir to dissolve.

Drop in the large claws and boil for 3 minutes. Immediately remove the claws with tongs or a spider and drop into the ice bath to stop the cooking. Bring the water back to a boil and add the tails. Boil for 2 minutes. Transfer to the ice bath. When the water has come back to a boil again, add the small claws. Boil for 1½ minutes, then transfer to the ice bath. Let cool.

The lobsters will be cooked just to rare at this point, so be prepared to make a mess as you shell them. If you can, set your cutting board over the sink so all the juices can drip into it.

There are a couple of ways to get to the tail meat. You can lay the tail on its back and cut it in half down the center with a heavy chef's knife. Pull out the meat. Discard the vein.

The messier method will keep the tail meat intact so you can cut pretty medallions. Hold the shell in your hand, with the back down, and squeeze hard to crack the shell. Then use both hands to pull the shell apart—be ready for squirting juices—and pull out the meat. Make a shallow cut down the back and remove the vein.

For the claws, start by twisting each claw from the arm, or knuckle. Grab the "thumb" of the claw, bend it back until you hear a crack, and then pull out the thumb and cartilage. Set the claw down on a cutting board, hold it by the tip, and smack it firmly with the back of a heavy chef's knife to crack the shell. Turn the claw over and smack it again. Pull off the tip of the shell. Shake the claw to release the meat, giving it a nudge or two if you need to.

Twist each arm to separate the knuckles. Cut each one open with kitchen shears to release the meat. Don't ever skip this step—this is the tastiest meat in the lobster.

CRAB POACHED
IN SCAMPI BUTTER SAUCE

Just thinking about sweet, tender crab swimming in this sauce gets my mouth watering. It's rich, so serve it as a first course. I love the way fresh pasta marries with the sauce, but you can substitute angel hair or even egg noodles.

The butter sauce is on the delicate side, so don't make it until you're ready to finish the dish and serve. If you leave it on the stove too long, the sauce will break.

Serves 4 as a first course

ACCEPT SUBSTITUTES

Any crabmeat will work in this dish. For a real treat, try it with shelled stone crab. Cooked meat from a Dungeness crab or a few Alaskan king crab legs is great too. Cooked king crab legs will come to you very highly seasoned. Consider cutting back on the salt in the pasta water if you're using their meat for this dish.

Scampi Butter Sauce (page 408)
12 ounces jumbo lump crabmeat, picked over

Coarse salt
½ pound fresh fettuccine
Chopped fresh parsley or basil leaves

Have the butter sauce at just below a simmer in a saucepan over low heat. Stir in the crabmeat carefully, trying not to break up the lumps. Then keep it warm on the back of the stove. The crabmeat's already cooked, so you're just warming it.

Meanwhile, bring a large pot of salted water to a boil. Add the pasta and cook to al dente.

Drain the pasta and divide among four plates. Spoon the crab and some of the sauce over the pasta and shower with the chopped herb of your choice. Serve right away.

VARIATION

If tomatoes are in season, seed a big juicy beefsteak, dice it, and use it to garnish the dish.

ABOUT POACHING FISH IN OIL

The process of poaching fish in oil is very simple. You heat the oil on top of the stove to about 125 degrees, which will feel hot when you put your finger into it but won't burn you. Then you add the fish, cover, and move the pan to a warm oven, about 175 degrees. These low, gentle temperatures will cook the fish through without releasing a lot of the protein—that release of protein is what dries fish out. No matter how gently you poach, though, you will see some tiny whitish beads of protein on the surface of the fish. It's inevitable, so don't be distressed. But these little beads aren't that attractive, so wipe them off with paper towels before serving the fish.

You'll be using a lot of oil here, but it doesn't need to be the finest quality. Good basic olive oil is what you want. And you can save the oil for more poaching. Let it cool, and the juices that have been released from the fish will settle on the bottom of the pan. Slowly pour the oil into a jar, leaving the juices in the pan. Keep the oil in the refrigerator.

OIL-POACHED HALIBUT
WITH GRIBICHE AND POACHED EGGS

Poaching halibut gently in olive oil leaves the fish moist, succulent, and full of flavor. It's an ideal technique for this fish.

Make the gribiche (a fancy name for the pickle garnish) at least 2 hours ahead of serving, the day before if you can swing it. And don't think that the poached egg is anything but essential—the yolk runs into the gribiche and makes a sauce. (The photograph is on page 202.)   Serves 4

ACCEPT SUBSTITUTES

You're looking for a white fish with big flakes:
haddock, cod, or sturgeon.

FOR THE GRIBICHE
⅓ cup diced tomato
3 tablespoons minced shallots
3 tablespoons minced cornichons
2 tablespoons capers
¼ cup extra virgin olive oil
2 tablespoons sherry vinegar
Juice of ½ lemon
Coarse salt and freshly ground white
    pepper
1 teaspoon chopped fresh tarragon
1 teaspoon chopped fresh parsley
1 scallion (white part only), minced

FOR THE FISH
4 (6- to 7-ounce) pieces halibut fillet
Coarse salt and freshly ground white
    pepper
Olive oil for poaching
Zest of 1 lemon (remove it with a
    vegetable peeler)

TO FINISH
⅔ cup minced onion
2 large garlic cloves, minced
1 pound baby spinach
Coarse salt
4 large eggs, poached (see box)

FOR THE GRIBICHE: Stir the tomato, shallots, cornichons, capers, olive oil, vinegar, and lemon juice together in a bowl. Season with salt and white pepper. Leave it at room temperature for 2 hours. (Or, better, cover and refrigerate overnight. Bring to room temperature before serving.)

MEANWHILE, FOR THE FISH: Forty-five minutes to 1 hour before cooking, season the halibut on both sides with salt and pepper. Refrigerate.

The real key to making poached eggs is getting truly fresh eggs. As they sit in your refrigerator (or in the case at the supermarket), the whites get thinner and runnier and the yolks get flatter.

Heat about 3 inches of water in a deep 10-inch skillet. Add a tablespoon or two of white vinegar and bring the water to a simmer over medium-high heat. Crack the eggs into custard cups or coffee cups.

When the water is just simmering, stir it several times so it's swirling, then slip each egg from its cup into the water; the eggs should be side by side but not touching. Lower the heat so that the water is just barely moving—if it boils or even simmers too vigorously, the eggs will become tough and may break apart.

When the whites are set and opaque but the yolks are still soft, about 4 minutes, lift the eggs, one by one, from the water with a slotted spoon. Slide them onto a cloth or paper towel to drain for a few seconds. If you are fussy about presentation, you may want to trim off any runaway bits of egg white with a small knife.

When poaching eggs ahead or for a crowd, you can hold them in a bowl of cold water for several hours in the refrigerator. Just slide them into a bath of simmering water for a few seconds to reheat before serving.

Heat the oven to 175 degrees.

Put the fish in an ovenproof skillet large enough to hold it without crowding. Pour in enough olive oil to cover the fish, then take the fish out and set aside on a plate. Add the lemon zest to the oil and heat it to about 125 degrees (warm enough to feel hot but not burn when you stick your finger in it; or just use a thermometer). Return the fish to the skillet, cover, and slide the pan into the oven. Poach the fish for 25 minutes.

TO FINISH: Just before serving, heat a large skillet over medium-high heat. Spoon in 2 tablespoons of the oil from the fish and add the onion. Sauté, stirring often, until the onion softens, about 3 minutes. Add the garlic and sauté until fragrant, about 20 seconds. Add the spinach and sauté, stirring constantly, until the spinach wilts. Season it with salt and scrape it into a strainer to drain.

Stir the tarragon, parsley, and scallion into the gribiche.

Make a bed of spinach on each of four dinner plates. Remove the fish from the oil with a fish spatula and blot it dry with paper towels. Set it on the spinach and place a poached egg on top of each piece. Spoon some gribiche onto each egg and around the plates. Serve it now.

TUNA PRESERVED IN OIL

I came across this method of cooking and preserving tuna on my travels through Italy, where I saw jars of tuna kept out on the counters of many of the houses I visited. But it's not just something thrifty; it's pretty damn delicious. As you'll see, it's a variation on the technique of poaching in oil.   Makes 1 pound

1 pound tuna, cut into large chunks   Olive oil
Coarse salt

Put the tuna on a plate and salt it generously on all sides. Let it sit at room temperature for 20 minutes.

Transfer the tuna to a heavy pot just large enough to accommodate it in one layer and cover it with olive oil. Set the pot over low heat and cook for 30 minutes. Keep your eye on the pot; you want the oil hot but not bubbling. Remove the tuna from the heat and let it cool completely in the oil.

Transfer the tuna and oil to a large jar, making sure the tuna remains covered in oil. Store in the refrigerator. It will keep for weeks.

SALMON PRESERVED IN OIL

I love tuna poached in oil so much that I had to try the technique with other fish. Salmon's the most successful; the fish becomes meltingly tender. Here it's perfumed with bay.   Makes 1 pound

5 small bay leaves
Olive oil

2 (8-ounce) pieces skinless wild salmon
fillet
Coarse salt

Put the bay leaves in a saucepan big enough to hold the fish in one layer. Pour in ¼ inch of oil and bring to a simmer over medium heat. Remove from the heat and cool to room temperature.

Meanwhile, put the salmon on a plate and salt it generously on all sides. Let it sit at room temperature for 20 minutes.

Set the salmon on the bay leaves and cover it with olive oil. Set the pan over medium-low heat and cook for 15 minutes. The oil should just start to bubble at the end of the cooking time. Remove the salmon from the heat and let it cool completely in the oil.

Transfer the salmon to a large jar, making sure the salmon remains covered in oil. Store in the refrigerator. It keeps for weeks.

USING TUNA OR SALMON PRESERVED IN OIL

You'll find a few recipes elsewhere in the book where either fish would be a natural. They're great in the Sicilian Tuna Salad Sandwich (page 338), Tuna Salad with Pickled Vegetables (page 335), and Niçoise Salad (page 336). You could also flake the fish and toss it with white beans and sliced red onions and serve over arugula. Or serve it on Croutons (page 475), garnished with chopped parsley.

STEAMING AND BOILING

STEAMED SALMON WITH FENNEL

The pure flavors of salmon and fennel shine in this comforting dish. Aromatic fennel is both the side dish and the base for a sauce that's simple and elegant.   Serves 4

ACCEPT SUBSTITUTES
Char is a natural here.

1 large fennel bulb

1 tablespoon toasted fennel seeds

3 large shallots, cut into thin slices

2 garlic cloves, minced

2 cups Quick Vegetable Stock (page 476) or water

Coarse salt

4 (6-ounce) pieces skinless wild salmon fillet

3 tablespoons unsalted butter, cut into 4 or 5 pieces

Juice of ½ lemon

Coarse sea salt for serving

Cut off the tops and remove the tough outer layer of the fennel bulb, then cut it into very thin strips; you'll be using these strips to line the steamer basket. Cut the rest of the fennel bulb into large dice.

Combine the diced fennel, fennel seeds, shallots, garlic, and vegetable stock in a saucepan. Season with salt and bring to a boil over medium-high heat. Cover, reduce the heat to medium-low, and simmer until the fennel is tender, 15 to 20 minutes. Drain, reserving the stock. Keep the vegetables warm.

Return the stock to the saucepan, place it on high heat, and reduce to ½ cup.

ABOUT STEAMING FISH

Steaming may be the easiest way to enter the world of seafood. Steaming is quick. The heat — steam — is even and enveloping, which gives you more leeway in timing. It's a rare occasion when steaming results in dry fish. And it's relatively no fuss; you don't have to turn the fish. It's a particularly attractive method to use in the summer, since it doesn't really heat up the kitchen. And cleanup is easy. You just need to take a bit of care lifting the steamer basket out of the pan. Steam burns can be nasty.

Meanwhile, pour about 2 cups water into a pan that holds your steamer basket snugly and bring to a boil over high heat. Line the basket with the sliced fennel strips. Season the salmon with salt and set it on the fennel. Cover the steamer, reduce the heat to medium, and steam the fish for 8 minutes for medium-rare.

While the salmon cooks, pour the reduced stock into a blender and add about ¼ cup of the reserved vegetables. Puree until very smooth. With the blender running, drop in the butter piece by piece. Add the lemon juice and taste for salt.

To serve, divide the remaining vegetables among four dinner plates and set the fish on top. Whir the sauce in the blender again so it's foamy, then pour it around the fish. Toss a pinch of sea salt onto each piece of fish and serve.

STEAMED BLACK SEA BASS WITH SIZZLING GINGER

This isn't a white-shirt meal, but it does capture all the sweetness you can get from the fish. Keep the head on the fish, please. It's integral for flavor. Set the table with extra plates for the bones.

See About Steamer Baskets (page 108).   Serves 2

ACCEPT SUBSTITUTES

Dorade (it will cook a bit more quickly)

Porgies or any small to medium whole fish

2 whole black sea bass (each about 1¼ pounds), scaled and gutted, gills and fins removed

2 large shallots, cut into thin slices

¼ cup chopped fresh ginger

¼ cup soy sauce

6 scallions, trimmed and halved lengthwise

FOR THE SIZZLING GINGER

2 tablespoons vegetable oil

4–5 slices fresh ginger, cut into very fine matchsticks

FOR SERVING

White rice

Make 3 deep diagonal cuts into both sides of each fish—into the flesh, but not down to the bone.

WHEN THE FISH DOESN'T FIT IN THE STEAMER

It happens—sometimes the fish is too long.

The easiest solution is to let the tail curl up, but if you still can't get the cover on snugly, cut off the tail. Please don't cut off the head. The gelatin it contributes to the cooking juices is the best you can get. And fish cheeks are pretty tasty morsels.

Toss the shallots and chopped ginger together and stuff into the cavities of the sea bass, dividing the mixture equally. Put the fish into a baking dish and pour in the soy. Get your hands in and rub the fish all over with the soy. Let the fish marinate for 20 minutes.

Divide the scallions between two salad plates—ones that will fit into the steamer baskets and then sit nicely on dinner plates when you serve the fish. Trim any scallion greens that hang off the plates and stuff them into the fish. Set the fish on their beds of scallions and set the plates into two steamer baskets.

Pour about 2 cups water into a skillet or pan that holds your steamer snugly and bring to a boil over medium-high heat. If there's any soy (or solids) left in the baking dish, add it to the water. Set the steamer baskets over the boiling water, cover, and steam for 10 minutes, or until the fish is cooked through and swimming in broth; when it's done, the fish will feel firm to the touch and the slashes will have opened wide. To double-check, you can stick the tip of a knife into the thickest part of a fish and leave it for a few seconds, then touch the knife to your lip; if the fish is cooked properly, it will feel hot. Your other cue for doneness is the eyes, which will have turned white and popped when the fish is done. Lift the plates out of the steamer baskets and set them on dinner plates.

FOR THE SIZZLING GINGER: Heat the oil in a small skillet over medium-high heat until it's smoking. Add the ginger and immediately take the skillet off the heat.

Spoon the hot oil over the fish and serve, with bowls of white rice on the side.

TEA-STEAMED SEA BASS

Cooking fish on the bone — particularly steaming it — lets the natural flavors of the fish shine. Here, I'm adding the smokiness of lapsang souchong tea.   Serves 2

ACCEPT SUBSTITUTES

Dorade (it will cook a bit more quickly)

Porgies or any small to medium whole fish

2 tablespoons lapsang souchong
  tea leaves
1 teaspoon coarse salt
2 whole sea bass (each about
  1¼ pounds), scaled and gutted,
  gills and fins removed

1 lemon, halved
Horseradish Cream (page 420)
Asian Cucumber Salad (page 458)

Grind the tea and salt to a fine powder in a spice grinder.

Make 3 deep diagonal cuts into both sides of each fish — into the flesh, but not down to the bone.

Sprinkle about half the tea mixture over both sides of the fish. Refrigerate for 30 minutes.

Pour about 2 cups water into a skillet or pan that holds your steamers snugly and bring to a boil over medium-high heat. Add the remaining tea mixture.

Put the fish into two steamer baskets, set over the steaming tea, cover, and steam for 8 minutes, or until the fish is cooked through. When it's done, the fish will feel firm to the touch and the slashes will have opened wide. To double-check, you can stick the tip of a knife into the thickest part of the fish and leave it for a few seconds, then touch the knife to your lip; if the fish is cooked properly, it will feel hot. Your other cue for doneness is the eyes, which will have turned white and popped when the fish is done.

Use a large spatula to transfer the fish to dinner plates. Squeeze on some lemon juice. Serve with the horseradish cream and cucumber salad.

STEAMED HALIBUT WITH CREAMY CORN AND RED PEPPER COULIS

Halibut has a tendency to dry out, so the moist heat of steaming is ideal. Here the fish's mild flavor is paired with sweet corn and sweet bell peppers. It's a simple and very pretty dish. Make the corn and coulis in advance if you want. Serves 4

ACCEPT SUBSTITUTES

Try this combination of flavors with the cod family, salmon steaks, or sea scallops.

4 (7-ounce) halibut steaks
Coarse salt and freshly ground white
    pepper

Creamy Corn (page 457)
Red Bell Pepper Coulis (page 427)
4 scallions, chopped

Pour about 2 cups water into a pan that holds a bamboo steamer basket snugly and bring to a boil over high heat.

Season the halibut with salt and white pepper, put it in the steamer basket, and set over the boiling water. Cover, reduce the heat to medium, and steam the fish for 4 to 5 minutes, until it is barely cooked through. It should still have some give when you poke it with your finger; you don't want it to flake.

To serve, spread some of the creamy corn into the center of four dinner plates. Set the fish on the corn, surround with the coulis, and shower the halibut with the chopped scallions.

VARIATION

Instead of steaming, marinate the halibut in Basil Oil (page 436) and sauté it, then serve with the corn and coulis.

STEAMED JUMBO SHRIMP

Bright orangey-pink shrimp, the flesh snappingly crisp after a short brine and brightly seasoned with your own Chesapeake seasoning, will have you licking your fingers and thinking of the shore. Serve as a first course or as a main, with boiled red-skinned potatoes and corn on the cob.

A quick brine seasons the flesh, and it also firms the texture, giving shrimp a snap. It's a great technique for enlivening shrimp that have been frozen and may be a bit limp.

Bamboo steamer baskets are best for cooking here, and they have the added appeal of working as serving bowls too.   Serves 4 as a main course, 6 as an appetizer

FOR THE BRINE
⅓ cup coarse salt
2 cups water
A tray of ice cubes (about 12)

2 pounds jumbo (11–15 count) shrimp
    in the shell
Homemade Chesapeake Seasoning
    (page 441) or about 2½ tablespoons
    Old Bay seasoning
2 cups water
¾ cup white vinegar

Melted unsalted butter for serving

ABOUT STEAMER BASKETS

I haven't been able to find a better piece of equipment than those inexpensive stacked bamboo steamers, which come with two baskets for steaming and a lid. They're so easy to clean, and they're attractive enough to serve from. I've got a couple of sets so I can make dishes like Stovetop Clambake (page 110). Bamboo steamers are sold in a variety of stores—I found mine in New York City's Chinatown—and they're readily available online.

FOR THE BRINE: Dissolve the salt in the water in a medium bowl. Add the ice cubes and shrimp and leave on the counter for 30 minutes.

Lift the shrimp out of the brine and toss with 2 tablespoons of the seasoning. Let sit while you bring the water for steaming to a boil.

Pour the water and vinegar into a pan that holds your steamer snugly and bring to a boil. Divide the shrimp between two bamboo steamer baskets, spreading them out into a single layer. Sprinkle the remaining ½ tablespoon seasoning over the shrimp. Set the steamers over the boiling water and vinegar, cover them, and steam for 5 minutes. The shells should be bright pink and the shrimp, when you squeeze them between your fingers, should feel firm.

Set the steamer baskets on dinner plates and bring them to the table. Set out small bowls of the steaming liquid and of melted butter so you and your guests can dip the shrimp after you shell them.

Do you really need the butter? Maybe not. But it rounds out all the flavors and makes you feel like you're outside, with a sea breeze in your face.

STOVETOP CLAMBAKE

Here's the thing about clambakes: if you make them outside in a pit or inside in a big pot, by the time the potatoes are cooked, the clams will have turned to leather. But when you use bamboo steamers, you can control all the cooking times and you've got a pretty nice way of serving too. (The photo is on page 158.)

You do need a four-basket setup to serve 2, though. If you want to serve 4, I suggest making one batch and transferring everything to a big serving platter, then repeating the process to make a second batch.

Ask your fishmonger for seaweed. Cover it with cold water and let it soak for about 15 minutes before you line the steamer baskets.   Serves 2

1 lobster (about 1½ pounds)
Seaweed (see headnote)
6 small creamer or red-skinned
   potatoes (about ⅓ pound),
   scrubbed
6 small onions (cipollini, if you can
   find them), peeled

1–1½ pounds steamer clams
½ pound kielbasa, cut into quarters
2 ears corn, shucked and cut into thirds
2 (12-ounce) cans or bottles lager beer
8 tablespoons (1 stick) unsalted butter
Juice of 1 lemon

Dispatch the lobster by cutting through the head (see page 46). Pull off the claws and crack the claws and knuckles with the back of a chef's knife. Twist off the tail, split it with a chef's knife, and remove the vein.

Line four bamboo steamer baskets with seaweed. Fill basket 1 with the potatoes and onions. Fill basket 2 with the lobster pieces. Fill basket 3 with the steamers. Fill basket 4 with the kielbasa and corn.

Pour the beer into a wide saucepan—one that the baskets will fit into snugly. Set basket 1 in the pan, cover, and bring to a boil over high heat. Once you've got the steam going, turn the heat down to medium-high and steam for 15 minutes.

Stack on the remaining baskets in order (so basket 4 is on top), cover, and steam for 15 minutes more.

Meanwhile, melt the butter and stir in the lemon juice. Divide the lemon butter between two ramekins.

Serve the clambake right from the steamer baskets.

STEAMED WEST COAST OYSTERS

With its elegant combination of shallot, ginger, and garlic, this dish showcases the unique flavor of oysters from the West Coast. So good, so full of the ocean.

Ask your fishmonger for seaweed, or shred the outer leaves from a head of green cabbage to use as a substitute for stabilizing the oysters

You can double the recipe, but keep steaming just one basket at a time. The bottom oysters will overcook if you stack the baskets.   Serves 2 as an appetizer

ACCEPT SUBSTITUTES

West Coast oysters, with their melony, cucumbery flavor, are really what you want, but you can substitute any large oyster.

2 teaspoons minced shallot
½ teaspoon minced fresh ginger
½ teaspoon minced garlic
¼ teaspoon minced red Thai chile (or serrano chile)

12 large oysters, such as Penn Cove, Quilcene, Hood Canal, or Olympia, scrubbed
Seaweed (see headnote)
Fresh cilantro leaves for garnish

Toss the shallot, ginger, garlic, and chile together in a small bowl.

Shuck the oysters, leaving them on the half-shell (see page 45), and place a pinch of the shallot mixture on top of each.

Fill a deep skillet—one that a bamboo steamer will fit into snugly—with about 1 inch of water and bring to a boil.

Meanwhile, arrange the seaweed loosely in the bottom of two steamer baskets. Set 6 oysters on top of the seaweed in each one, nestling them so they sit upright and the juices don't spill.

Cover one of the baskets and set it over the boiling water. Steam for 5 minutes. The oysters will be warmed through and the edges will have ruffled and curled. Remove the basket and cover it with a plate while you steam the second basket.

Place each steamer basket on a dinner plate, garnish the oysters with a few cilantro leaves, and serve.

Remember how you want to eat oysters. Have a fork to pick up the oyster and slurp it down. But never, never forget to pick up the shell and drink down whatever's left.

NEW ENGLAND STEAMED DINNER

Like the classic New England boiled dinner, this dish is simple. But there's no corned beef here. The flavors are of the potatoes, turnips, cabbage, and halibut, pure, almost innocent, and the dish satisfies just like chicken soup.   Serves 4

ACCEPT SUBSTITUTES

Fillets of thick-fleshed fish are what you want here;
other possibilities are cod, scrod, tilefish, sea bass, and turbot
(delicious, but expensive; fold the fillets into thirds).

5 slices thick-cut bacon, cut into
  ½-inch pieces
1 onion, chopped
2 carrots, cut into ⅓-inch chunks
2 turnips, peeled and cut into ½-inch
  chunks
½ pound creamer potatoes, scrubbed,
  ends trimmed, and halved
  (quartered if large)
1 teaspoon fresh thyme leaves
1 bay leaf

Coarse salt and freshly ground
  white pepper
1 pound cabbage, cut into 1-inch
  chunks
2 cups water
4 (5-ounce) skinless pieces
  halibut fillet

FOR SERVING
Horseradish Cream (page 420)
Fleur de sel or other coarse sea salt
Chopped fresh parsley (optional)

You'll need a wide deep pot that your steamer will fit into snugly. Drop the bacon, onion, carrots, turnips, and potatoes into the pot and add the thyme and bay leaf. Season with salt and white pepper and give the ingredients a stir. Scatter the cabbage on top and season with salt and pepper. Pour in the water, cover the pot, and bring to an active simmer over medium-high heat. Cook the vegetables for 8 minutes.

Meanwhile, spray the bottom of the steamer basket with pan spray. Season the halibut on both sides with salt and put it into the steamer.

Set the steamer over the vegetables and steam for about 8 minutes. Check the fish: the sides of the fillets should feel firm when you squeeze them, but the tops should still be slightly mushy. Halibut can be very dry if it's overcooked, so you are aiming for something slightly underdone—the fish will finish cooking with residual heat. Thicker fillets—about 1 inch thick—will take 9 to 10 minutes to steam.

To serve, divide the vegetables and broth among four wide soup plates. Set a piece of halibut on top of each. Plop a spoonful of horseradish cream on the fish and sprinkle the vegetables with a pinch of fleur de sel or other coarse sea salt. If you feel the need for color, shower the dish with chopped parsley. Pass the rest of the horseradish cream at the table.

STEAMED SALMON PACKETS
WITH PEANUT AND RED CURRY SAUCE

The Asian-inspired sauce is a riff on sesame noodles and pairs well with salmon. Cabbage leaves make edible wrappers for the packets.

You can find Thai red curry paste in the Asian section of most grocery stores and in Asian and specialty markets. It's fiery hot, so use it with discretion, folks. Don't use "natural" peanut butter for this dish. You need the sugar that you get in Jif or Skippy.

Serves 4

ACCEPT SUBSTITUTES

Char

2 heaped tablespoons peanut butter
   (chunky or smooth)
1 teaspoon Thai red curry paste
¼ cup coconut milk
1 teaspoon fish sauce
3 tablespoons chopped mixed fresh
   herbs (use a combination of
   cilantro, basil, and mint)

8 green cabbage leaves
4 (6-ounce) pieces skinless wild salmon
   fillet
Coarse salt
Carrot Slaw (page 454) or Asian Slaw
   (page 453)

Combine the peanut butter, red curry paste, coconut milk, fish sauce, and herbs in a small bowl. Stir until smooth. Let the flavors ripen while you prep the cabbage.

Fill a deep skillet—one that your steamer will fit into snugly—with about 1 inch of water and bring it to a boil over high heat.

Meanwhile, cut out the thick central rib of each cabbage leaf. Set the steamer over the steaming water and steam the cabbage leaves 2 at a time, covered, for about a minute, until they are limp.

Set 2 of the leaves out on your work surface, patching them together so you have something large enough to enclose a piece of salmon. (You may not use all the cabbage.) Smear a generous tablespoon of the red curry sauce over the center of each leaf. Season the salmon on both sides with salt and set the fillets on top of the cabbage. Smear the top of each fillet with another tablespoon of the sauce. Fold the top of the cabbage leaves toward you, then fold in the sides. Then fold the entire packet toward you, over the bottom free ends of the cabbage leaves. Repeat to make 3 more packets. If you want, you can make the packets in advance and refrigerate them until dinnertime.

Set the packets in the steamer, seam side down, cover, and steam for 10 minutes.

Take the salmon out of the steamer, and cut each packet in half on the diagonal with a serrated knife. Plate and serve with one of the slaws.

DUNGENESS CRAB BOIL

I prefer blue crabmeat when I'm making crab cakes, but Dungeness is my choice for a boil. The meat is so sweet and firm.

When it comes down to it, I like these best cold. That's when the flavors of the boil shine through. So I make this a day ahead of when I plan to serve it. That's not to say that hot crabs don't have their place; see the variation. (The photo is on page 160.)   Serves 4

3 gallons water

3 lemons

1½ cups coarse salt

¼ cup coriander seeds

3 tablespoons brown mustard seeds

1 tablespoon dill seeds

2 teaspoons crushed red pepper

1 heaped teaspoon allspice berries
   (about 24)

1 teaspoon celery seeds

1 teaspoon white peppercorns

1 teaspoon black peppercorns

1 large bay leaf, crumbled

4 Dungeness crabs (each about 1½
   pounds)

Louis Dressing (page 339)

Put the water in a very large pot. Cut the lemons in half, squeeze the juice into the water, and drop in the rinds. Add the salt, coriander, mustard, dill, crushed red pepper, allspice, celery seeds, white and black peppercorns, and bay leaf. Bring to a boil over high heat and boil for 5 minutes.

Add the crabs, cover, and bring back to a full boil. Turn off the heat and let the crabs sit for 15 minutes.

Remove the crabs and cool them down, then chill completely, preferably overnight.

Lift the top shell off the crabs and discard the feathery gills and the sand sacs. Cut the crabs in half and pull off the legs. Serve with the dressing—or pick the meat and make it the centerpiece of a Louis Salad.

Hot crabs and corn on the cob are the kind of thing you want to eat with friends, the juices running down your arms as you smack your lips.

I skip all the spices when I plan on serving these crabs hot. Combine the water, lemon juice and rinds, and salt in that big pot and bring it to a boil. (There's no need to boil for 5 minutes.) Add the crabs, cover, and bring back to a boil. Turn off the heat and let it all sit for 15 minutes.

Serve with lemon wedges and plenty of melted butter.

BETTER BOILED LOBSTER

I've boiled lobsters for years and years, each time pulling them out of the pot and seeing all that white stuff that looks like albumen floating in the water, and I thought there had to be a better way. There is. Follow this technique for richer, more lobstery-tasting boiled lobster.

This is a basic technique, so I'm giving guidelines, not amounts. I've based this on lobsters that weigh between 1¼ and 1½ pounds. For larger ones, increase the sitting time by 5 minutes per half pound.

Coarse salt
Live lobsters

Bring a large pot of well-salted water to a boil—at least 3 quarts for 2 lobsters. You want ocean saltiness here, so a good rule of thumb is ¼ cup of salt for each quart of water.

When the water is at a full boil, drop in the lobsters head first and cover the pot. Bring back to a boil and boil for 1 minute. Turn off the heat and leave the lobsters alone for 20 minutes.

If you're serving the lobsters hot, pull them out of the pot with tongs. Crack the claws in the kitchen, drain the lobsters, and serve.

If you've boiled the lobsters for a salad, pick them out of the pot and put them in a big bowl of ice water for 10 minutes to set the meat.

LOBSTER ROLL

It's lobster with some crunch, piled into a bun, and it's a summertime classic.

Remove the meat from a boiled lobster (about 1½ pounds) and cut it into chunks. Add ¼ cup diced fennel or celery, 3 tablespoons mayonnaise, some salt and pepper, and a squirt of lemon juice.

Butter 2 hot dog buns (top-loading ones are traditional, but I love potato buns) and toast them on a hot griddle or skillet. Then pile in the lobster salad and enjoy.

SHRIMP BOIL

Have plenty of napkins on hand for this deliciously messy dish.

You can serve the shrimp simply as is or with cocktail sauce or bowls of melted butter for dipping.

Serves 4

FOR THE "BOIL"
¼ cup coriander seeds
3 tablespoons brown mustard seeds
1 tablespoon dill seeds
2 teaspoons crushed red pepper
1 heaped teaspoon allspice berries
 (about 24)
1 teaspoon celery seeds
1 teaspoon white peppercorns

1 teaspoon black peppercorns
1 large bay leaf, crumbled
3 quarts water

6 tablespoons coarse salt
1 lemon, halved
2 pounds extra-large (16–20 count)
 shrimp in the shell

FOR THE "BOIL": Stir all the ingredients except the water together. You can make this mix well in advance and store it in a jar out of the light. It keeps for months.

Pour the water into a large pot. Add the salt, then juice the lemon into the water and drop in the lemon rind. Add the spice mix, bring to a boil over high heat, and boil for 5 minutes.

Add the shrimp and bring back to a full boil. Cover, turn off the heat, and let the shrimp sit for 4 minutes. Drain and serve.

BROILING

BROILED FISH FILLETS
WITH BUTTER AND HERBS

This is a classic restaurant technique, and the dish was a staple on the menu when I cooked at New York City's Le Cirque. It's a great way of getting delicious fillets on the table fast. Of course, you're not going to have a salamander—a super-hot restaurant broiler—in your kitchen, so I've adapted the technique for the oven broiler. (The photo is on page 207.)

As you'll see in the variations, this technique opens the door to all kinds of experimentation at home.

Serves 4

ACCEPT SUBSTITUTES

Just about any flat fillet—with skin or without—works well
with this technique. Consider flounder, gray sole, lemon sole,
rainbow trout, tilapia, even dorade.

FOR THE HERB MIX
2 tablespoons minced fresh parsley
1 tablespoon minced fresh dill
⅓ cup minced fresh chives

8 tablespoons (1 stick) unsalted butter, melted
4 (6-ounce) pieces fish fillet
Coarse salt and freshly ground white pepper
About 4 teaspoons fresh bread crumbs (see page 475)
Lemon wedges

Set an oven rack in the top position, slide in a cast-iron griddle, and turn on the broiler. Let the griddle heat for 15 minutes.

MEANWHILE, FOR THE HERB MIX: Toss the parsley, dill, and chives together in a small bowl.

Pour the butter into a soup plate. Dip each piece of fish into the butter to coat it on both sides, then lay the fish skin side down on a work surface and season with salt and white pepper. Divide the herb mix among the 4 fillets, sprinkling it evenly. Sprinkle each fillet with about 1 teaspoon bread crumbs and pat the coating onto the fish. Drizzle each fillet with a little of the butter.

The ridged broiler pan that came with your oven is not your best friend when it comes to broiling tender fish fillets. Those ridges and drip holes are designed for cooking meat. Broil a delicate piece of fish on the pan, and chances are it will fall apart when you try to take it off.

The best piece of equipment to use when you're broiling fillets—with or without skin—is a well-seasoned flat cast-iron griddle. Position it under the broiler and heat it up for 15 minutes, until it's searingly hot. When you put skin-on fillets on it, the heat from the griddle will crisp the skin, and the flat surface makes plating very simple. When you use it for skinless fillets, you get great caramelization on the bottom side.

When you're broiling skinless fillets, like flounder, you can also use a lightly oiled baking sheet. No need to heat the sheet in advance: set the fillets on the sheet and slide them under the heat. You'll find you have perfectly broiled fillets, and the smooth surface of the baking sheet makes sliding the fish off and onto the plate a snap.

For fillets with skin, a baking sheet will work, but it won't get as hot as the griddle and so the skin won't be as crisp. Oh, and those insulated cookie sheets won't work for broiling at all—you need a heavy professional baking sheet.

Set the fillets skin side down on the griddle. You'll hear an immediate and very satisfying sizzle. Broil the fish for about 3 minutes, until the crumbs are toasty and caramelized.

Serve with lemon wedges.

VARIATIONS

Make an herb mix with 3 tablespoons minced fresh cilantro, 3 tablespoons minced fresh basil, and 1 teaspoon grated lime zest. Combine 1 tablespoon sugar and 2 teaspoons coarse salt in a small bowl. Add 1 teaspoon Thai red curry paste to the butter when you melt it, and whisk to dissolve the paste completely. Coat the fish on both sides with the butter and season with the sugar and salt (no pepper needed). Coat with the herb mix, sprinkle with the bread crumbs, and drizzle with butter as in the master recipe. Broil, and serve with lime wedges.

Make some Parsley Pesto (page 422). Season the fish with salt and pepper and dip it in olive oil (no butter in this variation). Spread each fillet with about 2 teaspoons of the pesto, sprinkle with bread crumbs as in the master recipe, and broil. Serve with lemon wedges.

BROILED FISH FILLETS
WITH COMPOUND BUTTER

Simple and satisfying, this technique couldn't be easier when you've got some compound butter in the refrigerator.

What I'm giving you here is a kind of mix-and-match thing. Find the fish that looks best in the market and pair it with a butter of your choice.

THE FISH
Branzino fillets, skin on,
Fluke fillets,
Tilapia fillets, sliced in half down the
    center seam, *or*
Catfish fillets, sliced in half down the
    center seam

Olive or vegetable oil
Coarse salt and freshly ground white
    pepper

THE BUTTER (PAGES 410–413),
SOFTENED
    Porcini Butter,
    Black Olive and Anchovy Butter,
    Chile Cilantro Butter,
    Ginger Soy Butter, *or*
    Sun-Dried Tomato Butter

Set an oven rack in the top position, slide in a cast-iron griddle, and turn on the broiler. Let the griddle heat for 15 minutes.

Meanwhile, brush the skin side of the fish with oil and season with salt and white pepper. Smear the other side of the fish with a couple teaspoons of your chosen butter.

Set the fillets skin side down on the griddle. You'll hear an immediate and very satisfying sizzle.

BRANZINO: broil for 1 minute.

FLUKE: broil for 2 minutes.

TILAPIA: broil small pieces for 2 minutes, larger pieces for 3 minutes.

CATFISH: broil small pieces for 2 minutes, larger pieces for 3 minutes.

Remove the fillets with a fish spatula and serve hot.

BROILED FLOUNDER WITH ARUGULA PESTO

This recipe is a great way to start moving kids beyond fish fingers and into the land of grown-up fish dishes.   Serves 4

ACCEPT SUBSTITUTES

Just about any skinless flat fillet works with this technique.
Consider gray sole, lemon sole, even tilapia or catfish.

4 tablespoons unsalted butter, melted

4 (5- to 6-ounce) flounder fillets, about
   ½ inch thick

Coarse salt and freshly ground white
   pepper

2 teaspoons grated lemon zest

4 heaped tablespoons Arugula Pesto
   (page 423)

2 teaspoons dry bread crumbs

Lemon wedges

Pour the butter into a soup plate. Season the flounder on both sides with salt and white pepper. Dip both sides in the melted butter.

Rub ½ teaspoon of the lemon zest into the top (the side that had no skin) of each fillet. Spread on a heaping tablespoon of the pesto, going not quite to the edges, and sprinkle on ½ teaspoon of the bread crumbs. Set the fillets on a greased baking sheet. The fish can be prepared several hours in advance and refrigerated.

Set an oven rack about 5 inches below the heat source and heat the broiler.

Slide the baking sheet under the broiler and broil the fish for about 5 minutes—a minute or so longer if you've refrigerated the fish. The topping will be browned and you'll see a little oil bubbling around the edges of the fish.

Serve hot, with lemon wedges.

BROILED BLUEFISH DIJONNAISE

You might want to serve this with rice and a sauté of zucchini and tomato. Or maybe Peperonata (page 465). The photo is on page 199. Serves 4

ACCEPT SUBSTITUTES

Mackerel, shad, herring,
flounder, gray sole

¼ cup mayonnaise

2 tablespoons Dijon mustard

½ teaspoon dried thyme or oregano
   (optional)

4 (6-ounce) pieces bluefish fillet (skin
   on or off)

Coarse salt and freshly ground white
   pepper

Set a cast-iron griddle under the broiler, turn on the broiler, and heat it for 15 minutes. You want the griddle sizzling hot.

Meanwhile, stir the mayonnaise and mustard together in a small bowl. Crumble in the herb if you're using it.

Season the fish with salt and white pepper on both sides and paint one side with the mustard coating.

Put the fish on the griddle, painted side up, and broil for 3 to 4 minutes, until the coating is browned and bubbling. Serve it up hot.

NOTE: You can use your Foreman grill (see page 136) for this dish. Be sure to use skinless fillets, since the skin won't crisp enough. Cook for the same 3 to 4 minutes.

BROILED SWORDFISH

This is just how my mother used to cook swordfish when I was growing up, and I still think it's pretty damn good. Keep the skin on when you broil the fish and peel it off before serving.   Serves 4

4 (6- to 7-ounce) pieces swordfish
   steak
Coarse salt

Paprika (hot, sweet, smoked—it's up
   to you)
2 tablespoons unsalted butter

Set a cast-iron griddle on the top oven rack and heat the broiler.

Meanwhile, season the swordfish on both sides with salt and sprinkle one side with an even coating of paprika. Dot the fish with the butter.

When the griddle is searingly hot, set the swordfish on it, paprika side up, and broil until just cooked through, about 5½ minutes. Serve hot.

BROILED SALMON STEAKS

Here's another example of pure, very simple cooking—something easy for a week-night dinner. Serve these with buttery boiled potatoes and a salad.   Serves 4

4 (10- to 12-ounce) salmon steaks,
   1½ inches thick
Vegetable oil

About 3 tablespoons Cajun Spice Mix
   (page 442)

Rub the steaks generously with oil and coat them on both sides with the rub. You can do this well in advance and refrigerate until dinnertime.

Set a cast-iron griddle on the top oven rack and heat the broiler.

When the griddle is searingly hot, set the salmon on it. Broil for 4 minutes for medium-rare. Serve hot.

BROILED MACKEREL

Boy, do I love the flavor of broiled mackerel. The fish is so rich. Serve it on a bed of Puttanesca Sauce (page 430), if you want, or Tomato Concassé (page 428).

Be forewarned: your kitchen will smell very fishy when you cook mackerel this way. My solution: put out a bowl of bleach by the stove and it will pull the smell out of the air. (Make sure no one mistakes the bleach for water.)   Serves 4

4 (6- to 7-ounce) pieces mackerel fillet,   Olive oil
   skin on   Coarse salt

Rub the fish generously with olive oil and season it with salt.

Set a cast-iron griddle on the top oven rack and heat the broiler for 15 minutes.

When the griddle is searingly hot, set the mackerel on it, skin side down. Broil until lightly browned on top, about 3½ minutes. Serve hot.

BROILED HALIBUT STEAKS WITH BASIL BUTTER

As with broiled fillets, this is a very easy technique. The little bit of bread crumbs combines with the butter to make a sweet crust.

Try this with the Red Pepper and Tabasco Butter (page 409) too. It's great, particularly when you give the fish a squirt of lemon before you serve it.   Serves 4

ACCEPT SUBSTITUTES
Swordfish steaks and salmon fillets both shine when cooked this way.
Both should be 1 inch thick. Broil swordfish steaks for 4½ minutes,
salmon fillets (skin side down) for 3 minutes.

4 (6- to 7-ounce) halibut steaks,
    1½ inches thick
Coarse salt and freshly ground white
    pepper
Olive or vegetable oil

About 4 tablespoons Basil Butter (page
    409), softened
About 4 teaspoons fresh bread crumbs
    (see page 475)

Season the halibut with salt and white pepper on both sides. Pour a little oil on a plate and set the fish on top. Smear the top of each piece of fish with about 1 tablespoon of the butter, then sprinkle on about 1 teaspoon bread crumbs and pat them into the butter. You can prep the fish well in advance and refrigerate it until you're ready to broil.

Set an oven rack in the top position, slide in a cast-iron griddle, and turn on the broiler. Let the griddle heat for 15 minutes.

Set the fish onto the griddle, buttered side up. You'll hear an immediate and very satisfying sizzle. Broil for 6½ to 7 minutes. If you're unsure about doneness, poke inside with a knife. It should look slightly rare in the center; the carry-over heat will finish the cooking.

Remove the halibut with a fish spatula and let rest for 5 minutes before serving.

BROILED SARDINES

If you have the time and inclination, marinate the sardines. But even if you don't, they'll still be blistered, browned, and delicious.

Serve them with your favorite hummus and some pita breads, which you can warm under the griddle while you broil the fish. (The photo is on page 205.)

Serves 4

FOR THE MARINADE (OPTIONAL)
¼ cup olive oil
1 heaped tablespoon chopped garlic
2 teaspoons cumin seeds, toasted (see page 30)

8 sardines, scaled and gutted (see page 351)
Extra virgin olive oil
Coarse sea salt
About ½ teaspoon dried oregano (if not marinating the fish)
Lemon wedges

FOR THE MARINADE (OPTIONAL): Stir the oil, garlic, and cumin together in a dish large enough to hold the sardines in a single layer. Roll the sardines in the marinade, coating them, then cover with plastic and refrigerate for 3 to 4 hours.

Set a cast-iron griddle on the top oven rack and heat the broiler for at least 15 minutes.

When the griddle is searingly hot, remove the sardines from the marinade (if you haven't marinated them, rub the fish generously with olive oil and season with salt). Broil until the skin is blistered and browned and the tails are charred, about 4 minutes.

Drizzle the sardines with olive oil. Sprinkle on some salt and crumble on the oregano if you haven't marinated the sardines. The lemon wedges go on the plates. Serve while the sardines are nice and hot.

CITRUS BROILED SHRIMP

These are great on their own, but put out little bowls of melted butter for dipping if you want to go over the top. You'll get your fingers good and messy when you eat these shrimp, but it's so worth it.

I use this marinade for roast lobster too (page 210).   Serves 4

FOR THE MARINADE
Grated zest and juice of 3 oranges
Grated zest and juice of 1 grapefruit
½ cup olive oil
2 teaspoons fish sauce
2 shallots, minced
½ cup chopped fresh mint
½ teaspoon fresh thyme leaves

2 pounds extra-large (16–20 count)
    shrimp in the shell, deveined (see
    page 41)
Coarse salt
Melted butter for serving (optional)

FOR THE MARINADE: Whisk the zests and juices, olive oil, fish sauce, shallots, mint, and thyme together in a bowl.

Spread the shrimp out in a single layer in a baking dish. Pour in the marinade, cover with plastic wrap, and refrigerate for at least 4 hours, and up to 8 hours.

Set an oven rack in the top position and heat a cast-iron griddle under the broiler for at least 15 minutes.

Meanwhile, take the shrimp out of the marinade.

Put the shrimp in a single layer on the griddle pan and season them well with salt. Broil for 2½ minutes, or until barely cooked through.

Serve hot, with melted butter if you want.

GRILLING—STOVETOP AND OUTDOOR— AND SMOKING

JERK TUNA WITH MANGO SAUCE

Jamaican jerk seasoning may be traditional with chicken, but it's also a great way to spice up tuna. The colors and flavors of this dish will send you right to the beach.

I usually serve this with Coconut Rice with Carrots (page 468).   Serves 4

ACCEPT SUBSTITUTES

Yellowtail (hamachi) is an expensive alternative. Or try swordfish, for a change.

FOR THE MANGO SAUCE
1 ripe mango, peeled, pitted, and
   chopped
1 (1-inch) knob fresh ginger, peeled
   and grated
⅓ cup orange juice
Grated zest of ½ lemon
2 tablespoons fresh lemon juice, plus
   more if needed

4 (6-ounce) pieces tuna, about ½ inch
   thick
Coarse salt
4 teaspoons vegetable oil
4 teaspoons jerk seasoning (see Note)

FOR THE MANGO SAUCE: Combine all the ingredients in a food processor and process until smooth. Give the sauce a taste. It should be tangy, so add more lemon juice if you need it. This makes about 1½ cups.

Season the tuna with salt and rub each piece with 1 teaspoon of the oil. Rub ½ teaspoon of the jerk seasoning into each side of each piece.

Heat a Foreman grill (see page 136). Grill the tuna for 2 minutes for medium-rare. Or heat a grill pan over medium-high heat and grill the tuna for 1½ minutes on each side.

To serve, spoon the mango sauce onto dinner plates. Slice the tuna and fan the slices over the sauce.

NOTE: Jerk seasoning is available from Kalustyan's (www.kalustyans.com) and other online sources / specialty markets.

ABOUT STOVETOP GRILLING

Not all of us have a backyard or terrace and an outdoor grill that makes fish taste so good when you cook on it. Well, you can make do indoors with a stovetop grill.

These heavy, ridged cast-iron pans come in a variety of shapes, sizes, and prices, and all of them work equally well. Most affordable and useful are the reversible griddle/grills from Lodge, which are smooth on one side and ridged on the other and fit over two burners, but you'll also find pricier and prettier enameled grill pans in kitchenware stores. I leave the choice to you. The beauty of these pans is that you can get them blistering hot (unlike an electric grill).

The thing you need to keep in mind is that grilling is one smoky technique. A good hood over your stove will be more than helpful, and you should temporarily disable your smoke alarm.

TIPS FOR STOVETOP GRILLING

- Get the grill pan good and hot. The easiest way to do this is to put the pan in a 400-degree oven for about 20 minutes. Then transfer it to the stovetop. Or get it blistering hot over medium-high heat.

- There's no need to soak bamboo skewers when you grill indoors. You're just exposing them to heat, not flames.

- Let the fish tell you when it's ready to turn. Use my timing as a guide, but if the fish is sticking, wait. Forcing a spatula between fish and grill is only going to tear the fish.

- Marinades are most welcome.

GRILLED TUNA TACOS

Can I tell you these things rock? Meaty tuna gives the tacos the kind of kick you'd expect from skirt steak.

Makes 12 tacos

FOR THE CABBAGE

¾ pound napa or savoy cabbage, shredded

Juice of 1½ limes

Coarse salt

FOR THE RUB

1 tablespoon chili powder

2 teaspoons coriander seeds

¾ teaspoon cumin seeds

2 teaspoons vegetable oil

4 (5-ounce) pieces tuna, ¾ inch thick

Coarse salt

FOR SERVING

12 corn tortillas

Lime wedges

Ripe tomatoes, sliced into half-moons

Coarse sea salt

Guacamole (page 398)

Mango Salsa (page 394)

FOR THE CABBAGE: Combine the cabbage and lime juice in a mixing bowl. Salt it well and toss with your hands or a big spoon. Taste for salt. Cover with plastic wrap and refrigerate until you need it.

FOR THE RUB: Combine the chili powder, coriander seeds, and cumin seeds in a spice grinder. Process to a fine dust. Pour the rub out into a small bowl.

Heat up your Foreman grill or heat a cast-iron grill pan over medium-high heat.

Spoon the oil onto a plate and rub the fish in it, coating it on both sides. Season the fish on both sides with salt and the rub. Use all the rub, and work it into the fish.

THE LEAN MEAN GRILLING MACHINE

I'm not going to be the first guy to say this, but I wish I had invented the George Foreman Grill. It's incredibly convenient for cooking fish. These clamshell-shaped electric grills have a floating hinge that allows the top and bottom surfaces to maintain even contact with the fish, whatever its thickness. You don't get the char and caramelization that comes from grilling over charwood, but you never have the problem of sticking. And cleanup is a snap. You'll find that I use this grill in a lot of recipes.

Cook the fish for 2 minutes in the Foreman grill. If you're using a grill pan, grill for 1½ minutes per side. Put the fish on a cutting board and let it rest while you toast the tortillas.

Heat a heavy skillet over medium-high heat, or use the griddle you used for the tuna. Toast the tortillas until warmed through and browned in spots, about 30 seconds a side. Pile them in a cloth-lined basket as they're toasted.

To serve, cut the tuna into fingers and arrange on a platter with the lime wedges. Pile the cabbage in the center of another platter and surround with the sliced tomatoes. Season the tomatoes with salt.

Set the table with the guacamole and salsa, the basket of tortillas, the tuna and limes, and the cabbage and tomatoes, and let everyone dig in.

GRILLED SALMON

It doesn't get much simpler than this.

I'm giving you two sets of directions here: one for the grill pan and one for the broiler.   Serves 4

ACCEPT SUBSTITUTES

You won't find a fish that matches king salmon for flavor, but even with the salmon family, you have choices, and other options as well. What you should look for is a fillet that is about 1 inch thick, at its thickest. You'll need to adjust cooking times depending on the density and fat content of the fish.

Sockeye or coho salmon, char,
swordfish, mahi mahi, dorade

⅔ cup chopped fresh cilantro (no
   coarse stems)
¼ cup olive oil
4 (6-ounce) pieces skinless king
   salmon fillet
Coarse salt and freshly ground white
   pepper

FOR SERVING
4 handfuls arugula
1 tablespoon extra virgin olive oil
Coarse sea salt and freshly ground
   white pepper
Salsa Cruda (page 395)

Combine the cilantro and olive oil in a shallow dish large enough to hold the fillets in one layer. Add the fish and coat on both sides with the cilantro and oil. Refrigerate (covered or not) for at least an hour.

Heat a cast-iron grill pan over medium-high heat or heat a cast-iron griddle under the broiler, with the broiler rack 3 to 4 inches under the heating element.

Turn the fish again in the cilantro and oil and season on both sides with salt and white pepper.

TO COOK ON THE STOVETOP: Set the fillets on the grill pan—leave the rest of the cilantro and oil in the dish—and cook for 3 to 4 minutes per side, depending on the thickness of the fillets. Cooking a 1-inch piece for 3 minutes a side will result in perfect medium-rare salmon. You can stick the point of a knife into the center of the fish and peek: the center should look rare; residual heat will finish the cooking.

TO COOK UNDER THE BROILER: Set the fillets on the griddle and slide it back under the broiler. Broil for 3 to 4 minutes. Cooking a 1-inch piece for 3 minutes will result in perfect medium-rare salmon. You can stick the point of a knife into the center of the fish and peek: the center should look rare; residual heat will finish the cooking.

Either way, when the salmon is done, return it to the dish with the cilantro and oil and coat both sides.

To serve, toss the arugula with the extra virgin olive oil and season with sea salt and pepper. Divide the salad among four dinner plates, making a mound in the center of each plate. Lean a piece of fish against each salad and surround with the salsa cruda.

GRILLED TORO SALMON

Just as with any animal, the highest concentration of fat in a salmon is right around the belly, in that thin flap of flesh you see on a fillet. You'll hear about toro most often when you're ordering sushi or sashimi, when the word refers to tuna; I've just borrowed the name for this delicious salmon dish. Toro is extravagantly rich, the fish equivalent of foie gras, so I serve it as an appetizer with a little salad to cut the richness.

Unless you've made very good friends with your fishmonger, it's unlikely that you'll be able to buy this part of the salmon on its own. But you can certainly trim off the toro yourself when you buy a side of salmon for, say, gravlax (see pages 354 and 356). Or trim the belly off salmon steaks. Either way, leave the skin on.

I'm giving you proportions for 2 servings. You can double or triple this recipe at will.

Serves 2 as an appetizer

FOR THE SALAD
2 teaspoons minced shallot
½ teaspoon grated fresh ginger (use a
    Microplane)
1 tablespoon rice vinegar
1½ teaspoons soy sauce
2 tablespoons vegetable oil
Pinch of dried oregano
Pinch of sugar
2 handfuls sturdy greens, cut into
    wide strips (frisée, curly chicory,
    escarole, romaine, and even Belgian
    endive are great for this salad)
3–4 button or cremini mushrooms,
    cut into thin slices

FOR THE TORO
2 (3-ounce) pieces salmon belly (see
    page 38)
1 teaspoon grated fresh ginger
4 teaspoons soy sauce

- Clean the grate. The best method is to scrub it with a wire brush.

- Take the time you need to make sure the fire is very hot.

- Be aware that some "cold" spots are inevitable in your fire. Keep an eye out for them.

- Brush the grate with oil right before you put the fish on it. The best way to do this is to soak a paper towel with vegetable oil and use tongs to rub it on the grate. Bristles on basting brushes can melt.

- Timing can only be a guideline. Watch for cues as to how quickly your fish is cooking.

- Fish will tell you when it's ready to turn: you'll be able to slide the spatula under it easily. Don't force it. And remember that there's nothing wrong with grilling a piece of fish just about all the way through on one side and then turning and grilling it for just a flash on the second side.

- Two big spatulas can make it easier to turn a fillet or steak over. Press one of the spatulas on the top of the fish to hold it in place while you slide the other one underneath.

FOR THE SALAD: Whisk the shallot, ginger, vinegar, soy, and oil together in a small bowl. Crumble in the oregano, add the sugar, and whisk again. Let the dressing sit on the counter for at least 2 hours to give the oregano a chance to soften and mellow.

FOR THE TORO: Rub the salmon belly with the ginger and coat it on both sides with the soy. Refrigerate for 20 to 30 minutes.

Heat a Foreman grill (see page 136) or heat a cast-iron grill pan over high heat. Grill the salmon for about 4 minutes in the Foreman grill, until the skin is very crisp and the fish is cooked through. Or grill the salmon skin side down for 3 minutes on the grill pan, then turn and grill for 30 seconds.

To serve, toss the greens and mushrooms in the dressing and divide between two plates. Cut each serving of toro into 3 pieces and arrange, skin side up, on the salad.

VARIATION

If you've got an outdoor grill fired up, cook the toro there, with the rack as close to the coals as possible. Start with the skin side for 2 minutes, then turn and cook for 20 seconds.

GRILLED DORADE WITH HOISIN GLAZE

Simple pleasure here, and it's a very fast weeknight supper when you make this on a Foreman grill. The texture of dorade is firm and resilient, like a flatfish; it grills well.

Serves 4

ACCEPT SUBSTITUTES

Salmon, char, rainbow trout

4 (6- to 7-ounce) dorade fillets, skin on
Coarse salt and freshly ground white
  pepper

Olive oil
Hoisin Glaze (page 439)
Asian Slaw (page 453)

Season the fish with salt and white pepper and coat each fillet with oil. You can prep this well in advance and keep it cold in the refrigerator.

Grill the dorade on a Foreman grill for 3 to 4 minutes. Give the fish a poke — it will feel firm when it's cooked.

You can use a hot cast-iron grill pan too. Grill the fillets for 1½ minutes on the skin side, then turn and grill for another 1½ minutes or so.

Alternatively, prepare a grill. When the coals are hot, set the grate on the lowest level (closest to the coals) and get it very hot.

Brush the grate with vegetable oil. Grill the fillets for 1½ minutes on the skin side, then turn and grill for another 1 to 1½ minutes, until the fish feels firm.

When the fish is done, remove from the grill and brush the skin side with the glaze. Serve right away, with a side of slaw.

VARIATION

Skip the hoisin glaze and serve the fish on a bed of arugula tossed with olive oil and seasoned with salt and pepper. Surround with Simple Salsa (page 394).

SALMON STEAKS ON THE GRILL

The secret here, not that it's really a secret, is the dry rub.

These are big steaks, so I treat them as I would a whole fish on the grill—a bit farther away from the fire.

Serves 4

4 (1 pound) wild salmon steaks, tied
   (see page 38)
About 3 tablespoons Cajun Spice Mix
   (page 442) or Moroccan Spice Mix
   (page 440)
Vegetable oil

Rub the steaks with the spice mix of your choice and refrigerate for 2 hours.

Prepare a grill. When the coals are hot, set the grate about 4 inches above the fire and get it very hot. When the grate is ready, brush it with oil.

Brush the steaks with oil and grill for 5 minutes on the first side to get a great browned crust, then turn with a big metal spatula and grill for about another 5 minutes for medium-rare.

Let the steaks sit for a few minutes, then cut off the string and pull off the skin (you haven't actually grilled it, so it will be pretty flabby). Take the salmon off the bone and put it on a platter, or divide it among four plates.

Let me begin by saying that the grill I prefer for fish is one that will burn hardwood charcoal. It gives you superior flavor, and it generates the amount of heat you need to cook fish. High heat is one of those little tricks that will help prevent fish from sticking, and I don't think that gas grills ever get hot enough. Gas can be fine when you're grilling meat and chicken; they will be spending more time on the grill, and you want to be able to cook chicken all the way through without burning it. But for fish, go with charcoal.

That doesn't mean you need one of those top-of-the-line grills with bells and whistles. I got my grill at the grocery store. It's one of those inexpensive, lightweight kettle types, and it works just fine, thank you.

THE CHARCOAL

Hardwood charcoal, often called lump charcoal or charwood, is the way to go. Briquettes start out as sawdust, and they don't generate the heat that hardwood does. I buy mine at the grocery store.

The only time you need wood chips is when you're smoking fish (see pages 182–184). There are a couple of reasons for this. First, fish cooks very quickly, so there really isn't enough time for the smoke to impart any flavor. Second, because the fish is cooked so fast, you really shouldn't cover the grill—you'll have to monitor what you're cooking—and without the cover, you're just putting smoke in the air. And third, you'll see that I'm a fan of marinades and rubs and "lubricants" like spicy mayonnaise for fish on the grill; those are the flavors I want to come through and combine with the caramelization you get from grilling. When I'm smoking fish, I like the flavor imparted by fruit-wood chips, particularly cherry.

LIGHTING THE GRILL

Use a chimney starter, and please don't use lighter fluid, unless you want your fish to taste like gasoline. Stuff the bottom of the starter with a couple of pieces of crumpled newspaper. Fill the starter with hardwood charcoal and set it in the grill (have the grate to the side). Light the newspaper. Now you can just leave it alone until the coals at the top of the starter are covered with light gray ash. Lift up the starter and dump the hot coals onto half of the grill. Pile on some more charcoal to bring the level up to about 1 inch from the grate and set the grate on the grill. Once the second batch of charcoal is covered with ash, the grate should be really hot, and you'll be ready for grilling.

To test, hold your hand 5 inches above the grate. If you can keep it there for only 1 to 2 seconds, you have a hot fire.

REGULATING THE FIRE

You will be able to grill all the recipes in this chapter using just this setup. But if you are planning on doing a lot of grilling and you want to crank it all out quickly, I advise setting up the chimney starter again. Place it on a heavy rack, so the air can circulate, on a baking sheet, light it, and you'll have hot coals ready when you need them. Otherwise, as the fire starts to die down, add more charcoal and wait until it is covered with ash, then give the fire the 5-inches test.

Chicken-Fried Trout with Green Tartar Sauce and Asian Slaw (pages 272, 453, and 471).

Opposite: Clams and Chorizo (page 283). *Above:* Louis Salad (page 339).

Top: Oyster Shooters (page 279).
Above: Pineapple-Carrot Ceviche with Sea
Scallops (page 348). *Opposite:* Fennel-Onion
Gravlax with Orange Cream (page 356).

Opposite: Turbot Poached in Milk, with Noodles and Mustard Butter Sauce (page 88). *Above:* Grilled Shrimp with Charred Pineapple and Mango Salsa (pages 172 and 396). *Left:* Jumbo Lump Crab Cake (page 370).

Opposite: Bay Scallop Hush Puppies and Green Tartar Sauce (pages 260 and 417). *Above:* Chicken-Fried Soft-Shell Crab BLT (page 273).

Left: Lobster Fra Diavolo (page 379).
Above: Shrimp Risotto (page 387).

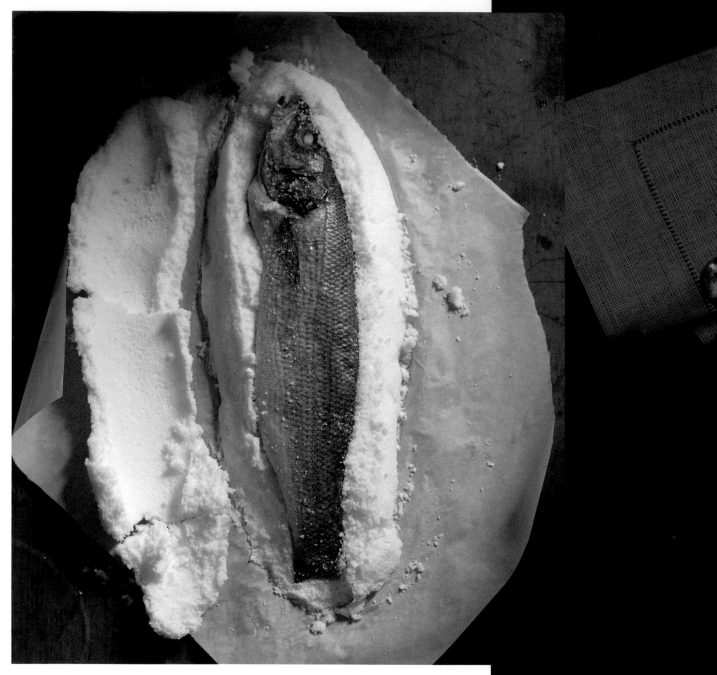

Above and right: Whole Branzino Roasted in Salt (page 189).

Opposite: Stovetop Clambake (page 110). *Above:* Catfish Sloppy Joe (page 373).
Following page: Dungeness Crab Boil (page 116).

RÉMOULADE SALMON ON THE GRILL

Mayonnaise is one of those traditional lubricants for fish on the grill. The fat in the mayo helps the fish keep from sticking, and it flavors the fish too. The mayonnaise base in this rémoulade makes it great for skinless fillets that might stick, and the sauce packs much more flavor than plain mayo.   Serves 4

ACCEPT SUBSTITUTES

Char, swordfish, rainbow trout

4 (6- to 7-ounce) pieces skinless wild
   salmon fillet
Coarse salt and freshly ground white
   pepper

Spicy Rémoulade (page 416)

Season the fish with salt and white pepper and coat each fillet evenly with some of the rémoulade. You can prep this well in advance and keep it cold in the refrigerator.

Prepare a grill. When the coals are hot, set the grate on the lowest level (closest to the coals) and get it very hot. Brush the grate with vegetable oil.

Grill the salmon for 4½ minutes on the skinned side, then turn and grill for another 2 minutes for medium-rare.

Pass the remaining rémoulade with the salmon.

TANDOORI SALMON ON THE GRILL

Grilling caramelizes the tandoori paste and that, combined with the smoke, makes this a killer dish. The creamy cucumber flavor of tzatziki is a great foil for tandoori, but so is the bright acidity of a cucumber salad or Asian slaw. *Serves 4*

ACCEPT SUBSTITUTES
Char, swordfish, rainbow trout

½ cup tandoori paste (see Note)
2 tablespoons plain yogurt
1 tablespoon unsalted butter, melted
4 (6- to 7-ounce) pieces wild salmon
   fillet (skin on or off)

Coarse salt
Tzatziki (page 399), Asian Slaw (page
   453), or Mom's Cucumber Salad
   (page 459)

Combine the tandoori paste, yogurt, and butter in a small bowl. Slather the fish with the paste, pack it into a sealable plastic bag, and refrigerate for 1 to 4 hours.

Prepare a grill. When the coals are hot, set the grate on the lowest level (closest to the coals) and get it very hot.

Wipe some of the tandoori paste from the fish, leaving just a light coating. Season lightly with salt.

Brush the grate with vegetable oil and set the fish on it, skin side down. Grill for about 2 minutes, until browned, then turn and grill for another minute for medium-rare.

Transfer the fish to a platter and let it rest for a few minutes before serving with the accompaniment of your choice.

NOTE: Commercial tandoori pastes are available in better grocery stores and specialty markets, and they vary in quality and flavor. My favorite is Bombay brand. You can also get it online from www.bombaybrand.com (it is listed as Tandoori BBQ/Grilling Paste). I've also used Patak's Spicy Ginger and Garlic Marinade and Grill Sauce, which is available from Kalustyan's (www.kalustyans.com).

Check the ingredients on whichever paste you use. If tamarind is one of the main ingredients, don't marinate the fish for longer than 1 hour.

GRILLED SWORDFISH WITH HOISIN GLAZE

The sweet earthiness of hoisin plays off the meatiness of swordfish.   Serves 4

ACCEPT SUBSTITUTES

Try this with any fish you can grill, like salmon, char, or mahi mahi.

4 (7-ounce) pieces swordfish
Coarse salt and freshly ground white
  pepper
Vegetable oil
Basic Bok Choy (page 451)

Hoisin Glaze (page 439)
Coconut and Green Curry Sauce
  (page 431) or Wasabi Butter
  Sauce (page 406)

Prepare an outdoor grill or heat a cast-iron grill pan. If using a grill, when the coals are hot, set the grate on the lowest level (closest to the coals) and get it very hot. Brush the grate with oil.

Season the fish with salt and white pepper and coat it well on both sides with oil. Grill for 5 minutes, then turn and grill for about 1 minute, until barely cooked through.

Divide the bok choy among four dinner plates. Set the fish on the bok choy, then spoon on the glaze, spreading it over the fish with the back of a spoon. Surround with the sauce and serve while it's hot.

GRILLED SALMON PAILLARDS

The fish is cooked very simply—just salt and pepper and some oil to make sure it doesn't stick—so you'll want a sauce or salad to accompany it. I'm giving you some possible combinations, but you can also come up with your own. This is a great lunch dish.

If the word "paillard" throws you, just think of this dish as grilled salmon cutlets.

Serves 4

1 (1¼- to 1½-pound) piece skinless
    wild salmon fillet, cut into paillards
    (see page 38)
Coarse salt and freshly ground white
    pepper

Olive oil
Red Wine Butter Sauce (page 407)

Season the fish with salt and white pepper and coat on both sides with olive oil.

Heat a cast-iron grill pan.

Grill the salmon for about 1 minute. Turn with a spatula and grill for another 30 seconds for rare.

Sprinkle the fish with some more salt and serve with a puddle of the sauce on each plate.

VARIATIONS

GRILLED MAHI MAHI PAILLARDS

Mahi grills beautifully. Cook for 1 minute on each side and serve with a squirt of lemon juice and a drizzle of your best extra virgin olive oil or with Garlic Butter Sauce (page 405).

GRILLED STURGEON PAILLARDS

The texture of sturgeon sliced and grilled is extraordinary, like the best veal cutlet you ever ate. Grill for 1 minute on each side and serve with some American paddlefish caviar or with Mustard Butter Sauce (page 406).

ABOUT GRILLING FISH PAILLARDS

Paillards, thin slices of fish cut on an angle, cook in a flash on a cast-iron grill pan. And when you cook so quickly, you get the true flavor of the fish.

The best fish for grilling this way are the meatier ones, salmon and mahi mahi and sturgeon, for example, which are sturdy enough to hold together when sliced thin. You would think tuna would be a prime candidate, but actually it dries out too quickly. Flatfish like flounder and more delicate fillets like tilefish just fall apart.

Let's face it, though: sometimes fish sticks to the pan. Here are a couple of tips that will help guarantee success.

- Make sure the fish is well coated with oil. Not swimming in it, but glistening all over.

- Make sure the grill pan is properly heated; it should be just about smoking.

- Don't force matters. The fish will release itself when the first side is cooked. If that means you are cooking the paillards for 1½ minutes on the first side and then just 30 seconds on the second, fine. When you serve, just make sure you have the side with the nice grill marks facing up.

I recommend a grill pan for paillards because you have more control, but you can certainly grill them outdoors. Follow the guidelines for setting up the grill (the grate as close to the coals as possible — you should be able to hold your hand 5 inches over the coals for barely 3 seconds — and the grate should be well oiled). On the outdoor grill, cook the paillards almost all the way through on the first side. Then turn the fish and leave it for just 5 seconds.

You'll find instructions for cutting fish paillards on page 38. Cutting the fish this way should give you slices that weigh about 2 ounces each, so plan on 3 or 4 slices per serving. Or ask your fish person to slice the fillets scaloppine-style.

TUNA BROCHETTES
WITH PROVENÇAL MARINADE

With flavors like garlic and anchovies in the marinade, you can't go wrong.
Soak the skewers in water for 20 minutes if you're grilling outdoors.   Serves 4

ACCEPT SUBSTITUTES

Shrimp and sea scallops are prime candidates for brochettes,
and they both work very well with this marinade.

24 extra-large (16–20 count) shrimp will serve 4.
Shell them, but leave the tails on; grill for 2 minutes per side.

24 sea scallops (1¼ to 1½ pounds) will serve 4.
Grill for 2 minutes per side.

Swordfish takes nicely to this marinade too
(ask for a belly cut); grill 2 minutes per side on all
four sides, for a total of 8 minutes.

FOR THE MARINADE
8 garlic cloves, cut into thin slices or
    put through a press
8 anchovy fillets
2 teaspoons fresh thyme leaves
1 teaspoon crushed red pepper
½ cup olive oil

1¾ pounds tuna, 1½ inches thick

FOR SERVING (PICK YOUR FAVORITE)
Wasabi Butter Sauce (page 406),
Garlic Butter Sauce (page 405), or
Bacon Vinaigrette (page 433)

FOR THE MARINADE: Mash the garlic, anchovies, and thyme together into a paste. You can do this in a small bowl with a fork, but it's easier in a mortar. Stir in the crushed red pepper and oil.

Cut the tuna into 1½-inch cubes. Divide into 4 portions and double-skewer them (see opposite page) on bamboo skewers.

Scrape the marinade into a baking dish or plastic container that will hold the skewers. Add the skewers, rolling them to coat the tuna with the marinade. Cover with plastic and marinate in the refrigerator for at least 2 hours and up to 6 hours.

Heat a grill pan or prepare an outdoor grill. If using a grill, when the coals are hot, set the grate on the lowest level (closest to the coals) and get it very hot, then brush the grate with vegetable oil.

Brush the solids off the fish and grill for about 45 seconds per side to sear it on all four sides. I like grilled tuna rare and tender.

Serve — on or off the skewers — with the sauce of your choice.

DOUBLE-SKEWERING BROCHETTES

Using two skewers for each one when you're making brochettes pretty much guarantees that the cubes of fish — or the shrimp or the scallops — won't rotate on the skewer when you turn them on the grill.

I find the easiest way to do this is to lay out one portion on the work surface and slide in the first skewer, off center, then slide in the second skewer, leaving a little space between them.

SWORDFISH BROCHETTES WITH ORANGE-CHIPOTLE MARINADE

The smoky heat of the chipotles accents the flavor you get from grilling, and it's nicely balanced by the acidity of the oranges. (The photo is on page 208.)

Serves 4

ACCEPT SUBSTITUTES

Shrimp and sea scallops are prime candidates for brochettes,
and they both work very well with this marinade.

24 extra-large (16–20 count) shrimp will serve 4.
Shell them, but leave the tails on. Grill for 2 minutes per side.

24 sea scallops (1¼ to 1½ pounds) will serve 4.
Grill for 2 minutes per side. These are terrific served with
Tomatillo and Poblano Sauce (page 426).

FOR THE MARINADE
2 oranges
Grated zest of 1 lemon
2 chipotles in adobo, minced
¼ cup olive oil

FOR THE BROCHETTES
1¾ pounds swordfish steak (ask for
 the belly cut), 1½ inches thick

FOR SERVING (PICK YOUR FAVORITE)
Wasabi Butter Sauce (page 406),
Garlic Butter Sauce (page 405), or
Bacon Vinaigrette (page 433)

FOR THE MARINADE: Grate the zest from the oranges and squeeze the juice. Measure out ½ cup orange juice for the marinade and drink the rest.

Combine the orange zest and juice, lemon zest, chipotles, and olive oil in a baking dish or plastic container that will hold the skewers. Whisk to combine.

Cut the swordfish into 1½-inch cubes. Divide into 4 portions and double-skewer them (see page 167) on bamboo skewers.

Add the skewers to the baking dish, rolling them to coat with the marinade. Make sure you've got minced chipotles on all sides. Cover with plastic and marinate in the refrigerator for at least 2 hours and up to 4 hours.

Heat a grill pan or prepare an outdoor grill. If using a grill, when the coals are hot, set the grate on the lowest level (closest to the coals) and get it very hot, then brush the grate with vegetable oil.

Grill the fish for 2 minutes per side on all four sides, for a total of 8 minutes.

Serve with the sauce of your choice.

GRILLED SQUID

At its best, grilled squid is tender and sweet, and almost creamy inside. The secret to keeping it tender is cutting off the tip of the body. That way you won't have any steam buildup, which would toughen the squid.

You can prepare the squid inside in a cast-iron grill pan or fire up your outdoor grill. (The photo is on page 204.)   Serves 4 as an appetizer

About 1½ pounds cleaned squid (see page 43)

Coarse salt and freshly ground white pepper

Olive oil

Chopped fresh parsley

Garlic Butter Sauce (page 405) or Asian "Vinaigrette" (page 432)

Heat a cast-iron grill pan to almost smoking or fire up an outdoor grill. If using a grill, when the coals are hot, set the grate on the lowest level (closest to the coals) and get it very hot, then brush the grate with vegetable oil.

Meanwhile, cut the tips from the squid bodies and discard. Dry the squid well with paper towels. Season the squid lightly with salt and white pepper. Drizzle with a little olive oil and toss to coat the squid.

Start by grilling the tentacles (which will take the longest) and the biggest squid bodies. Then add the smaller bodies. Press down on them with the back of a spatula to get good grill marks, then turn the pieces over. The squid bodies will seem to inflate and turn milky white and opaque as it cooks.

If you are grilling indoors, total grilling time for the bodies will be about 90 seconds; the tentacles may take up to 2 minutes. If you are grilling outdoors, total time for the bodies will be about 75 seconds; the tentacles will take about 1½ minutes.

Shower the squid with chopped parsley and serve with a bowl of the garlic butter sauce or the vinaigrette for dipping.

SEA SCALLOPS WITH JALAPEÑO-GRAPEFRUIT MARINADE

This tart marinade, which has a nice hit of heat, brings out the sweetness of the scallops (or shrimp).   Serves 4 (8 as an appetizer)

ACCEPT SUBSTITUTES

This is terrific with head-on shrimp. You'll need 16 to serve 4.
Leave the heads on and shell the bodies; leave the tails on. Cook for 2 minutes
on the first side and 1½ to 2 minutes on the second side.

Grated zest of 1 grapefruit

Juice of 2 grapefruits (about 1⅓ cups, and pulp is fine)

¼ cup minced jalapeño chiles (with seeds)

¼ cup chopped fresh cilantro

¼ cup chopped scallions

⅓ cup dry vermouth

3 tablespoons olive oil, plus more for brushing

16 large sea scallops, tough bits removed

Coarse salt and freshly ground white pepper

Soak 8 bamboo skewers in water for 20 minutes or so.

Stir the grapefruit zest and juice together with the jalapeños, cilantro, scallions, vermouth, and olive oil in a baking dish or plastic container that will hold the skewered scallops.

Double-skewer the scallops (see page 167), 4 scallops per serving. Immerse them in the marinade, cover, and refrigerate for 1 hour.

Prepare a grill. When the coals are hot, set the grate on the lowest level (closest to the coals) and get it very hot.

Meanwhile, take the scallops out of the marinade. Season them with salt and white pepper and brush them with vegetable oil.

Brush the grate with vegetable oil. Grill the scallops for 3 minutes per side. Scallops are like little sponges—they soak up the marinade, which will slow down the cooking. Don't expect these to get very brown, though you should have grill marks.

Serve on or off the skewers.

GRILLED SHRIMP

A combination of blue and white tortilla chips makes this presentation even prettier. (The photo is on page 151.) Serves 6 as an appetizer

(The photo is on page 151.)

ACCEPT SUBSTITUTES

I like head-on shrimp best on the grill, but you can certainly use other jumbo shrimp. You should double-skewer headless shrimp, though (see page 167).

1 garlic clove, finely chopped
1 teaspoon chopped fresh thyme
2 teaspoons extra virgin olive oil
12 head-on shrimp
Coarse salt and freshly ground white
   pepper

Charred Pineapple and Mango Salsa
   (page 396)
Tortilla chips

Combine the garlic, thyme, and olive oil in a stainless steel or glass bowl large enough to hold the shrimp. Shell the shrimp, leaving the heads and tails on. Pat the shrimp dry on paper towels, add to the bowl, and toss to coat. Season with salt and white pepper and toss again. Cover with plastic and refrigerate for at least 1 hour and up to 24 hours.

Prepare a grill. When the coals are hot, set the grate on the lowest level (closest to the coals) and get it very hot.

Remove the shrimp from the marinade and season on both sides with salt.

Brush the grate with vegetable oil. Grill the shrimp for about 1½ minutes on each side, until the shells turn pink and the fat part of the shrimp is white.

To serve, divide the salsa evenly among six plates, mounding it in the center of the plates. Make sure to spoon on some of the juices. Lean 2 grilled shrimp into each mound of salsa and surround with tortilla chips.

ABOUT HEAD-ON SHRIMP

Cooking shrimp with the heads on is like cooking fish on the bone: you get a lot more flavor and richness in the finished dish.

Head-on shrimp can be difficult to find, and usually when you find them, they're frozen. Don't be put off by that icy block of shrimp, though; shrimp do freeze well. You can get fresh, never-been-frozen, head-on wild shrimp from Louisiana from Farm-2-Market (see page 477).

If you need a substitute for head-on shrimp for the recipes in this chapter, go for jumbos (11–15 count) and leave the tails on when you shell them.

GRILLED SHRIMP WITH CHILI-CUMIN MARINADE

I'm going for smoky and delicious Southwestern flavors here. If you can, get head-on shrimp and grill them outdoors.   Serves 4 (6 as an appetizer)

ACCEPT SUBSTITUTES

Tuna and sturgeon, cut into cubes for brochettes;
both work great with this marinade.

FOR THE MARINADE
1 tablespoon chili powder
2 teaspoons cumin seeds, toasted and
  ground
¼ cup minced onion
2 teaspoons chopped garlic
2 tablespoons fresh lime juice
3 tablespoons vegetable oil

1½ pounds extra-large (16–20 count)
  shrimp, shelled, with the tails left on
Coarse salt and freshly ground white
  pepper
Charred Pineapple and Mango Salsa
  (page 396)

FOR THE MARINADE: Combine the chili powder, cumin, onion, garlic, lime juice, and oil in an 8-inch square baking dish (or something similar). Stir well. The marinade will look like a wet tapenade.

Divide the shrimp into 4 portions and double-skewer them (see page 167) on bamboo skewers. Season with salt and white pepper. Add the shrimp to the marinade, turning them so they're well coated. Cover with plastic and refrigerate for 2 to 4 hours.

Prepare an outdoor grill or heat a cast-iron grill pan. If using a grill, when the coals are hot, set the grate on the lowest level (closest to the coals) and get it very hot, then brush the grate with vegetable oil.

Grill the shrimp for 1½ to 2 minutes per side; if you want to check, the thickest part of the shrimp should be slightly translucent in the center.

Serve with the salsa.

BARBECUE SHRIMP ON THE GRILL

Get ready to lick your fingers!   Serves 6 as an appetizer

ACCEPT SUBSTITUTES
I like head-on shrimp best on the grill, but you can
certainly substitute jumbo shrimp. Or make brochettes with swordfish
or salmon (from steaks).

24 head-on shrimp
Barbecue Sauce for Fish (page 437)

Shell the shrimp but leave the heads and tails on. Double-skewer the shrimp (see page
167), 4 to a serving. Put the skewers in a baking dish or plastic container large enough
to hold the skewers and pour in the barbecue sauce. Get your hands in and make sure
all the shrimp are covered with sauce. Cover and refrigerate for at least 1 hour and up
to 4 hours.

Prepare a grill. When the coals are hot, set the grate on the lowest level (closest to the
coals) and get it very hot.

Brush the grate with vegetable oil. Grill the shrimp for about 1½ minutes per side.
The shells should be pink, and the flesh should feel firm.

Serve on the skewers or not.

CAJUN SHRIMP ON THE GRILL

The rub makes these shrimp good and spicy. Bring out some Sweet Pickle Relish Sauce (page 418) for dipping, or serve with Potato Salad Louis (page 466). You want something creamy for balance.   Serves 6 as an appetizer

ACCEPT SUBSTITUTES

I like head-on shrimp best on the grill, but you can certainly substitute jumbo shrimp.

24 head-on shrimp
½ cup Cajun Spice Mix (page 442)
Vegetable oil

Shell the shrimp but leave the heads and tails on. Double-skewer the shrimp (see page 167), 4 to a serving. Put the skewers in a baking dish or plastic container. Sprinkle on the spice mix, rubbing it all over the shrimp. Cover and refrigerate for 2 hours.

Prepare a grill. When the coals are hot, set the grate on the lowest level (closest to the coals) and get it very hot.

Brush the grate with vegetable oil. Brush the shrimp with oil and grill for about 2 minutes per side. The shells should be pink, and the flesh should feel firm.

Serve on the skewers or not.

GRILLED CLAMS AND OYSTERS

Don't forget these bivalves when you've got the grill going. It's a great way to start a meal, and it couldn't be easier to grill them.

Scrub the clams or oysters and set them on the grill until they pop open. That's it!

Serve with a spicy salsa or one of the compound butters on pages 409–413.

EASY BRANZINO ON THE GRILL

The spicy mayonnaise is playing two roles here. It flavors the fish, and it's also a great lubricant for thin fillets and helps prevent them from sticking to the grill.

Serves 4

ACCEPT SUBSTITUTES

Dorade is fine, and so is mackerel. You can also try salmon and char, but these thicker fillets will need longer grilling.

4 (6- to 7-ounce) branzino fillets, skin on

Coarse salt and freshly ground white pepper

Spicy Mayonnaise (page 415)

Season the fish with salt and white pepper and coat evenly with some of the mayonnaise. You can prep this well in advance and keep it cold in the refrigerator.

Prepare a grill. When the coals are hot, set the grate on the lowest level (closest to the coals) and get it very hot.

Brush the grate with vegetable oil. Grill the fillets for 2 minutes on the skin side, then turn and grill for about another 1½ minutes. If you're unsure about doneness, turn the fillet over and poke inside. It should be just opaque in the center.

Serve the remaining mayo with the fish.

WHOLE DORADE ON THE GRILL

Dorade is a great fish for the simplest of grilling preparations—just some oil, salt, and pepper. Using a basket makes turning the fish and taking it off the grill a snap. This tastes great with the red pepper coulis, but you could just as easily serve it with a squirt of lemon and a drizzle of olive oil. Serves 3

ACCEPT SUBSTITUTES

Black sea bass
Striped bass
Branzino
Barramundi

3 whole dorade (each about 1¼ pounds), scaled and gutted, gills and fins removed

Coarse salt and freshly ground white pepper
Olive oil
Red Pepper Coulis (page 427)

Season the fish inside and out with salt and white pepper and rub it all over with oil.

Prepare a grill. When the coals are hot, set the grate on the lowest level (closest to the coals) and get it very hot. (These are small fish, so I'm making an exception to my usual advice to keep whole fish farther away from the fire.)

Brush a fish basket with olive oil and pack the dorade into it. Grill the fish for 3 minutes, then brush the tops with oil and turn the basket over. Grill for another 3 minutes. Brush once more with oil, turn, and grill for about 1 minute. The skin should be crackling and browned. To test, insert a thin knife or a metal skewer into the thickest part of the fish and leave it for 30 seconds or so. When you remove it, the tip should feel pretty warm on the inside of your wrist.

Let the fish rest for a few minutes before you fillet it. Serve with the coulis.

With all the variables involved—from the kind of grill you're using to the material the grate is made of (heavy cast iron or lightweight steel) to the air supply that will feed your fire—grilling is an advanced technique. Put a whole fish on the fire, and you're adding more variables.

I look on it as a challenge—me against the apparatus—and it's the kind of challenge I live for. Friends have described me as some kind of dervish at the grill. Maybe I don't whirl, but I do move around the grill a lot, checking the fire, fanning the fire, tending to the fish. I always get in close, and sometimes I end up sizzling the hair on my arms. It's exhilarating. But this kind of cooking comes only with practice, so here are a few tips.

- Don't smother the fire. Keeping the grate about 4 inches from the fire allows air to circulate and feed the fire.

- Use a grill basket. This is the best friend you can have when you're grilling a whole fish. The basket keeps the fish intact when you turn it, so you don't have to juggle with a couple of big spatulas. And it makes the task of getting a delicate cooked fish off the grill and onto a platter much easier. Take the top off the basket, put the platter over the fish, and, holding the platter and the bottom of the basket, flip the fish out, as if you were turning a cake out of a pan.

- Oil the basket and lubricate the fish well before grilling. The simplest way is to brush the fish with olive or vegetable oil, but mayonnaise-based sauces flavor the fish as they keep it from sticking.

- Until you've got experience with the grill, stick with smaller (under 2½ pounds) fish, which will fit in a basket. Once you move to larger fish, make sure you've got two large, heavy spatulas. You'll need them both to roll the fish over on the grill to cook the second side and to support it when you take it off the grill.

IDEAS FOR IMPROVISATION

- Spice rubs—like the Moroccan Spice Mix (page 440) and Cajun Spice Mix (page 442)—add a nice layer of flavor. Make a few slits just through the skin of the fish, rub the spices all over the fish, and marinate for at least 1 hour. Oil the fish well before grilling.

- Mayonnaise is a classic lubricant. I've got friends on Martha's Vineyard who slather a bluefish they've just pulled out of the ocean with mayo and slap it on the grill until it's crusty and browned. Sauces like Spicy Mayonnaise (page 415) and Spicy Rémoulade (page 416) throw some more interesting flavors into the mix.

- A bed of herbs will perfume fish when you grill it. Try grilling mackerel on a bed of rosemary or try branzino or striped bass on dill.

- Wrappings—grape leaves, for example, or banana leaves—show up on the grill in more than a few cuisines. And there are plenty of folks out there who wrap a fish in foil before they grill it. Since these wrappings trap the moisture in the fish, you're really steaming the fish more than grilling it. If you want to go this route, I suggest slathering the fish before you wrap it with something moist and flavorful—Charmoula (page 438) is great, and so is Arugula Pesto (page 423) or Cilantro Aïoli (page 419).

WHOLE BRANZINO WITH CHARMOULA ON THE GRILL

Plan ahead so the fish will have plenty of time to marinate in the spice paste.

Serves 4

ACCEPT SUBSTITUTES

Little black sea bass is nice, and so is mackerel or barramundi.

2 whole branzino (each about Charmoula (page 438)
   2 pounds), scaled and gutted, gills
   and fins removed

Trim the tails with scissors (they'll just burn on the grill).

Make several shallow cuts through the skin on both sides of the fish. Put the fish in a large glass baking dish and slather them liberally with the charmoula. Pack the rest of the charmoula into the cavities. Let the fish marinate in the refrigerator for at least 5 hours and up to 8 hours.

Prepare a grill. When the coals are hot, set the grate about 4 inches above the fire and get it very hot.

Brush a fish basket with oil and pack the fish into it. Grill for 5 minutes, then turn and grill for another 5 minutes. Insert a thin knife or a metal skewer into the thickest part of the fish and leave it for 30 seconds or so. When you remove it, the tip should feel pretty warm on the inside of your wrist. If not, grill for another minute.

Let the fish rest for 10 minutes before you fillet and serve it.

A BIG WHOLE STRIPED BASS
(OR OTHER FISH) ON THE GRILL

Farmed striped bass is another fish that shines with even the simplest of preparations. This fish may be a little bigger than the bass you will usually find in the fish market, but it will give you an idea of timing when you experiment with bigger fish.

Serves 4

ACCEPT SUBSTITUTES
Char, smaller salmon, bluefish — all would be fine.

1 whole striped bass (about 3¾ pounds), scaled and gutted, gills and fins removed

Coarse salt and freshly ground white pepper
Olive oil
Simple Salsa (page 394)

Trim the tail with scissors (it'll just burn on the grill). Season the fish with salt and white pepper and brush it liberally with oil.

Prepare a grill. When the coals are hot, set the grate about 4 inches above the fire and get it very hot.

Brush the grate with oil. Grill the bass for 7 minutes. Slide two big metal spatulas under the fish to make sure it isn't sticking anywhere, and then roll the fish over. (If you need to, move it back over the hottest part of the fire.) Grill for another 7 minutes. Insert a thin knife or a metal skewer into the thickest part of the fish and leave it for 30 seconds or so. When you remove it, the tip should feel pretty warm on the inside of your wrist. If not, grill for another minute.

Let the fish rest for 10 minutes before you fillet it. Serve with the salsa.

GRILLED LOUP DE MER WITH FENNEL

Loup de mer, or "wolf of the sea," is the French name for branzino, and I couldn't resist using it for this dish with decidedly Provençal flavors.   Serves 4

ACCEPT SUBSTITUTES

Dorade works well with these flavors.

2 whole branzino (each about
   1½ pounds), scaled and gutted,
   gills and fins removed
Coarse salt and freshly ground white
   pepper

2 teaspoons minced garlic
1 large fennel bulb with long stalks
¼ cup Pernod
3 tablespoons olive oil, plus additional
   for the fennel

Trim the tails of the fish with scissors (they'll just burn on the grill). Make 3 shallow cuts on each side of each fish. Season the cavities with salt and white pepper and rub with the garlic.

Cut the stalks from the fennel bulb. Chop 1 stalk, and stuff it into the cavities of the fish. Cut the remaining stalks in half, then into thin strips. Slice the bulb lengthwise into ⅓-inch-thick slices. Save these for later.

Put the fish in a baking dish and season the outside with salt and white pepper. Pour in the Pernod and drizzle on the oil. Turn the fish in the marinade, cover with plastic, and refrigerate for about 4 hours, turning the fish once or twice.

Prepare a grill. When the coals are hot, set the grate about 4 inches above the fire and get it very hot.

Toss the reserved fennel stalks with some oil and use half to make a bed in a fish basket. Set the fish on top and cover with the rest of the stalks. Put the basket top on.

Grill the fish for 5 minutes, then turn and grill for another 5 minutes. Insert a thin knife or a metal skewer into the thickest part of the fish and leave it for 30 seconds or so. When you remove it, the tip should feel pretty warm on the inside of your wrist. If not, grill for another minute. Let the fish rest for 10 minutes.

Meanwhile, brush the sliced fennel with oil and season it with salt. Grill it for about 6 minutes per side.

Fillet the fish and serve it with the grilled fennel.

SMOKED TROUT

I don't think there's anything that can compare to the flavor and succulence of warm home-smoked trout.   Serves 6 (12 as an appetizer)

ACCEPT SUBSTITUTES

Make this with any trout — even rainbow.

FOR THE MARINADE
4 cups water
1 cup sliced shallots
5 garlic cloves, minced
¼ cup coarse salt
2 tablespoons sugar
¼ cup chopped fresh dill
2 tablespoons coriander seeds, toasted
   and cracked
Grated zest of 2 lemons

6 (12-ounce) boned and butterflied
   whole trout (head on)
Cherry wood chips
Vegetable oil

FOR SERVING
Horseradish Cream (page 420)
Mom's Cucumber Salad (page 459)
Carrot Slaw (page 454)

FOR THE MARINADE: Mix the water, shallots, garlic, salt, sugar, dill, coriander, and lemon zest in a bowl, stirring until the salt and sugar dissolve. If you have the time, let the marinade sit at room temperature for 1 to 2 hours.

Lay 3 of the trout, skin side down and opened up, in a 9-x-12-inch baking dish. Pour in half the marinade. Lay the remaining trout, skin side up this time and opened up, on top and pour in the rest of the marinade. Cover with plastic and refrigerate for 4 hours.

Prepare a grill. Soak a few handfuls of cherry chips in water while the coals heat.

Remove the trout from the marinade and pat dry. Close each fish back up, like a book, and brush the skin with vegetable oil.

When the coals are hot, bank them in one half of the grill. Open the vent(s) in the bottom of the grill. Put the chips on the glowing coals, place the grate over the coals, and set the fish on the cool side of the grate (not over the coals). Put the cover on the grill, vents closed to trap the smoke, and smoke the trout for 15 minutes. It won't hurt if you bend down and blow into the lower vent, or fan it some, to increase the smoke. The fish should be opaque throughout when it is done.

Take the trout off the grill, open them up again, and lay them skin side up on a board. Lift off the skin. Discard the skin and heads and serve right away, with the horseradish cream and the salads.

ADVANCE PREPARATION

I think these taste best right off the grill, but there's no reason you can't double the recipe and have more trout in the refrigerator for another day.

When you take the trout off the grill, open them and lift off the skin, but don't remove it completely — lay it back over the trout (it keeps the fish moist). Set the trout on a parchment-lined baking sheet. Let cool, then cover and refrigerate.

When you're ready to serve, wash 5 or 6 leaves of leaf lettuce and line a baking sheet with them (leave the water clinging to the leaves). Set the trout skin side up on top of the lettuce and heat in a 400-degree oven for 3 to 4 minutes.

SMOKED STURGEON

Unlike the Smoked Trout (page 182), smoked sturgeon is best the next day, after it has had time to chill.

Serves 6 as an appetizer

(page 182)

ACCEPT SUBSTITUTES

This also works with sablefish (smoke for 12 minutes).

FOR THE MARINADE
2 cups water
½ cup sliced shallots
2 garlic cloves, minced
2 tablespoons coarse salt
1 tablespoon sugar
2 tablespoons chopped fresh dill
1 tablespoon coriander seeds, toasted
  and cracked
Grated zest of 1 lemon

1 (1-pound) piece skinless sturgeon
  fillet
Cherry wood chips
Vegetable oil

FOR SERVING
Sliced ripe tomatoes
Chopped fresh parsley and basil
Coarse sea salt
Olive oil

FOR THE MARINADE: Mix the water, shallots, garlic, salt, sugar, dill, coriander, and lemon zest in a bowl, stirring until the salt and sugar dissolve. If you have the time, let the marinade sit at room temperature for 1 to 2 hours.

Set the sturgeon in a small nonreactive container and pour in the marinade. Make sure the fish is completely covered with marinade. Cover with plastic and refrigerate for 4 hours.

Prepare a grill. Soak a few handfuls of cherry chips in water while the coals heat.

Remove the sturgeon from the marinade and pat dry. Brush it all over with vegetable oil.

When the coals are hot, bank them in one half of the grill. Open the vent(s) in the bottom of the grill. Put the chips on the glowing coals, set the grate over the coals, and set the fish on the cool side of the grate (not over the coals). Put the cover on the grill, vents closed to trap the smoke, and smoke the sturgeon for 18 minutes. It won't hurt if you bend down and blow into the lower vent, or fan it some, to increase the smoke. The fish should be opaque throughout when it is done.

Let the sturgeon cool, then wrap it snugly in plastic and refrigerate overnight.

To serve, make a bed of sliced tomatoes on six salad plates. Sprinkle with chopped herbs and salt, drizzle with olive oil, and top with thin slices of the sturgeon.

VARIATION

This fish is delicious with scrambled eggs. Flake the fish and fold it into the eggs right before they're done. Top with a handful of chopped scallions.

BAKING AND ROASTING

TANDOORI SABLE

Tangy and sweet. This is the cooking method you want when you don't feel like starting up a grill for tandoori (see page 162). The photo — which in this case is tandoori salmon — is on page 193.   Serves 4

ACCEPT SUBSTITUTES

Salmon
Swordfish steaks (1 inch thick; sear for 90 seconds, then roast for about 8 minutes)

2 tablespoons ghee (see Note) or
  unsalted butter
½ cup tandoori paste (see Note)
2 tablespoons plain yogurt

4 (6-ounce) pieces skinless sablefish
  fillet
Coarse salt
Tzatziki (page 399)
Mint leaves for garnish

Melt 1 tablespoon ghee, and combine it with the tandoori paste and yogurt. Slather the fish with the paste, pack it into a sealable plastic bag, and refrigerate for 1 hour.

Heat the oven to 450 degrees.

Wipe some of the tandoori paste from the fish, leaving just a light coating. Season lightly with salt.

Heat a large cast-iron skillet over high heat. When the skillet's good and hot, add the remaining 1 tablespoon ghee. Lay the fish in the skillet and sear for 90 seconds. Turn the fish over and slide the skillet into the oven. Thin pieces will be cooked in about 3 minutes; thicker ones will take 5 minutes.

Serve, spooning a generous mound of tzatziki onto your dinner plates. Garnish with as much mint as you'd like.

NOTE: Ghee, India's version of clarified butter, is available in specialty markets, the international section of many grocery stores, and at Kalustyan's (www.kalustyans .com).

A lot of commercial tandoori pastes are available in better grocery stores and specialty markets, and they vary in quality and flavor. My favorite is Bombay brand, which is available online from www.bombaybrand.com, but I've also used Patak's Spicy Ginger and Garlic Marinade and Grill Sauce, available at Kalustyan's.

WHOLE FISH ROASTED IN SALT

Adding spices to the salt crust will perfume the fish. See pages 34 and 38 for instructions on preparing the fish for roasting, or have your fishmonger take on the job. You won't need to scale the fish—the scales help protect the fish, and they'll just pull off when you remove the salt. (The photos are on page 156.) Serves 2

ACCEPT SUBSTITUTES

All small whole fish will work here (also see the variations).

4 large egg whites
½ cup water
4 cups coarse salt
1 whole fish (1¼–1¾ pounds), gutted,
   gills and fins removed

FOR SERVING
Extra virgin olive oil
Chopped fresh herbs (parsley, chervil,
   or cilantro—your choice)
Lemon wedges or one of the butter
   sauces on pages 404–406

Heat the oven to 400 degrees. Line a baking sheet with parchment or aluminum foil for easy cleanup.

Whisk the egg whites and water in a large bowl until very frothy and about doubled in volume. Pour in the salt and mix well with your hands. You are going for something the consistency of wet sand; if your crust seems dry, add a few more tablespoons of water.

Pat out 1 cup of the crust mix on the baking sheet into the size and shape of your fish. Set the fish on top and cover with the remaining crust mix. Wet your hands and pat the crust all over, smoothing it out and making sure the fish is completely sealed.

Roast small fish for 30 minutes, large fish for 35 minutes.

Remove the fish from the oven and crack the crust along the sides with the back of a big spoon. Lift the crust up off the fish—carefully, because it will be hot.

Let the fish cool for a few minutes, then peel off the skin. Slide the top fillet off the bones and divide it between two plates. Grab the tail and lift up the bones. Brush or spoon any crust away from the sides of the remaining fillet, then lift it from the bottom crust and invert it onto a cutting board. Peel off the skin and divide the fillet between two plates. Sprinkle with oil and chopped herbs. Serve with lemon wedges or a butter sauce.

BRANZINO OR STRIPED BASS IN A SALT CRUST

Add 2 tablespoons caraway seeds to the crust mix for branzino; add 2 tablespoons fennel seeds for bass. Serve the branzino with just the oil and lemon, or maybe with the Basic Butter Sauce (page 404). Serve the bass with one of the flavored butter sauces (pages 404–406) or Bacon Vinaigrette (page 433).

DOVER SOLE IN A SALT CRUST

It's unlikely you'll ever see this served in a restaurant. It is a fussy dish to prepare, because the skin gets rubbery and you need patience to peel it. But you will also never taste a piece of sole as delicious as this.

Before sealing the fish in the crust, make an incision at the tail on both sides of the fish and scrape the skin back a little to give you a place to start when you peel off the skin after roasting. Start with 2 cups of the crust mix under the fish, then use the remainder on top. Roast for 25 minutes only. Serve with a squirt of lemon and the Basic Butter Sauce (page 404).

TURBOT IN A SALT CRUST

Double the recipe for the salt crust, since turbot has a huge surface, and roast for 30 minutes. Serve with one of the butter sauces (pages 404–406). Big as the fish is, it will serve just 3.

ABOUT ROASTING WHOLE FISH IN SALT

This is the technique you want to run to when you love the pure taste of fish. Roasting in a salt crust will heighten the fish's character, intensifying it. The combination of cooking the fish in its own juices and steaming it in the salt crust captures all the natural flavor and texture.

These recipes serve 2, but you can double or triple them, as long as you've got enough baking sheets.

Plan on plating the dish in the kitchen, because skinning and filleting the fish is a little fussy and slightly messy. You'll find step-by-step instructions for serving a whole fish on page 40.

ROAST CHAR

Whole roast fish seems like holiday food to me, an event for the table. Serve this tasty fish with rice or boiled potatoes to sop up the butter sauce, and maybe some asparagus. (The photo is on page 206.)   Serves 4

ACCEPT SUBSTITUTES

A sockeye salmon could stand in here.

Lemon Dill Butter (page 412), softened

2 fennel bulbs, trimmed and cut into thin slices

1 whole char (about 4½ pounds), scaled and gutted, gills and fins removed

Coarse salt and freshly ground white pepper

Stems from 1 bunch dill

Heat the oven to 375 degrees.

Butter a roasting pan with about 2 tablespoons of the butter. Scatter the fennel in the pan.

Cut 3 slashes into each side of the fish, going down almost to the bones. Season the fish inside and out with salt and white pepper and stuff the cavity with the dill stems. Stand the fish in the roasting pan, spreading out the belly to support it. Slather the fish with the rest of the butter.

Roast the fish for 45 minutes, basting it every 15 minutes (a bulb baster comes in handy for this).

Let the fish rest for 15 minutes before serving with the fennel and the juices in the pan.

ROAST TUNA

For this Sunday-dinner dish, I cook tuna—which I think of as the meat of the ocean
—the way I'd cook a big roast of beef. It's tender, rare, and full of flavor.

The key is making sure you don't overcook the tuna; it should be cold when you
put it in the oven. Serve it with sautéed hearty greens, something like kale or
spinach.

Serves 6

1½ pounds red-skinned or creamer
   potatoes, scrubbed and cut into
   bite-sized pieces
¼ cup olive oil
Coarse salt and freshly ground white
   pepper

1½ pounds onions, cut into chunks
3–4 sprigs thyme
1 (2½-pound) piece tuna, 3 inches thick
Black Olive and Anchovy Butter (page
   411), softened

Heat the oven to 400 degrees.

Put the potatoes in a heavy roasting pan with the olive oil and season with salt and
white pepper. Cook over medium-high heat, stirring occasionally, until the potatoes
start to caramelize, about 8 minutes. Add the onions and thyme, season with salt and
pepper, and cook for 5 minutes; the onions will show signs of softening.

Meanwhile, tie the tuna in two places around its width with kitchen string so it will
hold its shape. Season it all over with salt and pepper. Reserve about 1 tablespoon of
the butter and slather the rest over the top of the tuna.

Push the potatoes and onions to the sides of the roasting pan to make a space for the
tuna. Add the reserved butter to the space, set the tuna on top, and slide into the oven.
Roast for 20 minutes. If you like, baste with a bulb baster after 10 minutes. Let the
tuna rest for 10 minutes on a carving board.

Remove the string, cut the tuna into ½-inch slices, and serve with the potatoes and
onions.

Tandoori Salmon and Tzatziki (pages 188 and 399).

Opposite: Bouillabaisse for the American Kitchen (page 314).
Top: Lobster Gazpacho (page 329). *Above:* Shrimp and Branzino Stew, Caribbean-Style (page 321).

Above: Tuna Burger with Harissa Mayonnaise (page 367).
Opposite: Shrimp and Tilapia Burger (page 360).

Opposite: Trout Amandine (page 245).

Top, left: Lobster and Potato Salad (page 340). *Top, right:* Broiled Bluefish Dijonnaise (page 126).

Above, left: Shrimp Fritters (page 264). *Above, right:* Thai-Style Mussels (page 288).

Top: Sautéed Char with Hoisin Glaze and Wasabi Butter Sauce and Basic Bok Choy (pages 238 and 451). *Above:* Saumon au Frisée (page 342). *Right:* "Everything" Tuna (page 267).

Above: Oil-Poached Halibut with Gribiche and Poached Egg (page 96).
Opposite: Sole Stuffed with Crab (page 212).

Left: Grilled Squid with Garlic Butter Sauce (pages 170 and 405).
Below: Broiled Sardines (page 130) with hummus.

Above, left: Butter-Basted Halibut with Creamy Corn and Red Pepper Coulis (pages 251, 427, and 457).

Above, right: Roast Char (page 191).

Left: Almond-Crusted Barramundi with Spinach and Pickled Onions (pages 248 and 400).

Opposite: Broiled Flounder Fillet with Butter and Herbs (page 122).

Following page: Swordfish Brochette with Orange-Chipotle Marinade and Bacon Vinaigrette (pages 168 and 433).

SLOW-ROASTED SALMON WITH STEWED BABY ARTICHOKES

This slow roast at a low temperature keeps the salmon moist, almost creamy, and it intensifies the flavor of the fish in the best way.

Ask for a piece of salmon from the head end; a thick fillet is important here.

Serves 4

ACCEPT SUBSTITUTES

Char

1 (1½-pound) piece skinless wild
   salmon fillet, 2 inches thick
Coarse salt and freshly ground white
   pepper
2 tablespoons chopped fresh dill
2 tablespoons chopped fresh parsley
1 tablespoon chopped fresh tarragon

1 tablespoon chopped fresh thyme
Stalks from 1 fennel bulb, cut into long
   thin strips
½ cup olive oil
Stewed Baby Artichokes (page 446)
Coarse sea salt

Heat the oven to 250 degrees.

Season the top of the fish generously with salt and white pepper and leave it on the counter for 5 to 10 minutes. The top of the fish should be moist and a little sticky.

Mix the dill, parsley, tarragon, and thyme together.

Make a bed of the fennel stalks in a baking dish just large enough to hold the fish (a 1½-quart gratin is good). Set the fish on top and fold the belly over so you have an even thickness. Press the herbs onto the top of the fish and drizzle the oil evenly over it.

Roast for 40 minutes. (If you're not a fan of salmon that's pink in the center, roast it for another 15 minutes.)

Make a bed of the artichokes on four dinner plates. Top with the salmon, and serve garnished with coarse sea salt.

VARIATION

You could simplify the herb topping by replacing it with 5 to 6 tablespoons of chopped fresh basil.

CITRUS ROAST LOBSTER

Roasting lobster in its shell adds a layer of complexity to the flavor. I think of it as being more "lobstery." You'll want to start this marinating at least 4 hours ahead.

Serves 4

FOR THE MARINADE
Grated zest and juice of 3 oranges
Grated zest and juice of 1 grapefruit
½ cup olive oil
2 teaspoons fish sauce
2 shallots, minced
½ cup chopped fresh mint
½ teaspoon fresh thyme leaves

2 lobsters (each about 1½ pounds), dispatched and prepared for pan-roasting (see pages 46–47)
Coarse salt
Roast Asparagus (page 448)
Yellow Bell Pepper Coulis (page 427)

FOR THE MARINADE: Whisk the zests and juices, olive oil, fish sauce, shallots, mint, and thyme together in a bowl.

Pack the lobster pieces into a 9-x-13-inch baking dish, cut sides of the tails facing down. Pour in the marinade, cover with plastic, and marinate in the refrigerator for at least 4 hours and up to 8 (so you can start this in the morning).

Take the lobster out of the refrigerator. Heat the oven to 500 degrees, and oil a baking sheet.

Transfer the lobster pieces to the baking sheet. Season any exposed meat with salt. Roast for 10 minutes.

Serve with the asparagus and coulis.

BAKED BRANZINO

If you have individual gratin dishes — ones with a 2-cup capacity — pull them out and use them for this very simple dish. They will make dinner look a bit more elegant.   Serves 4

ACCEPT SUBSTITUTES

Make this with striped bass fillets or skinless mackerel or bluefish.
Mahi mahi is also quite nice in this preparation;
it will need to bake for 10 minutes, since it's denser.

Olive oil   Topping for Clams Oreganata
4 (6-ounce) pieces skinless branzino   (page 282)
   fillet   Lemon wedges

Heat the oven to 450 degrees.

Oil four individual gratin dishes or a large baking dish with olive oil. Set in the fish and drizzle lightly with oil. Top each portion with about 3 tablespoons of the oreganata topping.

Bake for 8 minutes. Peek inside one of the fillets if you're unsure about doneness. It should be barely opaque in the center.

Serve with lemon wedges.

SOLE STUFFED WITH CRAB

This is a simple marriage of the flavors of crab and sole. Serve it with sliced summer tomatoes and sautéed spinach to cut the richness. (The photo is on page 203.)

Serves 6

You can use any sole here, or flounder or turbot.

8 tablespoons (1 stick) unsalted butter

½ cup minced shallots

3 tablespoons all-purpose flour

1½ cups whole milk, heated

Coarse salt

1 tablespoon Dijon mustard

Juice of ½ lemon

2 tablespoons minced fresh parsley

Freshly ground white pepper

Cayenne

1 pound jumbo lump crabmeat

6 (5-ounce) Dover sole fillets

Dry bread crumbs

Set up a bowl of ice with some water, and set a smaller bowl on the ice.

Melt 3 tablespoons butter in a medium saucepan over medium heat. Add the shallots and cook until softened, about 2 minutes. Sprinkle in the flour and cook, stirring, until the roux smells toasty, about 6 minutes. Don't let it brown.

Take the pan off the heat and whisk in the milk, making sure you dissolve all the roux. Season generously with salt and return to the heat. Bring the sauce to a simmer, stirring often, then reduce the heat to low and simmer the sauce until it's very thick. Stir in the mustard, lemon juice, and parsley. Season with white pepper and cayenne, and check for salt. Fold in the crab, and scrape the mixture out into the bowl on the ice to cool it down quickly.

Melt the remaining 5 tablespoons butter and brush six individual gratin dishes (2-cup capacity) liberally with butter. Divide the crab stuffing among the gratins, mounding it in the center.

Cut the sole fillets down the center and then make a diagonal cut through each half. Drape 4 pieces of fish over the stuffing in each gratin, arranging them to cover the stuffing completely. Brush the fish with the remaining melted butter. You can bake the fish now or cover the dishes with plastic and refrigerate for a day.

Set an oven rack in the top position and heat the oven to 450 degrees.

Mix about 1 teaspoon salt with a pinch of cayenne and season the fish. Dust very lightly with bread crumbs, just a pinch or two for each casserole.

Bake until you can see the stuffing bubbling out and browning at the edges of the dish, about 10 minutes. If you've refrigerated the casseroles, baking time will be about 2 minutes longer.

SOLE BONNE FEMME

A "good woman" cooks simple dishes that are served up family-style. This French classic is usually made with just button mushrooms, but I like the deeper flavor that comes from adding dried ones too. Serves 4

ACCEPT SUBSTITUTES

Use any flatfish, like turbot or thin pieces of flounder.
Or try this with trout or slices of salmon fillet.

½ ounce (heaped ½ cup) dried
    porcini mushrooms
⅓ cup minced shallots
1 cup dry white wine
1 cup Quick Vegetable Stock (page
    476) or Fumet (page 296)
½ pound button mushrooms, cut
    into thin slices

1 cup heavy cream
Coarse salt
2 tablespoons unsalted butter
2 tablespoons all-purpose flour
Juice of ½ lemon
1½ pounds gray sole fillets
Freshly ground white pepper
3 tablespoons chopped fresh parsley

Cover the dried mushrooms with very hot water and soak for 20 minutes. Drain, rinse, and chop the mushrooms.

Heat the oven to 325 degrees.

Combine the shallots, wine, and stock or fumet in a small saucepan and bring to a boil over medium-high heat. Boil to reduce by a little more than half. Take off the heat.

Put the sliced mushrooms in a skillet with the cream and some salt. Bring to a simmer over medium heat and cook gently until the mushrooms are barely tender, about 3 minutes. Turn off the heat.

Melt the butter in a medium saucepan over medium heat. Add the flour and cook, stirring, until the roux smells toasty, about 5 minutes. Don't let it brown. Off the heat, add the wine reduction (with the shallots), the mushrooms and cream, and the dried mushrooms. Bring to a simmer over medium heat, stirring often. Reduce the heat and simmer for 5 minutes. Stir in the lemon juice.

Cut the sole fillets in half lengthwise. Season with salt and white pepper and roll them up. Set the rolls on end in a small gratin dish and spoon the sauce over them.

Cover with aluminum foil and bake for 25 minutes. If you're unsure about doneness, poke into one of the fillets in the center of the dish; it should be just barely translucent. Carry-over heat will finish the cooking.

Scatter on the parsley and serve from the gratin dish.

MACKEREL WITH PUTTANESCA AND POTATOES

I like making this satisfying, warming casserole in individual gratin dishes, but you can just as easily make it in one larger dish—just increase the cooking time by 5 minutes.

   Make the puttanesca and boil the potatoes a day ahead, and the dish will be a snap to put together.   Serves 4

ACCEPT SUBSTITUTES
Try this with bluefish or filleted fresh sardines.

Olive oil

1 pound white or red-skinned
   potatoes, boiled until just tender,
   peeled, and sliced

Coarse salt

4 tablespoons dry vermouth

4 (6- to 7-ounce) pieces mackerel fillet

Freshly ground white pepper

2 cups Puttanesca Sauce (page 430)

1 cup dry bread crumbs

2 tablespoons chopped fresh parsley

2 garlic cloves, minced or put through
   a press

Heat the oven to 450 degrees.

Oil four individual gratin dishes (2-cup capacity) generously with olive oil. Divide the potatoes among the dishes and season with salt. Sprinkle 1 tablespoon vermouth into each dish.

Season the fish with salt and white pepper. Lay the fillets on top of the potatoes and spread ½ cup of the puttanesca sauce over each, covering it completely.

Mix the bread crumbs, parsley, garlic, and 2 teaspoons olive oil together in a small bowl. Sprinkle the crumbs over the casseroles, dividing them as evenly as you can.

Slip the casseroles into the oven and bake until the potatoes are piping hot and the fish is cooked through, about 12 minutes.

BAKED SCALLOPS

This simple preparation highlights the sweetness of sea scallops.   Serves 4

1¾ pounds sea scallops, tough bits
   removed
Coarse salt and freshly ground white
   pepper

6 tablespoons Sun-Dried Tomato
   Butter (page 413) or Porcini Butter
   (page 410), softened
3 tablespoons dry bread crumbs

Place a rack in the upper third of the oven and heat the oven to 450 degrees.

Season the scallops with salt and white pepper. Smear about 2 tablespoons of the butter in the bottom of a 1½-quart gratin dish. Set the scallops in the dish in a single layer (it may be a snug fit) and spread the rest of the butter over the top of the scallops. Sprinkle on the bread crumbs.

Bake until bubbling and lightly browned, about 10 minutes. Let the scallops sit for a few minutes before serving.

COQUILLES ST.-JACQUES

This French classic, traditionally served in scallop shells as a first course, makes a fantastic main-dish casserole—particularly since I've simplified the preparation. You can make individual portions or bake it all in a big dish. And while it may look like a lot of work here, you can do it all in advance.   Serves 6

½ cup chopped shallots

2 pounds sea scallops, tough bits
   removed

Coarse salt and freshly ground white
   pepper

2 cups dry white wine

¼ cup water

Juice of ½ lemon

6 tablespoons unsalted butter

1½ pounds button mushrooms, halved
   if small, quartered if large

½ cup all-purpose flour

2 cups heavy cream

Butter a large skillet or sauté pan (be generous). Cut a piece of parchment to fit the pan, and cut a small vent hole in the center.

Scatter the shallots over the bottom of the pan. Season the scallops with salt and white pepper and set them in the pan in a single layer. Pour in the wine, cover with the parchment, and bring to a boil over high heat. Boil for 1 minute. Turn off the heat and let sit for 2 minutes.

With a slotted spoon, remove the scallops and shallots to a strainer set over a bowl (you want them to drain thoroughly). Reserve the cooking liquid, and save the parchment for the next step.

Put the water, lemon juice, and 2 tablespoons butter into another large skillet or sauté pan (or wipe out the one you used for the scallops). Bring to a boil over high heat. Add the mushrooms and a pinch of salt and cover with the parchment. Cook, shaking the pan once in a while, until the mushrooms are tender and the juices have reduced by half, about 10 minutes. Drain in a strainer set over a bowl, so you capture all the liquid.

Melt the remaining 4 tablespoons butter in a large saucepan over medium heat. Stir in the flour and cook, stirring constantly, until the roux smells toasty, about 3 minutes. Don't let it brown. Take the pan off the heat and whisk in the reserved cooking liquid from the scallops and the mushrooms.

Return the pan to the heat and cook, stirring constantly, until the sauce comes to a simmer. Pour in 1 cup cream, stir, and bring back to a simmer. The sauce should be very thick.

Cut the scallops into quarters. Add the scallops, shallots, and mushrooms to the sauce. Cook, stirring and scraping the bottom of the pan regularly, until the mixture comes back to a simmer. Don't expect to see tiny bubbles; you're looking for a few volcanic eruptions in the sauce. When you get one or two, stir, and then get another eruption right away, the sauce is ready. Scrape it out into a large bowl and let it cool. You can make the dish up to this point early in the day. Refrigerate it, covered, until you're ready to serve.

Heat the broiler.

Scrape the scallops and sauce into a large pot and heat over medium-low heat, stirring once in a while. The sauce will seem very thick at first, but it will thin a little as it warms. Remove from the heat.

Whip the remaining 1 cup cream into stiff peaks. Fold it into the sauce.

Divide the scallops and sauce among six individual gratin dishes or scrape into a large casserole. Even out the top and broil for 1 minute, or until bubbling and just starting to brown.

PACKETS OF BARRAMUNDI WITH SHRIMP AND MUSHROOMS

Serve this rich, juicy dish with boiled creamer potatoes.

If you have the time, simmer the shrimp shells in the fumet for 10 minutes for an even richer sauce.

Serves 4

ACCEPT SUBSTITUTES

Halibut

¾ pound button mushrooms,
  cut into thin slices

1 cup heavy cream

Coarse salt

2 tablespoons unsalted butter

1 shallot, minced

2 tablespoons all-purpose flour

1 cup Fumet (page 296)

Freshly ground white pepper

Juice of ½ lemon

2 tablespoons minced fresh parsley

2 tablespoons chopped fresh dill

4 (5-ounce) skinless barramundi fillets

8 extra-large (16–20 count) shrimp,
  shelled, with tail left on, and
  butterflied (see page 41)

Combine the mushrooms and cream in a saucepan. Season with salt and bring to a simmer. Cook at an active simmer for 3 minutes. Turn off the heat.

Melt the butter in a large saucepan over medium heat. Add the shallot and cook until translucent, about 1 minute. Sprinkle on the flour and cook, stirring, until the roux smells toasty, about 5 minutes. Take the pan off the heat and whisk in the fumet.

ABOUT FISH PACKETS

The technique of wrapping fish and other ingredients in a foil packet is actually the modern version of the classic French preparation *en papillote*. Cooking the ingredients together in a sealed package intensifies the flavors, marrying the fish with a side dish in a way that would never happen by just putting them together on a plate.

Return to the heat and cook, stirring, until the sauce comes to a boil. Stir in the mushrooms and cream, season with salt and white pepper, and bring to a simmer. Simmer until the sauce is reduced and silky, 15 to 18 minutes. Meanwhile, set up an ice bath (see page 474).

Stir the lemon juice and herbs into the sauce and taste for salt and pepper. Scrape the sauce into a bowl and set it in the ice bath. Chill, stirring with a rubber scraper from time to time, until the sauce is cold and very thick.

Place an oven rack in the top position and heat the oven to 450 degrees.

Tear off four 18-x-12-inch pieces of heavy-duty aluminum foil. Fold in thirds lengthwise and reopen. Butter the center of one piece of foil and place a fish fillet on it. Season it with salt and pepper. Place 1 shrimp on either side of the fish, cut side down. Curl the tail end of the shrimp over to where the head was (see page 41). Spoon one quarter of the sauce over the fish and seal the packet using the drugstore wrap (see page 39). Repeat with the remaining ingredients to make 3 more packets.

Place the packets on a baking sheet and bake for 20 minutes. Let the packets rest on the counter for 10 minutes.

Open each packet carefully in the kitchen — there's going to be a burst of hot steam and a lot of liquid — and slide the fish and shrimp out into a soup plate, with all the juices. Serve hot.

PACKETS OF BLUEFISH WITH PEPERONATA

Because of its oiliness, bluefish wants to be paired with assertive flavors. Here I use peperonata. Serve with rice or mashed potatoes.   Serves 4

ACCEPT SUBSTITUTES

Fatty fish are best here. Try mackerel or mahi mahi or swordfish.

Peperonata (page 465), at room
    temperature
Coarse salt and freshly ground white
    pepper

4 (6-ounce) pieces bluefish fillet
⅓ cup minced kalamata olives
1 tablespoon olive oil
1 tablespoon chopped fresh parsley

Heat the oven to 400 degrees. Tear off four 18-x-12-inch pieces of heavy-duty aluminum foil. Fold in thirds lengthwise and reopen.

Taste the peperonata for salt and pepper, and season it if necessary. Divide the peperonata among the pieces of foil, spooning it into the center of each. Season the fish with salt and pepper and set it on the peperonata.

Stir the minced olives and olive oil together in a small bowl and divide this olive paste among the pieces of fish, spreading it out with the back of a spoon. Use the drugstore wrap (see page 39) to close up the packets.

Set the packets on a baking sheet and bake for 15 minutes.

Open each packet carefully in the kitchen—there's going to be a burst of hot steam and a lot of liquid—and slide the fish and peperonata out into a soup plate, with all the juices. Sprinkle with the parsley and serve.

PACKETS OF HADDOCK WITH ZUCCHINI, TOMATOES, AND PARSLEY PESTO

All fresh flavors here. The dish is sweet and good in a tabbouleh kind of way.

If you can find leida or avocado squash at your farmers' market, go for it; these have better flavor. Otherwise, zucchini will be fine.   Serves 4

ACCEPT SUBSTITUTES

Any flaky white fish is great for this dish: cod or scrod, halibut, turbot
(fold the fillets in thirds), or black sea bass (fold the fillets in half).

2 small zucchini or other green
   squash (see headnote), cut into thin
   slices
Olive oil
Coarse salt
16 cherry or grape tomatoes, halved

4 (6-ounce) pieces haddock fillet, about
   1 inch thick
Freshly ground white pepper
4 generous tablespoons Parsley Pesto
   (page 422)
Extra virgin olive oil, for drizzling

Heat the oven to 400 degrees.

Tear off four 18-x-12-inch pieces of heavy-duty aluminum foil. Fold in thirds lengthwise and reopen. Toss the zucchini with a drizzle of olive oil and some salt and divide it among the pieces of foil, spooning it into the center of each piece. Toss the tomatoes with a drizzle of oil and some salt and spoon over the zucchini.

Season the fish with salt and white pepper and set it on top of the vegetables. Spread a generous tablespoon of the pesto on top of each piece of fish. Use the drugstore wrap (see page 39) to close up the packets.

Set the packets on a baking sheet and bake for 15 minutes.

Open each packet carefully in the kitchen—there's going to be a burst of hot steam —and slide the fish and vegetables out into a soup plate, with any juices. Drizzle with extra virgin olive oil and serve.

PACKETS OF SCROD WITH CLAMS AND POTATOES

Think of this as a baked chowder.   Serves 4

ACCEPT SUBSTITUTES

Any flaky white fish will be great for this dish: cod, halibut, turbot
(fold the fillets in thirds), or black sea bass (fold the fillets in half).

2 tablespoons plus 2 teaspoons
   unsalted butter
¼ pound bacon, cut into ½-inch
   pieces
1 medium onion, diced
2 celery ribs, diced
½ teaspoon fresh thyme leaves
¾ pound red-skinned potatoes,
   scrubbed and cut into matchsticks
   (use a mandoline or vegetable
   slicer)

1 cup bottled clam juice
Coarse salt and freshly ground white
   pepper
4 (6-ounce) pieces scrod
2 teaspoons chopped fresh parsley
   and dill
16 littleneck clams, scrubbed

Heat the oven to 400 degrees.

Heat a large deep skillet over medium heat. When the pan is hot, add 2 tablespoons
butter and the bacon. Cook, stirring, until the bacon is just starting to brown, 2 to 3
minutes. Add the onion, celery, and thyme and cook, stirring once or twice, until the
onion has softened, about 5 minutes. Add the potatoes and clam juice, season with
salt and white pepper, and give it all a stir. Bring to a boil, then cover, reduce the heat
to low, and simmer until the potatoes are just tender and the juice has thickened,
about 8 minutes. Remove from the heat.

Tear off four 18-x-12-inch pieces of heavy-duty aluminum foil. Fold in thirds lengthwise and reopen. Divide the potatoes among the pieces of foil, spooning them into
the center of each. Make sure you divide the juice too. Season the fish with salt and

set it on the potatoes. Sprinkle the fish with the chopped herbs and dot with the remaining 2 teaspoons of butter. Nestle 4 clams around each piece of fish and seal the packets using the drugstore wrap (see page 39).

Set the packets on a baking sheet and bake for 12 minutes.

Open each packet carefully in the kitchen—there's going to be a burst of hot steam and a lot of liquid—and slide the fish and clams and potatoes out into a soup plate, with all the juices. If a clam hasn't opened wide, help it along with a knife. Serve hot.

SEARING AND SAUTÉING

SEARED TUNA TONNATO

Tonnato is an Italian sauce traditionally served with thin slices of veal, turkey, or chicken. Combine it with flash-seared tuna and you've got a great summer dish. With the classic preparation, the veal is covered with the tuna sauce. I think the plate looks terrific when the slices of tuna and tomato are fanned out on top of the sauce.

Real summer tomatoes are essential. Go for big Jersey beefsteaks or an heirloom like Green Zebra or Black Krim.

Serve as a light lunch or as a first course for dinner.   Serves 4

ACCEPT SUBSTITUTES

You might want to try this with swordfish, sturgeon, or sable.

FOR THE TONNATO
1 (6-ounce) can tuna packed in olive oil
4 anchovy fillets, chopped
2 tablespoons capers
Grated zest of ½ lemon
3 tablespoons fresh lemon juice
2 large egg yolks
½ cup vegetable oil
Coarse salt and freshly ground white pepper

2 (8-ounce) pieces tuna, each about ½ inch thick
Coarse salt and freshly ground white pepper
Vegetable oil
About 1 tablespoon capers
2 ripe tomatoes, sliced

ABOUT SEARING

This technique—heating a cast-iron skillet to almost smoking and searing fish in it for only a few moments—is something you'd expect to use when you were cooking a piece of beef, maybe a filet mignon or a rib eye. It's also eminently suitable for tuna, that meat of the ocean, giving it a full-flavored caramelized crust while leaving the inside rare and tender.

FOR THE TONNATO: Put the tuna, with the oil from the can, into a food processor. Add the anchovies, capers, lemon zest and juice, and egg yolks. Pulse until smooth, scraping down the sides when you need to. With the processor running, drizzle in the vegetable oil to make a silky-smooth sauce. Season with salt and white pepper—go light on the salt—and scrape the sauce into a container. Cover and refrigerate until you're ready to serve.

Set a large cast-iron skillet or griddle on the stove and crank the heat up to high. You want to get the pan hot enough to just about set off the smoke alarm.

Season the tuna with salt and pepper and brush it with vegetable oil. Sear the tuna for 45 seconds per side. The outside will be browned and the tuna will be cooked very rare. You want this. Transfer the tuna to a plate and refrigerate until it's well chilled.

To serve, spread the sauce onto four dinner plates and scatter some capers on top. Season the tomatoes with salt. Cut the tuna into thin slices. Arrange the tuna and tomato slices on top of the sauce, fanning them out.

FENNEL-CRUSTED TUNA WITH WILTED CABBAGE AND ORANGE-SOY VINAIGRETTE

A dish can be rich and refreshing as well, and that's what you have here. Meaty tuna is stacked against barely wilted cabbage, with a citrusy tang provided by the vinaigrette.

While I think toasted seeds taste better, you don't need to toast them in advance here—the high heat you use to sear the tuna will take care of that layer of flavor.

Serves 4

2 tablespoons fennel seeds

2 teaspoons coriander seeds

½ teaspoon white peppercorns

2 (12-ounce) pieces tuna, each about
  1½ inches thick

Coarse salt

2 teaspoons vegetable oil

Wilted Cabbage (page 452)

Orange-Soy Vinaigrette (page 435)

Combine the fennel seeds, coriander seeds, and peppercorns in a spice grinder and grind to a fine powder. Pour out onto a plate.

Season the tuna with salt and coat it with the ground spices.

Heat a large cast-iron skillet over medium-high heat until very hot. Spoon in the oil and slide it around the skillet. Add the tuna and cook for 45 seconds to 1 minute on each side. You're just searing the tuna.

Transfer the tuna to a cutting board and let it rest for a minute or so.

To serve, make a mound of cabbage in the center of each of four dinner plates. Surround the cabbage with a ring of the vinaigrette—be generous. Slice the tuna and lay the slices against the cabbage.

TUNA AU POIVRE
WITH FENNEL SALAD

Here's an example of how well a classic steak recipe can be adapted to showcase tuna. I've replaced the traditional black peppercorns with a mix of white pepper and coriander seeds.

Serve with a light red wine, maybe a pinot noir.   Serves 4

ACCEPT SUBSTITUTES

Yellowtail is an expensive option, swordfish an acceptable one.
Cook the swordfish until it's just pink inside. Or try sturgeon.

2 tablespoons white peppercorns

4 teaspoons coriander seeds

4 (6-ounce) pieces tuna

Coarse salt

4 teaspoons vegetable oil, plus
 additional for searing

Fennel Salad (page 461)

Basil Oil (page 436)

Put the peppercorns and coriander seeds on a cutting board or work surface and crack them by rocking a heavy skillet back and forth over them.

Season the tuna with salt and rub each piece with 1 teaspoon of the oil. Press the fish into the cracked spices to coat it on both sides.

Heat a large cast-iron skillet over high heat. When the pan is very hot, almost smoking, add a drizzle of oil and sear the tuna for 30 seconds on each side. (You can also grill the tuna on a Foreman grill for 1 minute, but you won't get the crust you will from searing.)

To serve, mound the fennel salad on four dinner plates. Slice the tuna and fan the slices over the salad. Drizzle some basil oil around each plate.

Here's a technique that belongs in the repertoire of any fish cook. Sautéing is fast, and it's simple enough for weeknight cooking. It's plain cooking—you can sauté in oil alone, but I add a little butter for flavor—so the recipes give you ideas about serving. You'll find some great combinations and side dish suggestions.

The technique is simple: season the fish on both sides with salt and pepper. Spread some all-purpose flour out on a plate and lay the fish on it, skin side down (whether or not the fillet still has skin). Heat a sauté pan and add some oil—just a slick. Pick up the fish and pat off any excess flour; you want just a light coating. Add the fish to the pan, floured side down. Press down with your spatula, which will start to set the skin or caramelize the flesh, then add some butter, which you've cut into small pieces so it will melt quickly. Baste the fish, turn it over, and cook on the second side. Transfer the fish to paper towels to blot off any excess fat, and serve.

TIPS FOR SAUTÉING

- While a sauté pan—with its flat bottom and straight sides, which reflect heat back into the pan—is designed for this kind of high-heat cooking, you can sauté fish in just about any "frying" pan. The sloping sides of a frying pan may make it easier for you to get in with your spatula and turn the fillets, and a well-seasoned cast-iron skillet is a pan you can use to fry or sauté anything. The most important consideration is the weight of the pan. It should be heavy. You're much more likely to burn food in a flimsy pan.

- Use two sauté pans when you're sautéing more than two fillets. You'll have much more control than you would trying to fit all the fish into one large pan, and the fish will cook more evenly. If you don't have two pans, cook in batches.

- Put the fish into the pan vertically, rather than horizontally—with a narrow end toward you—and lower the end nearest you into the pan first. That way you're less likely to be spattered if you drop the fillet.

- The heat may cause the fish to buckle and curl a little when you put it into the pan, so press down lightly and evenly on it with your spatula.

- Do most of the cooking skin side down. You're building flavor through caramelization. The process is different from browning meat—which you do on both sides. If you brown fish to that extent, it will be overcooked.

- You could sauté the fish with oil alone, but butter adds such an appealing flavor, and it brings out the sweetness of the fish. It's added later in the process so it will brown but not burn.

- Thinner fillets will cook more quickly than thicker, obviously. You'll see it happening—follow the visual cues in the recipes.

- Once you've turned the fillets, test for doneness by pressing down in the center of a fillet with your finger. Well-done fish should feel firm and compact, not spongy. Keep in mind that the fish will continue to cook from residual heat when you take it from the pan.

- Serve floured side up, since that's the side with the more appealing crust.

SAUTÉED TURBOT WITH LEEKS AND RED WINE BUTTER SAUCE

Buttery leeks combined with nutty-tasting turbot—a fish that is particularly easy to cook since it leaves you margin for error because it doesn't dry out readily—cries out for big red wine.   Serves 4

ACCEPT SUBSTITUTES

So many different fish work with this combination of flavors.
Here are some of my favorites:

Flounder: Cook for 1 minute on the first side,
about 20 seconds on the second.

Char (skin on): Cook for 4 minutes on the first side, to make
sure the skin is very crisp, about 30 seconds on the second side.

Salmon: Cook for 3 minutes on the first side,
2 minutes on the second for rare.

4 (6-ounce) pieces turbot fillet
Coarse salt and freshly ground white
   pepper
All-purpose flour

Vegetable oil
2 tablespoons unsalted butter
Basic Leeks (page 462)
Red Wine Butter Sauce (page 407)

Heat two sauté pans over high heat. Meanwhile, season the fish on both sides with salt and white pepper. Dust the skinned side of the fish lightly with flour.

Add a slick of oil to each pan. Set in the fillets, floured side down, and reduce the heat to medium-high. Press down on the fish with your spatula, listening for the sizzle that tells you you're making a good crust. Add 1 tablespoon butter to each pan, breaking it into smaller pieces so it will melt quickly. Once the butter melts, tilt the pan and baste the fish. Cook for about 1½ minutes on the first side. Turn, and cook the fish for another 1½ minutes. Turn off the heat and let the fish sit for 30 seconds or so. Transfer to paper towels to drain briefly.

To serve, make a bed of the leeks on each of four dinner plates. Set the fish on the leeks and surround with a ring of the sauce. Pass a bowl with the rest of the sauce.

SAUTÉED MAHI MAHI
WITH BEETS AND SKORDALIA

Sautéed mahi mahi is a perfectly nice fish. It has terrific texture, but it has a tendency to be boring, so I pair it with intense flavors. Skordalia, a Greek condiment that rings loud notes of garlic and olive oil, and sweet tangy beets bring the fish to life. Make sure you brown the mahi well: caramelization is key to this preparation. Serves 4

ACCEPT SUBSTITUTES

This combination works with a great variety of fish, so try it with what's freshest. Here are some ideas:

Flounder: Cook for 1 minute on first side, about 20 seconds on the second.

Char (skin on): Cook for 4 minutes on the first side, to make sure the skin is very crisp, about 30 seconds on the second side.

Salmon: Cook for 3 minutes on the first side, 2 minutes on the second for rare.

4 (6-ounce) pieces mahi mahi fillet
Coarse salt and freshly ground white
   pepper
All-purpose flour
Vegetable oil

2 tablespoons unsalted butter
Skordalia (page 397)
Basic Beets (page 450), drained and
   cut into bite-sized pieces

Heat two sauté pans over high heat. Meanwhile, season the fish on both sides with salt and white pepper. Dust the skinned side of the fish lightly with flour.

Add a slick of oil to each pan. Set in the fillets, floured side down, and reduce the heat to medium-high. Press down on the fish with your spatula, listening for the sizzle that tells you you're making a good crust. Add 1 tablespoon butter to each pan, breaking it into smaller pieces so it will melt quickly. Once the butter melts, tilt the pan and baste the fish. Cook for about 3 minutes on the first side. Turn and cook the fish for another 3 minutes. Transfer to paper towels.

To serve, make a bed of the skordalia on each of four dinner plates. Set the fish on top and surround with the beets.

VARIATION

You can pair the skordalia and beets with fried fish for equally delicious results. Try it with Fish Fingers at Home (page 268) made with cod or mahi mahi.

SAUTÉED MACKEREL WITH TOMATO CONCASSÉ AND CUMIN BUTTER SAUCE

The sweetness of the tomato and earthiness of the cumin work well with just about any grilled or sautéed fatty fish.

Serves 4

ACCEPT SUBSTITUTES
Rouget, bluefish, or other oily fish.

4 (6-ounce) mackerel fillets, skin on
Coarse salt and freshly ground white
   pepper
All-purpose flour

Vegetable oil
2 tablespoons unsalted butter
Tomato Concassé (page 428), warmed
Cumin Butter Sauce (page 405)

Heat two sauté pans over high heat. Meanwhile, season the mackerel on both sides with salt and white pepper. Dust the skin lightly with flour.

Add a slick of oil to each pan. Set in the fillets, floured side down, and reduce the heat to medium-high. Press down on the fish with your spatula, listening for the sizzle that tells you you're making a good crust. Add 1 tablespoon butter to each pan, breaking it into smaller pieces so it will melt quickly. Once the butter melts, tilt the pan and baste the fish. Cook for about 2 minutes on the first side. You'll see the fish cooking from the bottom up. When it is almost cooked through, turn it over and turn off the heat. Let the fish sit for 30 seconds or so. Transfer to paper towels.

To serve, make a bed of the tomatoes on four dinner plates, using about ⅓ cup for each serving. Top with the fish and spoon a ring of the sauce around the tomatoes.

VARIATION

Sardines are terrific with this combination of flavors, but grill or broil them.

SAUTÉED CHAR WITH FENNEL PUREE AND SOY-ORANGE SAUCE

Here's an improvisation on the theme of fennel and orange, paired with a quick sauté of char. The sauce has an acidic sweetness—the result of the reduction—that offers a clean contrast to the fish and the fennel. Serves 4

ACCEPT SUBSTITUTES

Salmon is a natural, with or without skin. Trout is also a very acceptable substitute here; the fillets are often smaller and thinner, so adjust the cooking time.

4 (6-ounce) pieces char fillet, skin on	2 tablespoons unsalted butter
Coarse salt and freshly ground white pepper	Fennel Puree (page 460)
	Soy-Orange Sauce (page 424)
All-purpose flour	2 oranges, peeled and segmented
Vegetable oil	(see page 474; optional)

Heat two sauté pans over high heat. Meanwhile, season the char on both sides with salt and white pepper. Dust the skin lightly with flour.

Add a slick of oil to each pan. Set in the fillets, floured side down, and reduce the heat to medium-high. Press down on the fish with your spatula, listening for the sizzle that tells you you're making a good crust. Add 1 tablespoon butter to each pan, breaking it into smaller pieces so it will melt quickly. Once the butter melts, tilt the pan and baste the fish. Cook for about 3 minutes on the first side. You'll see the fish cooking from the bottom up. When it is almost cooked through, turn it over and turn off the heat. Let the fish sit for 30 seconds or so. Transfer to paper towels.

To serve, make a bed of fennel puree on each of four dinner plates. Set the char skin side up on top of the fennel and spoon the sauce around. Garnish with orange segments, if you like.

SAUTÉED CHAR WITH HOISIN GLAZE AND WASABI BUTTER SAUCE

The sour sweetness of this sauce is incredibly appealing, and it makes converts of people who say they don't like fish. (The photo is on page 200.)   Serves 4

ACCEPT SUBSTITUTES

I've made this with striped bass and swordfish with
great success. Salmon is another natural here.
Experiment with other fillets — skin on or off.

4 (6-ounce) pieces char fillet, skin on
Coarse salt and freshly ground white
  pepper
All-purpose flour
Vegetable oil

2 tablespoons unsalted butter
Basic Bok Choy (page 451) or Wilted
  Cabbage (page 452)
Hoisin Glaze (page 439)
Wasabi Butter Sauce (page 406)

Heat two sauté pans over high heat. Meanwhile, season the char on both sides with salt and white pepper. Dust the skin lightly with flour.

Add a slick of oil to each pan. Set in the fillets, floured side down, and reduce the heat to medium-high. Press down on the fish with your spatula, listening for the sizzle that tells you you're making a good crust. Add 1 tablespoon butter to each pan, breaking it into smaller pieces so it will melt quickly. Once the butter melts, tilt the pan and baste the fish. Cook for about 3 minutes on the first side. You'll see the fish cooking from the bottom up. When it is almost cooked through, turn it over and turn off the heat. Let the fish sit for 30 seconds or so. Transfer to paper towels.

To serve, divide the bok choy or cabbage among four dinner plates. Set a piece of fish on top of each portion and paint it with some of the hoisin glaze. Spoon on the butter sauce.

SAUTÉED CHAR WITH MOROCCAN SPICES, LENTILS, AND HARISSA TOMATO SAUCE

Earthy and spicy, this is an ideal dish for a cool night. I like the texture of the lentils and the balance of legumes and heat. You could simplify by just heating some canned chickpeas.   Serves 4

ACCEPT SUBSTITUTES

Salmon is a natural here, but you can try rainbow trout,
or even catfish or tilapia.

4 (6-ounce) pieces char fillet, skin on
Coarse salt
Moroccan Spice Mix (page 440)
All-purpose flour

Vegetable oil
2 tablespoons unsalted butter
Harissa Tomato Sauce (page 429)
Basic Lentils (page 463)

Heat two sauté pans over high heat. Meanwhile, season the char on both sides with salt and the spice mix. You want a light but noticeable coating of the spice. Dust the skin lightly with flour.

Add a slick of oil to each pan. Set in the fillets, floured side down, and reduce the heat to medium-high. Press down on the fish with your spatula, listening for the sizzle that tells you you're making a good crust. Add 1 tablespoon butter to each pan, breaking it into smaller pieces so it will melt quickly. Once the butter melts, tilt the pan and baste the fish. Cook for about 3 minutes on the first side. You'll see the fish cooking from the bottom up. When it is almost cooked through, turn it over and turn off the heat. Let the fish sit for 30 seconds or so. Transfer to paper towels.

To serve, spoon a bed of the tomato sauce onto one half of each plate and a bed of lentils onto the other half. Set the fish on top.

SAUTÉED BLACKFISH WITH MUSHROOMS AND CELERY ROOT AND POTATO PUREE

It may seem as if there's a lot of oil in the mushrooms, but what you're doing is making a sauce at the same time. It will drizzle down the fish and into the puree and tie everything together. If you can't find celery root, just make your favorite mashed potatoes.

Pour a pinot noir with this dish.   Serves 4

ACCEPT SUBSTITUTES

Striped bass

FOR THE MUSHROOMS
10 ounces mushrooms, diced
Coarse salt and freshly ground white
    pepper
⅓ cup peanut or olive oil
⅓ cup minced shallots
2 tablespoons sherry vinegar
¾ teaspoon fresh thyme leaves

4 (6- to 7-ounce) pieces skinless
    blackfish fillet (see Note)
Coarse salt and freshly ground white
    pepper
All-purpose flour
Peanut or vegetable oil
2 tablespoons unsalted butter

Celery Root and Potato Puree (page
    456)
Truffle or porcini oil (optional)

FOR THE MUSHROOMS: Heat a large skillet over medium-high heat. When the pan's hot, add the mushrooms and season with salt and white pepper. Sauté the mushrooms in their juices—the salt will get them to release the juices pretty quickly —until just tender, about 5 minutes. Push the mushrooms to the sides of the pan, and add the oil and shallots to the well you've made in the center. Leave the pan alone for a minute or so to get the oil hot and sizzling, then stir. Cook until the shallots are translucent and the mushrooms very tender, about 2 minutes. Add the vinegar, stir, and turn off the heat. Stir in the thyme and check the salt and white pepper. Move the skillet to the back of the stove.

FOR THE FISH: Heat two sauté pans over high heat. Meanwhile, season the fish on both sides with salt and white pepper. Dust the skinned side lightly with flour.

Add a slick of oil to each pan. Set in the fillets, floured side down, and reduce the heat to medium-high. Press down on the fish with your spatula, listening for the sizzle that tells you you're making a good crust. Add 1 tablespoon butter to each pan, breaking it into smaller pieces so it will melt quickly. Once the butter melts, tilt the pan and baste the fish. Cook for about 4 minutes on the first side. You'll see the fish changing color, going from pink to white at the edges. Turn the fish over, turn off the heat, and let the fish sit for 30 seconds or so. Transfer to paper towels.

To serve, make a mound of the puree in the center of four dinner plates. Set the fish on the puree and top the fish with the mushrooms, making sure you add all the juices in the pan. Drizzle on some truffle or porcini oil if you want to up the ante.

NOTE: The pinbones in blackfish are notoriously difficult to remove. Ask your fishmonger to do it for you, or make an incision down the center of each fillet and cut them out.

SAUTÉED ROUGET WITH TUNISIAN SAUCE

The rich sauce, reminiscent of puttanesca but much more refined, transforms little rouget into a special-occasion dish. This is a dish for real fish lovers. Rouget, with its pretty red skin, has a strong flavor that travels up to your nose, much the way truffles do.

This is also a dish for folks who love cooking. Let me tell you right off the bat that the sauce is time-consuming, but not very difficult. The biggest job is cleaning the fish, which must be scaled, filleted, and pinboned. Think about asking your fishmonger to do this for you and to pack up the bones for the sauce, and maybe you should slip him a tip as thanks.

Serves 6

FOR THE SAUCE

Heads and frames from 12 rouget (red mullet; see headnote)

5 tablespoons olive oil

1 cup chopped onion

½ cup chopped garlic

1 tablespoon cumin seeds

1 tablespoon coriander seeds

4–5 sprigs thyme

1 bay leaf

1 cup dry white wine

3 cups canned chopped tomatoes

Coarse salt and freshly ground white pepper

5 anchovy fillets, chopped

2 tablespoons chopped kalamata olives

2 tablespoons drained small capers

1 pound waxy (creamer or red-skinned) potatoes, boiled until tender, then chilled

3 tablespoons olive oil

Fillets from 12 rouget (red mullet), pinbones removed

Coarse salt and freshly ground white pepper

All-purpose flour

Vegetable oil

FOR THE SAUCE: Cut the heads from the fish frames. Wash the heads and frames very well, making sure you remove all traces of blood. Cover with cold water and soak for about 30 minutes, then rinse the heads and bones and dry them on paper towels.

Heat the oven to 500 degrees.

Heat a very large (14-inch) ovenproof skillet or a roasting pan over high heat. When the pan's hot, add 3 tablespoons olive oil and the fish heads. Brown the heads lightly on one side, then turn them over, add the fish frames, and sauté for a minute or so.

Slide the pan into the oven and roast for 10 minutes.

Return the pan to high heat on top of the stove, stirring and scraping, for about 2 minutes. Scrape the bones out into a bowl.

Add the remaining 2 tablespoons olive oil to the pan, along with the onion and garlic. Sauté, stirring and scraping the pan, until the onion starts to soften, about 2 minutes. Add the cumin and coriander seeds, thyme, and bay leaf and sauté until the onion is translucent, another 3 minutes or so. Return the bones to the pan, along with any juices in the bowl, and pour in the wine. The wine will bubble up right away, so stir and scrape the pan quickly to finish deglazing.

Add the tomatoes and season with salt (lightly) and white pepper. Bring to a boil, then reduce the heat and simmer for 10 minutes.

Working in batches, pulse and process the bones and tomatoes in a food processor to a coarse puree, then strain. You're processing to make sure you get some of the solids (bits of fish from the bones, for example), which will give the sauce body. Strain the sauce once more to remove any bits of fish solids or other; the sauce should have the consistency of heavy cream.

Pour the sauce into a saucepan and bring to an active simmer over medium heat. Simmer for a few minutes to reduce to about 1½ cups. You can make the sauce to this stage a day in advance; cover and refrigerate.

Peel and slice the chilled potatoes. Heat the olive oil in a skillet large enough to hold the potatoes in a single layer. Add the potatoes. You can either just warm the potatoes through in the oil or brown them on both sides—up to you.

Bring the sauce back to a simmer. Stir in the anchovies, olives, and capers.

Season the fillets with salt and white pepper and dust the skin side lightly with flour.

Heat a skillet over medium-high heat. When the pan's hot, pour in a slick of vegetable oil. Add as many fillets, floured side down, as will fit without crowding. Sauté, pressing down on the fillets to set the skin, until the fish is almost opaque on top, about 2 minutes. Turn the fish and cook for 30 seconds, then transfer to paper towels. Repeat with the remaining fillets, adding more oil to the skillet as necessary.

Divide the potatoes among six dinner plates. Set the fillets skin side up on top of the potatoes, and spoon a ring of sauce around. Pass the remaining sauce.

SAUTÉED STRIPED BASS
WITH ORANGE-SOY VINAIGRETTE

Light and elegant, this seems like a summer dish to me.   Serves 4

ACCEPT SUBSTITUTES

Try this with barramundi or sturgeon.

4 (5- to 6-ounce) striped bass fillets,
  1¼ inches thick, skin on
Coarse salt and freshly ground white
  pepper
All-purpose flour
Vegetable oil

2 tablespoons unsalted butter
Orange-Soy Vinaigrette (page 435)
3 oranges, peeled and segmented
  (see page 474)
Basic Bok Choy (or Cabbage)
  (page 451)

Heat two sauté pans over high heat. Meanwhile, season the bass on both sides with salt and white pepper. Dust the skin lightly with flour.

Add a slick of oil to each pan. Set in the fillets, floured side down, and reduce the heat to medium-high. Press down on the fish with your spatula, listening for the sizzle that tells you you're making a good crust. Add 1 tablespoon butter to each pan, breaking it into smaller pieces so it will melt quickly. Once the butter melts, tilt the pan and baste the fish. You'll see the fish cooking from the bottom up. Once it is cooked about two thirds of the way up, turn it over and turn off the heat. Let the fish sit for about 1 minute. Transfer to paper towels.

Place the fish on four dinner plates. Surround with a drizzle of the vinaigrette. Garnish with the orange segments. Serve with the bok choy, and pass the remaining vinaigrette at the table.

TROUT AMANDINE

I did a lot of camping and fishing when I was young, and this dish—sweet, tender fillets garnished with buttery shards of almond—brings back memories of cooking over a campfire. (The photo is on page 198.)

You can easily double this recipe. Sauté the fish in two skillets, but make the sauce in one of them.   Serves 2

ACCEPT SUBSTITUTES

Any trout will be delicious, but you might also want to try
this with sole or with tilefish.

2 white trout fillets, skin on
Coarse salt and freshly ground white
  pepper
All-purpose flour
Vegetable oil

7 tablespoons unsalted butter
½ cup sliced almonds
2 tablespoons chopped fresh parsley
Juice of ½ lemon

Season the trout on both sides with salt and white pepper. Dust the skin side lightly with flour and pat off any excess.

Heat a large skillet or sauté pan over medium-high heat. When the pan's hot, pour in a slick of vegetable oil. Add the trout, floured side down, and press down on the fish with a spatula to set the skin. Add 1 tablespoon butter. Sauté until the skin is crispy and browned, about 2 minutes. Turn over and sauté for 30 seconds. Transfer to two dinner plates.

Melt the remaining 6 tablespoons butter in the skillet. Add the almonds and sauté, stirring, until they're lightly browned. Add the parsley. Turn off the heat and squeeze in the lemon juice. Spoon the sauce over the fish and serve immediately.

SOLE PICCATA

Lemon and white wine — the flavors of that famous Italian-American chicken dish — work so well with sole. This is fast and delicious. Serves 4

ACCEPT SUBSTITUTES

Try this with turbot, sturgeon, or even trout.

4 (6- to 7-ounce) gray sole fillets
Coarse salt and freshly ground white
  pepper
All-purpose flour
Vegetable oil
4 tablespoons unsalted butter

½ cup minced shallots
4 thin lemon slices
¼ cup dry white wine or dry
  vermouth
2 teaspoons capers

Heat a large skillet over high heat. Meanwhile, season the fish on both sides with salt and white pepper and dredge in flour. Pat off the excess.

When the pan's hot, pour in a slick of vegetable oil. Add 2 fillets and 1 tablespoon butter, breaking it into bits so it will melt quickly. Cook the fish until golden, about 1½ minutes; turn and cook for another minute. Transfer the fish to dinner plates. Pour out the fat and repeat for the remaining 2 fillets.

Pour the fat out of the skillet and return it to the heat. Add 1 tablespoon butter and the shallots and lemon slices. Sauté, stirring, until the shallots soften, about 1 minute. Pour in the wine and stir to dissolve any browned bits in the pan. Put one lemon slice on each piece of fish, then add the last tablespoon of butter to the skillet, along with the capers. Tilt and shake the pan to melt the butter and thicken the sauce. Spoon over the fish and serve right away.

PECAN-CRUSTED TURBOT

Nicely nutty fillets pair well with the clean taste of orange.   Serves 4

ACCEPT SUBSTITUTES

This is a great method for cooking flatfish. Try it with flounder, sole, or fluke. Catfish or tilapia are good too. Larger pieces of fish will take longer to cook.

2 cups pecans

2 large egg whites

4 (4- to 5-ounce) pieces turbot fillet

Coarse salt and freshly ground white
   pepper

½ cup all-purpose flour

Vegetable oil

4 oranges, peeled and cut into
   segments (see page 474)

Soy-Orange Sauce (page 424; optional)

Grind the nuts in batches in a food processor to a fine meal. (You're doing this in batches so you have more control and to ensure you don't make pecan butter.) Pour into a shallow bowl.

Beat the egg whites in a second shallow bowl until frothy.

Season the turbot on both sides with salt and white pepper. Dredge in the flour and pat off the excess. Dip the fish in the egg whites, then in the nuts—press well to make an even coating. You can prep the fish a few hours ahead and keep it in the refrigerator on a rack set over a baking sheet.

Heat two medium skillets over medium heat. You're cooking on medium heat so you can toast the nuts but not burn them before the fish cooks through. When the pans are hot, pour in a slick of oil. Cook the fish for 2½ minutes on the first side, or until nicely browned, then turn and cook for another 1½ minutes.

Serve the fish garnished with the orange segments and a drizzle of the soy-orange sauce, if you want.

ALMOND-CRUSTED BARRAMUNDI WITH SPINACH AND PICKLED ONIONS

Watch your heat as you cook this fish. The trick is to make a toasty crust without burning the nuts and still cook the fish all the way through. Remember, you can always cook the fish longer on the second side if the nuts brown quickly. (The photo is on page 206.)

Serves 4

ACCEPT SUBSTITUTES
Sturgeon and swordfish both pair well with these flavors.

1 cup sliced almonds
¼ teaspoon cayenne
4 (5- to 6-ounce) skinless barramundi fillets
Coarse salt and freshly ground white pepper
1 tablespoon olive oil

1½ pounds leaf spinach, stemmed
All-purpose flour for dredging
1 large egg white, whisked until frothy
Peanut or vegetable oil
2 tablespoons unsalted butter
Pickled Onions (page 400)

ABOUT NUT CRUSTS

Nuts and fish have a good time together on a plate.

Bound to a fillet with a little egg white, a nut crust doesn't just add flavor and crunch. The fat from the nuts insinuates itself into the fish, giving you a richer feel in your mouth; the dish almost becomes self-basting.

You can take the idea for this crust in a lot of directions. The only pitfall, really, is cooking too quickly or using too-thick fillets; in those cases, the nuts will brown before the fish is cooked through.

SOME TIPS FOR IMPROVISATION

- Pecans, hazelnuts, almonds, cashews—all make great crusts. Walnuts are a bit too oily, and their flavor will overpower most fish.

- For very mild fish, make a crust on one side of the fillet only. More assertive fish—tilapia, say—can stand up to being encased completely.

- Spice is nice. Try adding a little of one of the spice mixes (pages 440–442) to the crust mixture. Or you might mince some fresh rosemary and add that.

- Avoid oily fish like salmon, bluefish, mackerel, swordfish, and tuna.

Put the nuts and cayenne into a food processor and pulse until finely chopped. Scrape out onto a plate. Set aside.

Season the fish with salt and white pepper and let it sit while you cook the spinach.

Heat a large skillet over medium-high heat. When the pan's hot, add the olive oil and spinach. Season with salt and white pepper. Sauté the spinach until tender, then scrape it into a colander and let it drain while you cook the fish.

Dredge the skinned side of the barramundi in flour and pat off the excess. Dip the floured side in the egg white, let the excess drip off, and dredge that side in the nuts, pressing down to make sure they adhere.

Heat two large skillets over medium-high heat. When the pans are hot, pour in a slick of peanut or vegetable oil and add the fish, crust side down, and the butter—1 tablespoon in each skillet. Reduce the heat to medium and cook the fish until the crust is browned, with a few dark flecks, 3 to 4 minutes. Turn the fish over and cook for another 1 to 2 minutes.

Make a bed of spinach on four dinner plates. Set the fish on the spinach, crust side up, and top with some pickled onions. Serve right away.

DORADE IN A POTATO CRUST

In this classic recipe, tender fish fillets are wrapped in a crisp golden brown jacket of potatoes.

Prepping the fish is a bit fussy, but you do it well in advance of cooking, so you can take your time.   Serves 4

ACCEPT SUBSTITUTES

So many fish would work here: sole, striped bass, mahi mahi, slices of sturgeon.
Just make sure the fish is no more than ⅓ inch thick.

2 large russet potatoes
½ pound (2 sticks) unsalted butter,
   melted
4 (6-ounce) skinless dorade fillets

Coarse salt and freshly ground white
   pepper
Parsley Pesto (page 422)
Vegetable oil
Peperonata (page 465)

Peel and rinse the potatoes, then cut them the long way into paper-thin slices on a mandoline or vegetable slicer. Put the potato slices in a bowl with the butter and microwave for 20 seconds to soften them.

Tear off a piece of plastic wrap and lay it on your work surface. Lay down a row of 4 slices of potato, long sides facing you and overlapping slightly, then lay down another row, again with the long edges facing you, overlapping the first row. Set a fillet on the center of the potatoes, season with salt and white pepper, and smear with about 1 teaspoon parsley pesto. Use the plastic wrap to lift the potato slices over the fish, enclosing it completely. Wrap the plastic snugly around the package. Repeat with the remaining fillets. Discard the remaining potato slices, but keep the butter. Refrigerate the fish packets for at least 2 hours.

Heat two sauté pans over medium-high heat. Unwrap the packets. When the pans are hot, drizzle in a slick of vegetable oil. Add the fish packets, pressing down on them with the back of a spatula. Spoon in 2 to 3 tablespoons of the reserved butter and sauté the packets, turning often, for 10 minutes, or until the potatoes are a rich golden brown. If the potatoes seem to be browning too quickly, lower the heat.

Blot the packets dry with paper towels and serve with the peperonata. Pass the remaining parsley pesto.

BUTTER-BASTED HALIBUT WITH CREAMY CORN AND RED PEPPER COULIS

This summer dish — a mix of sweet corn and sweet peppers and a slab of sweet fish marinated in cilantro — delights the eye as well as the taste buds. (The photo is on page 206.)   Serves 4

ACCEPT SUBSTITUTES

You've got a lot of options here: scrod or cod, snapper (skin-on fillets), black sea bass (skin-on fillets), or sea scallops.

1½ cups packed fresh cilantro leaves

¾ cup canola oil

Coarse salt

4 (5- to 6-ounce) pieces halibut fillet

Freshly ground white pepper

8 tablespoons (1 stick) unsalted butter

Creamy Corn (page 457)

Red Pepper Coulis (page 427)

Lemon wedges

Bring a large saucepan of salted water to a boil. Drop in the cilantro, blanch for 30 seconds, and drain. Refresh the cilantro in a bowl of cold water and drain again. Squeeze the cilantro until it's very dry. Start with just your hands, then put the cilantro into a triple thickness of paper towels and use the towels to help you get out all the moisture.

Put the cilantro into a blender with the oil and a pinch of salt. Puree until very smooth.

Season the fish on both sides with salt and white pepper. Put it into a sealable plastic bag and pour in the cilantro oil. Work the oil around so the fish is completely coated. Seal the bag and marinate in the refrigerator for at least 1 hour.

When you're ready to cook, remove the fish from the bag and scrape the excess marinade from the fillets.

Heat a 12-inch skillet over medium-high heat. Have a big spoon ready next to the stove as well as a few layers of paper towels. When the pan's good and hot, cut 4 tablespoons of the butter into pieces and add them to the skillet. When the butter has melted and stopped sizzling, add the fish, putting the pieces in the far side of the pan, leaving space in the part nearest you. Turn the heat down to medium and press down on the fish with a spatula; this helps get the fish started on its way to browning.

After about 30 seconds, cut the remaining 4 tablespoons butter into pieces and add them to the skillet. As the butter melts, tilt and pull the skillet toward you and start basting the fish, using that big spoon to pour the bubbling butter over the fish. You're pulling the skillet toward you so the fish will get the benefit of the heat, even though you have the pan tilted; lower the pan once in a while as you're cooking the fish. As you cook and baste, the butter will brown and its nuttiness will flavor the fish. Cook, basting constantly, for 6 minutes. Then turn the fish over, turn off the heat, and let the fish sit for 1 minute. If you stick a knife in to check, the halibut will look slightly rare in the center. That's good; carry-over heat will finish the cooking.

Use a spatula to take the fish out of the skillet and set it on the paper towels. Use another paper towel to blot it.

To serve, spread some of the creamy corn into the center of four dinner plates. Set the fish on the corn, surround with the coulis, and give each piece of fish a squirt of lemon.

ABOUT BUTTER-BASTING FISH

Remember the days of rich butter sauces served on fish? Elegant, delicious sauces like *beurre noisette* that made you smack your lips. Well, we're not eating those sauces so much these days, but with butter-basting, you'll find that you get that nutty taste of browned butter without all the fat.

Melt some butter in a large skillet and add the fish, skin side down. Press down on the fish with a spatula to set the skin in the hot butter. Then add more butter, enough so you can baste the fish effectively. As the fish cooks, the butter browns, and the almost continuous basting bathes the fish in the flavor of browned butter.

BUTTER-BASTED SEA SCALLOPS WITH GREEN BEANS AND CHORIZO AND TRUFFLE VINAIGRETTE

Sherry (which you'll find in the vinaigrette) and chorizo is a classic combination of flavors. Add the dimension of buttery scallops, and you've got a winner.   Serves 4

ACCEPT SUBSTITUTES

There really isn't a substitute for sea scallops, but this combination of flavors works well with cod, scrod, dorade, barramundi, or tilefish. Use 6-ounce portions.

1½ pounds sea scallops, tough bits removed

Coarse salt and freshly ground white pepper

4 tablespoons unsalted butter

1 sprig thyme

Green Beans and Chorizo (page 449)

Truffle Vinaigrette (page 434)

Blot the scallops dry with paper towels and season on both sides with salt and white pepper.

Heat a large heavy skillet over high heat. When the pan's good and hot, add 1 tablespoon butter and swirl it around. Set the scallops in the skillet and add the remaining 3 tablespoons butter, in pieces, and the thyme. Cook the scallops, basting almost constantly, until they are just firm, about 2 minutes. They should have a good brown crust on the bottom and be translucent in the center. (If you want the scallops more well done, turn them and cook for 30 seconds more.)

To serve, make a mound of the green beans in the center of four dinner plates. Spoon dollops of the vinaigrette around each pile of beans and set a scallop, brown crust up, on each dollop of sauce. Serve right away, with the remaining vinaigrette on the side.

BUTTER-BASTED SALMON WITH TEA

This is like a picnic at the dinner table. The salmon has the smokiness of a hot dog, the horseradish gives you the bite of mustard, and the cucumbers provide the sharpness of a pickle relish. That said, it is one elegant dish.   Serves 4

ACCEPT SUBSTITUTES

Char

4 (7-ounce) pieces wild salmon fillet,
  skin on
Coarse salt
2 teaspoons lapsang souchong tea
  powder (see Note)

8 tablespoons (1 stick) unsalted butter
Mom's Cucumber Salad (page 459)
Horseradish Cream (page 420)

Season the fish on both sides with salt, then rub all over with the tea powder. Wrap the fish tightly in plastic and refrigerate for 2 hours.

Heat a 12-inch skillet over medium-high heat. Have a big spoon ready next to the stove as well as a few layers of paper towels. When the pan's good and hot, cut 4 tablespoons butter into pieces and add them to the skillet. When the butter has melted and stopped sizzling, add the fish, skin side down, putting it in the far side of the pan, leaving space in the part nearest you. Turn the heat down to medium and press down on the fish with a spatula; this helps set the skin, getting it started on its way to being crisp and delicious.

After about 2 minutes, cut the remaining 4 tablespoons butter into pieces and add them to the skillet. As the butter melts, tilt and pull the skillet toward you and start basting the fish, using that big spoon to pour the bubbling butter over the fish. You're pulling the skillet toward you so the fish will get the benefit of the heat, even though you have the pan tilted; lower the pan once in a while as you're cooking the fish. As you cook and baste, the butter will brown and its nuttiness will flavor the fish. As the fish cooks, the flesh will turn milky pink. After 5 minutes, it should feel firm. If you have any doubts, use a knife to poke into your portion; the salmon should be rosy inside. Use a spatula to take the fish out of the skillet and set it on the paper towels. Use another paper towel to blot the salmon.

To serve, pile a mound of cucumber salad in the center of each dinner plate. Set a piece of salmon on top, skin side up, and spoon a ring of horseradish cream around the cucumber salad.

NOTE: I love the pure smoke flavor of lapsang souchong tea. To make the powder, just spoon some tea leaves into a spice grinder and process to a fine dust. Keep it in a glass jar out of the light.

FRYING

CRISPY CALAMARI

When you go to a restaurant with friends, chances are that you'll order some calamari for the table. Even if you've ordered the dish for yourself, someone else will reach over and pick. Keep that in mind at home. Bring your guests into the kitchen and turn the calamari out onto a platter. Just make sure you have plenty of napkins handy.

The secrets to crispy? It's the Wondra—and keeping the oil temperature constant. You'll want to start soaking the calamari at least 3 hours ahead.

Serves 4 as an appetizer

1 pound cleaned calamari (squid)
About 1 cup milk
Peanut or vegetable oil for deep-frying
2 cups Wondra flour
Coarse salt and freshly ground black pepper

Cayenne
Spicy Mayonnaise (page 415), Green Tartar Sauce (page 417), or Cocktail Sauce (page 421)

Even though the calamari was sold to you cleaned, run your finger inside each tube to make sure the quill has been removed. Check the tentacles for the beak, and if it's still there, snip it out with scissors. Rinse the calamari and drain it. If it's not cleaned, follow the instructions on page 43. Slice the bodies into rings about ⅓ inch wide. Cut off the very long tentacles and discard them.

Place the calamari in a bowl and cover with the milk. Refrigerate for at least 3 hours or as long as 24. You want the calamari very cold before you fry them.

Heat at least 3 inches of oil in a wide deep pot (a cast-iron Dutch oven is ideal) to 350 to 365 degrees.

Meanwhile, put the flour in a bowl and season it with salt, black pepper, and cayenne. Drain the calamari.

Working in batches, dredge the calamari in the seasoned flour and fry until golden, about 45 seconds, turning and stirring the pieces at least once. Scoop the calamari out with a spider or a slotted spoon and drain on paper towels.

Turn out onto a platter and have a bowl of the sauce of your choice nearby for dipping.

ABOUT DEEP-FRYING

To my mind, there's nothing that compares to the flavor of good fried fish. Even on a cold winter's night, frying up a batch of popcorn shrimp makes me think of summer. Yeah, it can be a little messy in the kitchen, with cleanup taking a bit longer than it might with other cooking methods, but the results are so worth the effort.

An electric deep-fryer is the cleanest method. If you have one, use it, following the manufacturer's directions. If you don't, here's what to do.

Fill a cast-iron Dutch oven, a wok, or a wide saucepan with at least 3 inches of oil. Make sure, though, that the pot is never more than half filled with oil. The oil will bubble up whenever you add fish to it, and if it overflows, you've got a mess.

Heat the oil over medium-high heat to 365 degrees. You can test it with a deep-frying or candy thermometer, or you can stick a chopstick into the oil. If small bubbles start rising around the chop-stick as soon as it hits the bottom of the pan, the oil is ready for frying. But if you are new to frying, use a thermometer. Bubbles will still rise around the chopstick when the oil's at 390 degrees, and that would destroy your fish. Best to be safe.

The temperature of the oil will drop whenever you add something to it. It's a good idea to heat up your spider or slotted spoon in the oil before you add what you're frying, and then start stirring as soon as you add it. And let the oil come back to temperature before you add more of what you're frying.

Keeping a small bowl of bleach near the stove while you fry will cut the smell (put a piece of tape across the top to make sure it's not mistaken for another liquid). And once the oil has cooled, you can pour it through a funnel into an empty bottle. Or you can pour it into a bag of cat litter and then discard it.

BAY SCALLOP HUSH PUPPIES

Crisp, golden brown nuggets of corn bread have the surprise of a sweet scallop in the center. Serve these little bites as soon as you fry them. (The photo is on page 152.)

Serves 4 to 6 as an appetizer

ACCEPT SUBSTITUTES

Fresh or frozen bay scallops are both fine.
You could also use sea scallops cut into quarters.
Or try this recipe with rock shrimp.

½ cup half-and-half or whole milk
1 tablespoon white vinegar
½ cup cornmeal
½ cup all-purpose flour
1 teaspoon baking soda
1 teaspoon coarse salt
Freshly ground white pepper
Peanut or corn oil for deep-frying

1 large egg, lightly beaten
1 pound bay scallops, tough bits removed

FOR SERVING
Grated lemon zest
Lemon wedges
Green Tartar Sauce (page 417)

Whisk the half-and-half or milk and vinegar together in a measuring cup. Let it sit while you get everything else ready. It will thicken and look slightly curdled.

Whisk the cornmeal, flour, baking soda, salt, and a generous dose of white pepper together in a large bowl.

Heat at least 3 inches of oil in a wide deep pot (a cast-iron Dutch oven is ideal) to 350 to 365 degrees. Set a rack over a baking sheet next to the stove.

When you're ready to fry, add the half-and-half or milk and the egg to the dry ingredients and stir until smooth. Fold in the scallops.

Lift out the scallops one by one and drop them into the hot oil; you can use a teaspoon for this. Don't crowd them in the pot. Fry until golden, 60 to 90 seconds. Lift the hush puppies out with a spider or slotted spoon and drain briefly on the rack.

Serve hot, with a shower of lemon zest, some wedges of lemon, and a bowl of the tartar sauce for dipping.

SHRIMP TEMPURA

Flour is a funny thing. It reacts differently depending on the weather and humidity, on the temperature, and on how it is stored. So how much liquid you'll use for this batter will vary every time you make it.

Traditionally these crispy bites would be served with something spicy, like the dipping sauce I use with Shrimp Fritters (page 264). But you may want to think outside of the box and dip them in Louis Dressing (page 339) or Green Tartar Sauce (page 417). Whatever you serve them with, you should eat these when they're almost too hot to touch.

Serves 4

1 cup all-purpose flour
½ cup cornstarch, plus additional
    for dredging
1 teaspoon coarse salt
1 large egg, lightly beaten
2 ice cubes

1–1¼ cups very cold seltzer
Peanut or vegetable oil for deep-frying
1½ pounds extra-large (16–20 count) or
    jumbo (11–15 count) shrimp, shelled,
    with tails left on, and deveined

Whisk the flour, cornstarch, and salt together in a medium bowl. Make a well in the center and add the egg. Start whisking in the egg and then the ice cubes and seltzer; continue whisking and adding seltzer until the batter is completely smooth and has the consistency of lightly whipped cream. It should have body but still be pourable. Refrigerate while you heat the oil.

Heat at least 3 inches of oil in a wide deep pot (a cast-iron Dutch oven is ideal) to 350 to 365 degrees. Set a rack over a baking sheet next to the stove.

Dredge a few shrimp in cornstarch, patting off the excess. When the oil is hot, use a bamboo skewer to lower a shrimp into the tempura batter. Let the excess batter drip off, then lower the shrimp a bit more than halfway into the oil. Hold it there for about 3 seconds, then give the skewer a little shake to release the shrimp. Repeat with a few more shrimp, but don't crowd the pot. Fry, turning the shrimp with a spider or slotted spoon so it fries evenly, until the batter is crisp and light gold, about 3½ minutes. Remove with the spider and drain on the rack for a few seconds.

Use the spider to scoop out any bits of cooked batter from the oil before frying more shrimp.

Serve right away, as they come out of the fryer.

POPCORN SHRIMP

Rock shrimp are truly convenient because they come shelled. Their soft texture is a great contrast to the crisp coating on these little nuggets.

Serves 4 to 6 as an appetizer

ACCEPT SUBSTITUTES

You can substitute shelled small (36–45 count) shrimp for the rock shrimp. You'll need 2 pounds.

2 cups milk or buttermilk

1 large egg

1½ pounds rock shrimp

Coarse salt and freshly ground white pepper

Peanut or vegetable oil for deep-frying

1 cup all-purpose flour

1 cup cornmeal

Spicy Rémoulade (page 416), Green Tartar Sauce (page 417), or Cocktail Sauce (page 421)

Whisk the milk and egg together in a medium bowl.

Season the rock shrimp with salt and white pepper and stir into the milk. Refrigerate for at least 1 hour and up to 8 hours. You want the shrimp very cold before you fry them so they won't overcook.

Heat at least 3 inches of oil in a wide deep pot (a cast-iron Dutch oven is ideal) to 350 to 365 degrees. Combine the flour and cornmeal in a shallow bowl.

When the oil is hot, drain the shrimp. Drop a handful of shrimp into the flour and cornmeal and toss to coat well. Add to the oil and fry for about 1½ minutes, until golden brown. Remove with a spider or slotted spoon and drain on paper towels. Repeat with the remaining shrimp.

Serve hot, sprinkled with some more salt if you want, and with the sauce of your choice.

POPCORN SCALLOPS

These are every bit as addictive as popcorn shrimp.   Serves 4 to 6 as an appetizer

If you can't find bay scallops, you can buy sea scallops
and cut them into quarters before you soak them.

2 cups milk or buttermilk
1 large egg
1½ pounds bay scallops, tough bits
    removed
Coarse salt and freshly ground white
    pepper
Peanut or vegetable oil for deep-
    frying

1 cup all-purpose flour
1 cup cracker crumbs (pulse saltines in
    the food processor)
Spicy Rémoulade (page 416), Green
    Tartar Sauce (page 417), or Cocktail
    Sauce (page 421)

Whisk the milk and egg together in a medium bowl.

Season the scallops with salt and white pepper and stir into the milk. Refrigerate for at least 1 hour and up to 8 hours. You want the scallops very cold before frying so they won't overcook.

Heat at least 3 inches of oil in a wide deep pot (a cast-iron Dutch oven is ideal) to 350 to 365 degrees. Combine the flour and cracker crumbs in a shallow bowl.

When the oil is hot, drain the scallops. Drop a handful of scallops into the flour and cracker crumbs and toss to coat well. Add to the oil and fry for about 1 minute, until golden brown. Remove with a spider or slotted spoon and drain on paper towels. Repeat with the remaining scallops.

Serve hot, sprinkled with some more salt if you want, and with the sauce of your choice.

SHRIMP FRITTERS

I'm going with Asian flavors for this starter of shrimp fried in a light and sassy batter. (The photo is on page 199.)   Makes about 24 fritters

FOR THE DIPPING SAUCE
⅓ cup fish sauce
⅓ cup fresh lime juice
2 tablespoons sugar
2 teaspoons minced garlic
1 small habanero chile, cut into thin
    rings (or 2 serranos, minced, with
    seeds)

FOR THE FRITTERS
2 large eggs
⅓ cup cold seltzer or club soda
2 tablespoons fresh lime juice

¾ cup self-rising cake flour (see Note),
    plus more if needed
1¼ pounds large (21–30 count) shrimp,
    shelled and chopped, or 1 pound
    rock shrimp
½ cup minced red onion
½ cup minced red bell pepper
¼ cup chopped fresh cilantro
Peanut or vegetable oil for deep-frying

FOR SERVING
1 head Boston or other tender lettuce
Fresh mint or cilantro leaves

FOR THE DIPPING SAUCE: Stir the fish sauce, lime juice, sugar, garlic, and chile together in a small bowl. Let the sauce sit for at least 30 minutes to allow the flavors to meld.

FOR THE FRITTERS: Whisk the eggs in a medium bowl to break them up. Pour in the seltzer or club soda and lime juice and whisk until smooth; the mixture will foam up. Add the flour and whisk until you have a smooth batter. Stir in the shrimp, onion, red pepper, and cilantro.

Heat at least 3 inches of oil in a wide deep pot (a cast-iron Dutch oven is ideal) to 350 to 365 degrees. Set a rack over a baking sheet next to the stove.

When the oil is hot, drop in heaping tablespoons of batter. Don't crowd them, or the oil temperature will drop too much and the fritters will be greasy. Fry the fritters, turning them with a spider or slotted spoon so they cook evenly, until golden brown and cooked through, about 3 minutes. Remove with the spider to the rack to drain. Spoon out any little bits of fritter from the oil before adding the next batch.

If the fritters really break apart when you add them to the oil, it means the batter is a bit too thin, so stir in another tablespoon or two of flour.

To serve, set out the bowl of sauce. Pile the fritters onto a platter and surround with the lettuce leaves and a pile of herb leaves so everyone can wrap a fritter and some herb leaves in lettuce and dip into the sauce.

NOTE: You can substitute regular cake flour, but add ½ teaspoon baking powder and ¼ teaspoon coarse salt.

CLAM FRITTERS

Fritters, like most fried foods, are the kind of things you serve in the kitchen, with guests gathered around. Enjoy these crisp dumplings right out of the fryer.

Makes about 16 fritters

36 littleneck clams, scrubbed
1 large egg
¼ cup minced poblano chile
¼ cup minced onion
2 tablespoons minced fresh parsley

1 tablespoon chopped fresh dill
1 cup plus 3 tablespoons self-rising cake
    flour (see Note), plus more if needed
Peanut or vegetable oil for deep-frying
Cocktail Sauce (page 421)

Shuck the clams into a strainer set over a bowl so you'll capture the juice. Let the clams drain thoroughly, then chop.

Whisk the egg and ⅓ cup of the clam juice in a bowl. Stir in the chile, onion, parsley, dill, and clams. Fold/stir in the flour to make a thick batter with no lumps.

Heat at least 3 inches of oil in a wide deep pot (a cast-iron Dutch oven is ideal) to 350 to 365 degrees. Set a rack over a baking sheet next to the stove.

When the oil is hot, drop in heaping tablespoons of batter. Don't crowd them, or the oil temperature will drop too much and you'll end up with greasy fritters. Fry the fritters, turning them with a spider or slotted spoon so they cook evenly, until golden brown and cooked through, about 4 minutes. Remove with the spider to the rack to drain. Spoon out any little bits of fritter from the oil before adding the next batch.

If the fritters really break apart when you add them to the oil, it means the batter is a bit too thin, so stir in another tablespoon or two of flour.

Serve these very hot, with a bowl of the cocktail sauce for dipping.

NOTE: You can substitute regular cake flour, but add ¾ teaspoon baking powder and ¼ teaspoon coarse salt.

"EVERYTHING" TUNA

My all-time favorite bagel is the everything bagel, the one with a little bit of each possible topping. I started playing around and turned those ingredients into a crust for tuna. (The photo is on page 201.)

Have your fishmonger cut the tuna. For each portion, you want a block of fish that's 1½ × 1½ × 3 inches.   Serves 4

FOR THE CRUST
¾ cup white sesame seeds
¾ cup black sesame seeds
1 cup poppy seeds
¾ cup dried minced onions
¾ cup dried minced garlic
1 tablespoon coarse sea salt

4 (7- to 8-ounce) pieces tuna (see headnote)
Coarse salt
1 large egg white
Canola oil for deep-frying
Soy sauce
Wasabi paste

FOR THE CRUST: Combine the white and black sesame seeds, poppy seeds, onions, garlic, and salt in a jar and mix well.

Season the tuna with salt.

Beat the egg white in a shallow bowl until frothy. Pour about 1 cup of the crust mixture onto a plate. Store the remaining mix in a glass jar out of direct light.

Dip each piece of tuna into the egg white and let the excess drip off, then coat the fish on all sides with the crust mixture, patting it to make sure it adheres. Put the tuna on a rack set over a plate or baking sheet and refrigerate while you heat the oil.

Pour about 3 inches of oil into a large deep saucepan and heat it to 365 degrees. Fry the tuna one piece at a time (if you do more, the oil temperature will drop too far and too quickly) until the dried onions brown, 1 minute to 1 minute and 15 seconds. Drain the fish on a rack.

Cut each portion into slices about ⅓ inch thick, and serve with soy sauce and wasabi paste.

FISH FINGERS AT HOME

These are the classic: the fish you get when you order fish and chips, the good old fried fish that kids love.

There are too many possible accompaniments for me to recommend just one or two. A mayonnaise-based sauce like Green Tartar Sauce (page 417) or Spicy Rémoulade (page 416)? Sure. Or just a sprinkle of malt vinegar? Fine by me. But do make your favorite French fries or potato salad.   Serves 4

ACCEPT SUBSTITUTES

Grouper (from Hawaii), halibut, and mahi mahi are other classic fish for
this kind of frying; cut the fillets into 1-x-1-x-3-inch fingers.

FOR THE BATTER
1 large egg
1½–1¾ cups cold seltzer or club soda
2 cups self-rising cake flour (see Note)

1½ pounds cod fillet
Coarse salt and freshly ground white
  pepper
Peanut or vegetable oil for deep-frying

FOR THE BATTER: Crack the egg into a medium bowl and whisk to break it up. Pour in 1½ cups seltzer or club soda and whisk well. It'll froth up. Whisk in the flour until completely smooth. The batter should have the consistency of lightly whipped cream. If it's too thick, whisk in more seltzer or club soda by the tablespoon.

ABOUT FRYING FISH FINGERS

There are a few tricks to achieving a cracklingly crisp crust on deep-fried fish fingers.

First is the consistency of the batter, which should be that of lightly whipped cream; be ready to adjust the amount of seltzer you add to get there (it all depends on your flour and the humidity that day).

Second is monitoring the temperature of the oil. Use your thermometer. The more oil you're frying in, the less chance there is of the temperature dropping a lot when you add the fish. So if you've decided to use a saucepan, fry just 2 or 3 pieces at a time.

Third is using a bamboo skewer to lower each piece of fish partway into the oil and hold it there for a few seconds. This sets the crust, and you won't have batter-coated fingers either.

Cut the cod into fingers that are about 1¼ × 1¼ × 3 inches. Season with salt and white pepper and keep in the refrigerator until you're ready to fry.

Heat at least 3 inches of oil in a wide deep pot (a cast-iron Dutch oven is ideal) to 365 degrees. Set a rack over a baking sheet next to the stove.

When the oil is hot, drop a few pieces of fish into the batter, pushing them down to coat completely. Use a bamboo skewer to lift out the fish one piece at a time and let the excess batter drip off. Lower the fish, still on the skewer, a bit more than halfway into the oil and hold it there for about 3 seconds, then give the skewer a little shake to release the fish. Fry, turning the fish with a spider or slotted spoon so it fries evenly, until rich golden brown, about 4 minutes. Remove the fish with a spider and let drain on the rack. Repeat with the remaining fish.

Serve hot.

NOTE: You can substitute regular cake flour, but add 1½ teaspoons baking powder and ½ teaspoon coarse salt.

VARIATION

Bluefish, dipped in buttermilk and mustard and dredged in flour, makes great fish fingers. Salting the fish in advance firms it up, so it's less likely to fall apart when you fry.

Cut 1½ pounds of skinless bluefish fillets into fingers about 1 x 3 inches. Salt them and place them in a single layer on a plate. Refrigerate for at least 4 hours.

Whisk ½ cup buttermilk with ¼ cup Dijon mustard in a medium bowl. Set up a plate with all-purpose flour for dredging. Dip the fish in the buttermilk, then coat well with flour. Place the coated fish on a rack.

Follow the instructions in the fish finger recipe for frying. Serve with Sweet Pickle Relish Sauce (page 418) or make sandwiches on soft potato buns, with shredded iceberg lettuce and the relish. It's enough to serve 4.

CATFISH TACOS

Here's my spin on these California treats. Traditionally they would be made with cod or mahi mahi, but I think they're a great use for catfish.

The beer batter has a malty essence that will be as rich as the beer you use. The cornmeal batter is sweeter, because of the corn, and it has a bit more texture. But both these batters come out of the fryer crisp and stay crisp, so take your pick.

Makes 6 tacos

ACCEPT SUBSTITUTES

Try tilapia or a firm fish like sturgeon.

BEER BATTER
1 cup Bisquick
1 cup beer (your choice)

OR

CORNMEAL BATTER
½ cup Bisquick
½ cup yellow cornmeal
⅔ cup milk

Peanut or vegetable oil for deep-frying
2 (8-ounce) catfish fillets, cut into thirds
Coarse salt and freshly ground white pepper

FOR SERVING
Sliced radishes
Sliced avocado, squirted with the juice of ½ lime
6 corn tortillas
¾ pound napa cabbage, shredded, salted, and tossed with the juice of 1½ limes
Mango Salsa (page 394)

FOR THE BATTER: Whisk the ingredients together in a medium bowl until smooth. Let sit at room temperature for 30 minutes.

Heat at least 3 inches of oil in a wide deep pot (a cast-iron Dutch oven is ideal) to 365 degrees. Set a rack over a baking sheet next to the stove.

Season the fish with salt and white pepper.

When the oil is hot, use a bamboo skewer to lower the fish one piece at a time into the batter. Let the excess drip off, then lower the fish a bit more than halfway into the oil. Hold it there for about 3 seconds, then give the skewer a little shake to release the fish. Fry in batches, turning the fish with a spider or slotted spoon so it fries evenly, until rich golden brown, about 4 minutes. Remove the fish with the spider and let drain on the rack.

To serve, put the fish on a platter with the radishes and avocado. Set out a basket of tortillas and bowls of the cabbage and salsa, and dig in.

CHICKEN-FRIED TROUT

Chicken-fried steak may be a little stodgy, but when you adapt this Southern classic for fish—adding zing to the buttermilk soak with scallions, lemon zest, and chili paste—you've got something that's moist and tender and, yes, light.

Serve this fish with a mayonnaisey sauce and some slaw and sliced ripe tomatoes, or make sandwiches. (The photo is on page 145.)   Serves 4

ACCEPT SUBSTITUTES

Cod fillets take happily to this marinade. So do tilapia and catfish; cut the fillets down the center before marinating, and keep in mind that the thinner halves will cook more quickly. Mahi mahi rocks when you chicken-fry it. Its dense fillets take longer to cook, though; count on 2 minutes per side.

FOR THE MARINADE
1 cup buttermilk
¼ cup minced red onion
¼ cup chopped scallions
3 tablespoons chopped fresh dill
1 teaspoon minced garlic
1 teaspoon grated lemon zest
½ teaspoon chili paste (sambal oelek)

4 (7-ounce) trout fillets
Coarse salt and freshly ground white
    pepper
All-purpose flour for dredging
Corn or peanut oil for frying
Spicy Rémoulade (page 416) or Green
    Tartar Sauce (page 417)

FOR THE MARINADE: Combine the buttermilk, onion, scallions, dill, garlic, zest, and chili paste in a baking dish. Whisk or stir well.

Lay the fillets in the marinade, making sure you've got them completely coated. Cover with plastic and marinate in the refrigerator for at least 1 hour and up to 8 hours.

When you're ready for dinner, remove the fish from the marinade and season it with salt and white pepper. Coat the fillets well with flour.

Heat ¼ inch of oil in a heavy skillet (this is a good time to pull out your cast-iron pan) until very hot but not smoking. Fry the fish in batches for about 1½ minutes on the first side, then turn and fry for another 45 seconds. The crust should be golden.

Drain on paper towels, and serve with the rémoulade or tartar sauce.

CHICKEN-FRIED SOFT-SHELL CRABS

The soft acidity of buttermilk works so well with the sweetness of crabs, and this technique makes a great crisp crab. Serves 4 to 6

FOR THE MARINADE

1 cup buttermilk

¼ cup minced red onion

¼ cup chopped scallions

3 tablespoons chopped fresh dill

1 teaspoon minced garlic

1 teaspoon grated lemon zest

½ teaspoon chili paste (sambal oelek)

12 ("hotel") soft-shell crabs, cleaned (see page 42)

Coarse salt and freshly ground white pepper

¾ cup all-purpose flour

¾ cup cornmeal

Corn or peanut oil for frying

Spicy Rémoulade (page 416) or Green Tartar Sauce (page 417)

FOR THE MARINADE: Combine the buttermilk, onion, scallions, dill, garlic, zest, and chili paste in a baking dish. Whisk or stir well.

Lay the crabs in the marinade, making sure you've got them completely coated. Cover with plastic and marinate in the refrigerator for 1 hour. The crabs will weep into the marinade; this is fine.

Remove the crabs from the marinade and season with salt and white pepper. Combine the flour and cornmeal and dip the crabs, patting to coat well. Lay them on a rack over a baking sheet. Refrigerate for about 1 hour to set the coating.

Heat ¼ inch of oil in a heavy skillet (this is a good time to pull out your cast-iron pan) until very hot but not smoking. Fry the crabs in batches for about 2 minutes on the first side, then turn and fry for another minute. The crust should be golden. Be prepared: the crabs will spit when you fry them; a splatter screen will come in handy.

Drain on paper towels, and serve with the rémoulade or tartar sauce.

THE SOFT-SHELL CRAB BLT

If you're a BLT fan, get ready for something awesome. (The photo is on page 153.)

Spread some potato rolls or hamburger buns with butter and toast them on a griddle. Smear the rolls with tartar sauce or maybe just mayonnaise and build a sandwich with a chicken-fried soft-shell crab, bacon, lettuce, tomato, sliced avocado, and a few grinds of the pepper mill.

SHRIMP TOAST

If you think these mainstays of Chinese restaurants have to be heavy and chewy, think again. This version is light and packed with bright flavors.

You can double the recipe and make a big batch, in which case it's worth using a Dutch oven to fry in. Otherwise, just fry a couple at a time in a saucepan, using less oil. **Serves 6 as an appetizer**

½ pound shelled medium (31–35 count) shrimp
4 teaspoons minced shallot
1 tablespoon minced fresh ginger
2 teaspoons minced garlic
2 teaspoons soy sauce
1–2 teaspoons chili paste (sambal oelek)

1 teaspoon sesame oil
⅓ cup chopped scallions
6 slices Pepperidge Farm Very Thin bread, crusts removed
Peanut or vegetable oil for deep-frying

Put the shrimp in the freezer for 20 minutes to make sure they are very cold.

Combine the shrimp, shallot, ginger, and garlic in a food processor. Pulse to make a coarse puree. Scrape down the sides. Add the soy sauce, chili paste, and sesame oil and process to a smooth puree, scraping down when you need to. Scrape the shrimp paste into a bowl and stir in the scallions.

Divide the shrimp paste among the 6 slices of bread, piling it in the center and tapering down to the edges. Cut on the diagonal to make 12 pieces.

Heat 3 inches of oil in a saucepan to 350 to 365 degrees. Fry the shrimp toast in batches, shrimp side down, until you see that the edges have turned golden. Turn and cook for a few seconds more, until the bread is golden. Drain on paper towels and serve hot.

FRIED OYSTERS

There are few things more delicious than a briny oyster that's been fried to a golden brown. Have plenty of napkins on hand when you serve these.

Serves 4 to 6 as an appetizer

1 pint shucked oysters
1 cup milk
Vegetable oil for deep-frying
½ cup Wondra flour

½ cup cornmeal
Green Tartar Sauce (page 417) or Spicy
    Rémoulade (page 416)

Drain the oysters and put them in a bowl with the milk. Refrigerate for at least 2 hours.

Heat at least 3 inches of oil in a wide deep pot (a cast-iron Dutch oven is ideal) to 350 to 365 degrees. Set a rack over a baking sheet next to the stove.

Drain the oysters. Mix the Wondra flour and cornmeal together in a bowl.

Working in batches, dredge the oysters in the dry mix, coating them well. Drop into the oil and fry in batches, turning once or twice with a spider or slotted spoon, until golden brown, about 3 minutes. Remove with the spider and drain on the rack.

Serve with the sauce of your choice.

OYSTER PO'BOY

Some people may vote for the muffaletta, but for me, the oyster po'boy is the great sandwich of New Orleans.

You need French bread, crusty on the outside and soft inside. Cut it open and slather it with green tartar sauce or spicy rémoulade (my choice). Pack it with hot fried oysters, give them a few shots of Louisiana Hot Sauce or Tabasco, and pile on some shredded iceberg lettuce.

SHELLFISH APPETIZERS AND FIRST COURSES

SOME OTHER APPETIZERS IN THE BOOK

The cooking techniques I use in this chapter are particularly suited to shellfish, so I've gathered them together. However, you'll find other dishes throughout the book that make ideal appetizers and first courses. Any of the grilled shrimp on pages 172–175, for example, could be served as a first course. Or you and your guests could just stand around and eat them with your fingers right off the grill.

Also take a look at the following:

OYSTER SHOOTERS

Amaze your friends! Have fun at parties!

No amounts here. The thing about oyster shooters is that you keep making them as long as the oysters, vodka, and cocktail sauce hold out. (The photo is on page 148.)

Cocktail Sauce (page 421)   Tabasco sauce

Oysters, shucked   Iced vodka

Put a little cocktail sauce in the bottom of a shot glass. Nestle 1 oyster on top, add a little more cocktail sauce, and top it with a shot of Tabasco and 1 ounce iced vodka.

Throw back the oyster as though it were a shot.

CLAMS CASINO

This classic is all about the flavor of bacon marrying with clams. Look for bacon that isn't too smoky (I particularly like the uncured center-cut bacon from Niman Ranch), so the flavors of the clams will still sing.

Makes 24 pieces

ACCEPT SUBSTITUTES

Fat Gulf oysters, maybe Apalachicolas, combine well with the casino topping. There's enough here for a dozen big oysters. Bake them at 500 degrees for 8 minutes.

½ pound bacon, chopped

1 cup finely chopped red bell pepper

½ cup finely chopped poblano chile
 or green bell pepper

Coarse salt

⅓ cup minced shallots

1 tablespoon minced garlic

Juice of ½ lemon

24 littleneck clams, scrubbed

Panko (Japanese bread crumbs),
 for sprinkling

Put the bacon in a large skillet, turn the heat to medium-high, and cook, stirring often, until the fat is rendered and the bacon bits are just starting to brown, about 5

ABOUT PURGING CLAMS AND MUSSELS

Mollusks often have sand in their bellies, and purging—which is giving them the chance to get rid of that sand—is something you have to do if you've harvested clams or mussels yourself. Those you purchase from a market have usually been purged already, but it won't hurt to do it again.

You've probably heard about the trick of adding a handful of cornmeal to the water when you soak mollusks. And it does work: the clams or mussels exchange whatever sand they have inside them for the cornmeal. But here's the problem: now they're filled with cornmeal, and when you cook them, you've got polenta. I don't care for that.

I soak clams and mussels just in well-salted water to purge them, and it works fine. Use cool water and enough salt so you can really taste it: ¼ cup of coarse salt to each quart of water is a good guide to follow.

Soak for about 30 minutes.

minutes. Add the peppers and a pinch of salt (be careful with the salt) and crank the heat up to high. Sauté for 1 minute, then add the shallots and garlic. Sauté until the garlic is fragrant, another 30 seconds or so. Turn off the heat and stir in the lemon juice.

Scrape the topping into a bowl or container and let it cool. Refrigerate for at least 1 hour or up to 1 week.

Heat the oven to 450 degrees. Pour enough coarse salt onto a baking sheet to make a base for the clams; you don't want them tipping over and spilling their juices.

Shuck the clams, leaving them in the bottom shells but running your knife under the clams to release them. Cover each clam with a heaping teaspoon of the topping—be generous—and a light dusting of panko, and nestle into the salt.

Bake for 10 minutes. Let the clams cool for a few minutes before serving. They're piping hot.

CLAMS OREGANATA

Whenever I need a refresher course on all things Italian-American, I check in with the Parisi brothers, who I worked with back in my days at the Water Club in Brooklyn. Mike has never let me down, and Pat will probably try to claim credit for this recipe.

The topping is also fantastic on baked fish (see page 211). Makes 24 pieces

Coarse salt
24 topneck clams, scrubbed

FOR THE TOPPING
1 cup dry bread crumbs
2 teaspoons minced garlic
¼ cup chopped fresh parsley
1 tablespoon crumbled dried oregano

1 teaspoon fresh thyme leaves
3 tablespoons freshly grated Parmesan
3 tablespoons olive oil
1 tablespoon fresh lemon juice
Coarse salt and freshly ground white pepper

Pour enough coarse salt onto a baking sheet to make a bed for the clams. Shuck the clams over a bowl, so you can capture and reserve the juice; leave them in the bottom shells but run your knife under the clams to release them. Set the clams on the baking sheet as you shuck them. Refrigerate until you're ready to serve.

FOR THE TOPPING: Combine the bread crumbs, garlic, parsley, oregano, thyme, Parmesan, olive oil, lemon juice, and ¼ cup of the reserved clam juice (if you're making this topping for fish, use bottled clam juice). Season with salt and white pepper and mix well. You can make the topping well in advance; cover it with plastic and refrigerate.

Heat the oven to 450 degrees.

Top each clam with a generous tablespoon of the topping. Bake for 8 minutes. Let the clams cool for a few minutes before serving; they're piping hot.

CLAMS AND CHORIZO

Here's something quick, easy, and delicious to share with drinks. Plan on having a sliced baguette on hand to sop up the sauce. (The photo is on page 146.)   Serves 4

2 tablespoons olive oil
1 (3-ounce) Spanish chorizo, casing
   removed, chopped
4 garlic cloves, coarsely chopped

2 sprigs thyme
12 littleneck clams, scrubbed
⅓ cup amontillado or dry sherry

Heat a large skillet over medium-high heat. Add the oil and chorizo and sauté, stirring often, until the chorizo starts to brown. Add the garlic and thyme and sauté until the garlic is fragrant, about 1 minute. Add the clams, pour in the sherry, and cover the skillet. Cook, shaking the pan often, until the clams open. This can take 5 to 10 minutes, depending on the mood of the clams (some just don't want to open right away), so check periodically and remove the clams as they open.

Serve in a wide shallow bowl with the pan juices scraped out over the clams.

CLAM BLOODY MARY MIX

Here's something to make when you're shucking a lot of clams and the recipe doesn't call for the juice. Get out a big pitcher and pour in 2 cups V8 and 1 cup clam juice (you can also make this with bottled, but fresh is better). Stir in 2 packed tablespoons prepared horseradish, 10 dashes Tabasco sauce, 5 dashes Worcestershire sauce, and ¼ teaspoon celery seeds.

This is enough for 4 big Bloody Marys. Make them with vodka or make them with gin, but don't forget the essential garnishes: a big piece of lime and a big piece of lemon squeezed into each drink. A celery stick makes the perfect stirrer.

CLASSIC STEAMED MUSSELS

A little wine, some shallot and garlic, a hint of mustard, and a shower of herbs—these are all flavors I love in a bowl of steaming mussels. Make sure there's bread on the table so diners can sop up the juices.

Don't be shy with the mint; it's great with the mustard and mussel juices.

Serves 4

¼ cup olive oil

6 tablespoons minced shallots

1 tablespoon minced garlic

2 pounds mussels, scrubbed and debearded

½ cup dry white wine

½ cup bottled clam juice

Juice of 1 lemon

2 tablespoons Dijon mustard

⅔ cup chopped mixed fresh parsley and mint

Heat a deep wide pot over high heat.

When the pot is good and hot, add the oil, shallots, and garlic and cook for 30 seconds, stirring. Add the mussels, wine, and clam juice and immediately slap on the lid and shake the pot. Cook, shaking the pot often, until the mussels open, about 4 minutes (the larger the mussels are, the longer they will take to cook). Transfer the mussels to a large bowl with a large spider or slotted spoon and cover them with a kitchen towel to keep them warm.

Reduce the heat to medium-high. Reduce the liquid by half, then turn off the heat. Whisk in the lemon juice, mustard, and half the herbs. Add the mussels (and any juices in the bowl) back to the pot and stir well, then divide the mussels and sauce among four big soup plates.

Garnish with the remaining herbs and serve immediately.

MUSSELS WITH FENNEL

The diced fennel adds texture to this improvisation on steamed mussels.   Serves 4

¼ cup olive oil

2 teaspoons toasted fennel seeds

1 fennel bulb, trimmed and cut into
  small dice

½ cup minced shallots

2 tablespoons minced garlic

Coarse salt and freshly ground white
  pepper

2 pounds mussels, scrubbed and
  debearded

1 cup dry white wine

4 plum tomatoes, cut into small dice

Heat a very large skillet over medium-high heat. When the pan's good and hot, add the olive oil and fennel seeds. Cook for 1 minute. Add the fennel and cook for 2 minutes. Add the shallots and garlic, season with salt and white pepper, and crank the heat up to high. Cook for 1 to 2 minutes, until the shallots have softened (the fennel will still have some tooth to it).

Add the mussels and wine and slap the lid on the skillet. Hold the lid down and give the skillet a good shake. Cook, shaking the pan regularly, until all the mussels have opened. Count on this taking about 4 minutes.

Remove the mussels from the pan with a large spider or slotted spoon to a colander set over a bowl. Cover the mussels with a kitchen towel to keep them warm while you finish the sauce.

Lower the heat under the skillet to medium-high and reduce the pan juices by half. Add the tomatoes and any liquid that's accumulated in the bowl under the mussels and cook for about 8 minutes, until the tomatoes start to thicken. Return the mussels to the skillet, stir them into the sauce, cover, and cook for about a minute to get them good and hot.

Divide the mussels among four bowls, pour the sauce over them, and serve right away.

MUSSELS WITH FENNEL AND POTATOES

This salad makes an elegant first course or, with a green salad and some bread, a fine little lunch.

Follow the instructions for Mussels with Fennel. While you reduce the sauce, shell the mussels.

Once the tomatoes have started to thicken, add 1 pound red-skinned or creamer potatoes that you have boiled, peeled, and sliced. Cook for a minute or two to heat them, folding rather than stirring, so you don't break up the potatoes. Fold in the mussels, 1 tablespoon white wine vinegar, 1 tablespoon chopped fresh basil, and 1 tablespoon olive oil.

You can serve this right away or at room temperature. This is enough for 4.

ABOUT COOKING MUSSELS

Here's the ideal: sitting down at the table with bowls piled high with plump, tender mussels for a crowd, a communal "shell bowl" in the center of the table. Your hands get messy as you reach into the bowl again to pull out another mussel and pop it into your mouth. And you and your guests smile, because each one is cooked perfectly.

That's attainable as long as you've got a clear plan of attack. Mussels cook quickly, and that means they'll overcook quickly, and an overcooked mussel is tough and stringy. The easiest way to avoid this problem is by using as wide a pan as possible over very high heat. That will expose all the mussels to the hot surface of the pan so they cook together at the same speed. Too small a pan, and the mussels on the bottom are ready first and then keep on cooking while the ones on top wait for the heat to reach them. So, here are a couple of things to keep in mind.

The pan you want is the one that will hold all the mussels in just about one layer. If you don't have a skillet that big, use two skillets—dividing all the ingredients—and then finish the sauce in one of them.

Have a big bowl ready, set near the stove, and have a clean kitchen towel nearby, so you can keep the mussels warm while you finish the sauce. Some recipes call for draining the mussels in a colander set in the bowl.

A spider, a large wire skimmer set onto a bamboo handle, is the best tool for pulling the mussels out of the pan and into the colander. It's inexpensive and handy. You can find them in Chinatown markets, and since they come in several sizes, get a big one.

MUSSELS WITH BLACK BEAN SAUCE

The earthiness and tang of this sauce are a great complement to the sweetness of the mussels. This dish comes together very quickly, so have everything ready to go. I call it bing-bang-boom cooking.   Serves 4

¼ cup vegetable oil

2 tablespoons minced fresh ginger

1 tablespoon minced garlic

¼ cup fermented black beans, rinsed (see Note)

1 teaspoon chili paste (sambal oelek)

2 pounds mussels, scrubbed and debearded

½ cup water

1 tablespoon sherry vinegar

1 tablespoon unsalted butter, cut into pieces

2 tablespoons fresh cilantro leaves

2 tablespoons chopped fresh basil

Juice of ½ lime

Heat a very large skillet over high heat. When the skillet is good and hot, add the oil and ginger and stir-fry for 15 seconds. Add the garlic and stir-fry for 15 seconds. Add the black beans and chili paste and stir-fry for 15 seconds. Add the mussels, water, and vinegar and put the lid on the skillet. Hold the lid down and give the skillet a good shake. Cook, shaking the pan regularly, until all the mussels have opened. Count on this taking about 4 minutes.

Remove the mussels from the pan with a large spider or slotted spoon to a colander set over a bowl. Cover the mussels with a kitchen towel to keep them warm while you finish the sauce.

Boil the liquid in the skillet—pour any juices that accumulate in the bowl under the mussels back into the pan—until it looks syrupy, about 2 minutes. Whisk in the butter, then stir in the herbs and lime juice. Dump the mussels back into the skillet and stir to coat with the sauce.

To serve, divide the mussels and sauce among four bowls.

NOTE: Fermented black beans are available in Asian markets and can also be ordered from Kalustyan's (www.kalustyans.com).

THAI-STYLE MUSSELS

This is a killer dish. Save the rice until you've finished eating the mussels, then stir it into the sauce and get out your spoon. (The photo is on page 199.)

Serves 4

4 fresh kaffir lime leaves (see Note)
1 (14-ounce) can coconut milk
1 tablespoon fresh lime juice
1 tablespoon fish sauce
2 red chiles, minced (with the seeds)
¼ cup vegetable oil
⅓ cup minced shallots
4 garlic cloves, cut into thin slices

2 pounds mussels, scrubbed and debearded
¼ cup chopped fresh cilantro
1 tablespoon chopped fresh mint

FOR SERVING
Jasmine or white rice

Bruise the lime leaves by squeezing and rubbing them between your fingers. Combine the coconut milk and lime leaves in a small saucepan. Bring to a simmer over medium-low heat. Turn off the heat, stir, and leave this to infuse for 30 minutes.

Combine the lime juice, fish sauce, and chiles in a small bowl.

Heat a deep wide pot over high heat. When the pot's good and hot, add the vegetable oil, shallots, and garlic and cook for 30 seconds, stirring. Add the mussels and cover the pot immediately. Cook, shaking the pot often, until the mussels open, about 4 minutes, depending on the size of the mussels. Transfer the mussels to a big bowl with a large spider or slotted spoon and cover them with a kitchen towel to keep them warm.

Reduce the juices in the pot by half, until they're syrupy looking. Add the lime juice and chile mixture and bring to a boil. Cook for 30 seconds. Add the coconut milk and lime leaves and bring to a boil. Boil for 1 minute. Return the mussels to the pot and bring to a boil. Stir in the herbs.

Divide the mussels and sauce among four big soup bowls. Serve immediately, with the rice on the side.

NOTE: Kaffir lime leaves are available fresh in some specialty markets and stores like Whole Foods.

STUFFED MUSSELS

You can make these tasty morsels well in advance and bake them right before serving. Fatty Mediterranean mussels work well here.   Serves 6

2 pounds mussels, scrubbed and
   debearded
½ cup dry white wine
2 garlic cloves
¼ cup fresh parsley leaves
1 cup dry bread crumbs

2 tablespoons grated Pecorino
1 teaspoon dried oregano
Crushed red pepper
1 teaspoon fresh lemon juice
Olive oil
Lemon wedges

Heat a large skillet over high heat. When the pan's good and hot, add the mussels and wine and cover immediately. Hold the lid down and give the skillet a good shake. Cook, shaking the pan regularly, until all the mussels have opened. Count on this taking about 4 minutes.

Drain the mussels in a colander set over a bowl and let them cool down.

Heat the oven to 425 degrees.

When the mussels are cool enough to handle, shell them, saving the clean halves of the shells — the halves without the bit of muscle still attached. Drop the mussels into the liquid in the bowl to keep them moist.

Mince the garlic and parsley together to make a paste — quick work in a mini-processor. Scrape the parsley paste into a mixing bowl. Add the bread crumbs and Pecorino, crumble in the oregano, and add a pinch of crushed red pepper. Mix the stuffing, then add the lemon juice and 2 to 3 tablespoons of the mussel liquid. You're looking for something the consistency of damp sand; the stuffing should just hold together when you pinch it.

Return the mussels to the clean shells and pile on the stuffing. Set the mussels on a baking sheet and drizzle them with olive oil. You can prepare the mussels in advance to this point. Cover the baking sheet with plastic and refrigerate.

Bake the mussels for 12 to 15 minutes, until lightly browned and piping hot. Let them sit for a few minutes before serving, so folks don't burn their fingers. Pass the lemon wedges.

SHRIMP SCAMPI

Scampi is the Italian name for langoustines, but the word also refers to an old-time favorite from Italian-American kitchens: shrimp cooked in garlic butter. I laugh every time I think of the name, because it's as close to "Shrimp Shrimp" as it can get.

Crusty bread belongs with this shrimp, but if you want, serve it over thin spaghetti or linguine.   Serves 6

1½ pounds jumbo (11–15 count)
  shrimp, shelled, with tails left on
Coarse salt and freshly ground white
  pepper

2 tablespoons olive oil
1 cup dry white wine or dry vermouth
Scampi Butter (page 408)
Chopped fresh parsley or basil leaves

Season the shrimp with salt and white pepper.

Heat a large heavy skillet over medium-high heat. When the pan's good and hot, increase the heat to high and add 1 tablespoon oil and half the shrimp. Sauté for about 1 minute, then turn the shrimp and sauté for another 30 seconds. The shrimp will not be fully cooked; you'll finish cooking them in the sauce. Transfer the shrimp to a plate. Add the remaining 1 tablespoon oil and shrimp to the skillet. Sauté the shrimp for 1 minute, turn them over, and sauté for another 30 seconds. Transfer these to the plate with the other shrimp.

Pour the wine into the skillet, bring to a boil, and reduce it by half. Reduce the heat to medium and whisk in the butter bit by bit to make a creamy sauce. Return the shrimp to the skillet and cook for 1 minute.

Serve garnished with the herb of your choice.

CELERY SHRIMP

Reminiscent of a traditional shrimp boil, this dish sings with the flavor of celery goosed with a hint of heat. It is prepared like a stir-fry, *à la minute*.

Serve it with crusty bread

Serves 4

¼ cup vegetable oil

2 teaspoons ground toasted coriander
   seeds

1 teaspoon celery seeds

6 dried red chiles (Thai, if you can
   find them), coarsely chopped

2 thin slices fresh ginger, cut into very
   fine strips

1 cup sliced onion

1 cup sliced celery

2 teaspoons minced garlic

1 pound extra-large (16–20) shrimp in
   the shell

Coarse salt

½ cup dry vermouth

Heat a large sauté pan over high heat. When the pan's good and hot, add the oil, coriander, celery seeds, and chiles and fry for a few seconds. Add the ginger and fry for 30 seconds. Add the onion and celery and stir-fry for about 1½ minutes. Add the garlic and stir-fry until fragrant, about 30 seconds.

Add the shrimp, season well with salt, and stir-fry until the shrimp are turning pink, about 2 minutes. Pull the pan off the heat and pour in the vermouth—watch out, this may flame. Then cover the pan and cook, shaking the pan, for 1 minute. Turn off the heat and let the shrimp sit for a minute or two before serving.

STUFFED SQUID

Serve these with boiled potatoes dressed with extra virgin olive oil and sea salt.

Serves 4

6 ounces sea scallops, tough bits removed, chilled in the freezer for 30 minutes

⅛ teaspoon freshly grated nutmeg

Coarse salt and freshly ground white pepper

Cayenne

½ cup heavy cream

2 tablespoons unsalted butter, softened

1½ pounds cleaned squid

2 tablespoons chopped fresh dill

¼ cup olive oil

1 cup chopped fennel

⅓ cup chopped shallots

1 cup chopped tomatoes (cherry tomatoes are fine here)

¼ cup dry white wine

Have ready a bowl set in a larger bowl of ice water.

Put the scallops into a food processor. Add the nutmeg and season with salt, white pepper, and a pinch of cayenne. Pulse until you have a fairly smooth paste, scraping down the sides when you need to. With the motor running, pour in the cream in a steady stream, then add the butter in pieces.

Scrape the mousse out into the bowl in the ice bath and spread it out so it chills quickly.

Poke a little hole into the tips of the squid tubes with the point of a paring knife; set aside. Finely chop enough of the tentacles to measure ¼ cup. Add them to the mousse, along with the dill.

Pack the mousse into a pastry bag and fill the squid tubes about two-thirds full. Close them with toothpicks.

Heat a large skillet over medium-high heat. When the pan's hot, add the oil, fennel, shallots, and tomatoes. Season with salt and white pepper and sauté for 2 minutes to get the cooking started. Set the squid on top of the vegetables, pour in the wine, cover, and reduce the heat to low. Cook for 1 hour, turning the squid once or twice.

Remove the squid to a plate and keep warm. Crank up the heat under the skillet and cook until the sauce is reduced and syrupy.

Pull the toothpicks out of the squid and slice the tubes on an angle. Serve with the sauce spooned over.

CHOWDERS, SOUPS, AND STEWS

FUMET

This is it, folks: classic fish stock. Make extra and freeze it in 1-cup amounts so you'll be sure to have it on hand. Some of the prepared stuff is fine (see page 32), but it will never compare in flavor to fumet you've made yourself.

Make life easy on yourself and ask your fishmonger to split the fish heads.

Fumet doesn't spend a lot of time on the heat, because longer cooking would bring out the impurities and cloud the stock. Cut the aromatics very thin, to get the most out of them. The fennel adds a fresh edge; add it if you have it.

Olive oil will add richness, but it's not essential. Makes about 4 cups

1 large onion, cut into very thin slices
2 large shallots, cut into very thin slices
2 celery ribs, cut into very thin slices
Stalks and fronds from 1 fennel bulb, cut into very thin slices (optional)

2 tablespoons olive oil (optional)
3 pounds fish frames and heads (see box on opposite page)
Coarse salt
1 cup dry white wine
3 cups water

ABOUT CUSTOMIZING FUMET

Let's face it: you can throw a lot of things into the pot when you're making fumet. You might not have all the ingredients the recipe calls for, or you may have more of one than another. Or you may want to adjust the flavors of the stock to match the finished dish.

Take the Shrimp and Branzino Stew, Caribbean-Style (page 321) as an example. First, fennel and shallots aren't classic ingredients in Caribbean cooking, so you could replace them with leeks and more onion. Make the stock with branzino frames, or the frames of whatever fish you're featuring in the stew. And you'll be adding shrimp to the stew, so use the shrimp shells in the stock for a bigger kick.

Here are some do's and don't's for customizing.

DO

- Use the frames and bones of the fish you're using in the finished dish.

- Add a leek if you have one, whole or just the greens.

- Throw in some parsley stems or sprigs if you're in the mood. It can't hurt.

- Drizzle a little oil over the vegetables to lubricate them, get the cooking process going, and add a bit of richness to the stock.

DON'T

- Add carrots or tomatoes. Fumet should be clear, and carrots and tomatoes add color.

- Cook too long. The fumet will become bitter.

Layer the onion, shallots, celery, and fennel, if using, in a wide stockpot—you want lots of surface area. Drizzle with olive oil if you're using it.

Take out your heaviest knife and chop into the spine of the fish frames, on both sides, at about 2-inch intervals. You're just cracking the bones open, not trying to cut the frames into pieces. Wash the heads and frames under cold water to get rid of as much blood as possible. Season the frames and heads with salt and set them on top of the vegetables.

Cover the pot and set it over medium-low heat. Sweat the aromatics and bones for about 15 minutes, until the bones are just opaque.

Add the wine and water—the liquid should barely cover the bones—and bring to a simmer. This will take about 12 minutes. When you have a slow simmer with lazy bubbles, set the timer and simmer for 15 minutes.

Cover the pot and take it off the heat. Let it sit for 1 hour.

Strain, pushing down on the solids to get all the liquid out of them. The fumet will keep for 3 days in the refrigerator and 3 months in the freezer.

FISH BONES FOR FUMET

I think snapper makes the best fumet, but you should be thoughtful about which snapper you choose. American red snapper, even wild-caught, is on the Monterey Bay Aquarium Seafood Watch list of fish to avoid. But there are other options, like black snapper or Pacific snapper.

Avoid oily fish when you're making fumet, or the stock will be murky and heavy tasting.

Make sure you remove the gills and any trace of blood or guts.

BEST FISH FOR FUMET	ACCEPTABLE FISH FOR FUMET
Snapper	Cod
Grouper	Scrod
Sole	Haddock
Flounder	Branzino
Turbot	Sablefish
Halibut	
Striped bass	
Black sea bass	
Mahi mahi	
Rouget	

LOBSTER AND CORN BISQUE

This blush-pink soup is a fine dinner for a winter's night. As is traditional, you're doing everything you can to extract flavor in this bisque, including leaving the shells in the soup base when you puree it, then straining it. The result is a very silky, elegant, high-end soup.

Serves 6

2 lobsters (each about 2 pounds)

⅓ cup cognac, plus 3 tablespoons if you have female lobsters with roe

2 large onions, diced

2 celery ribs, diced

2 shallots, diced

2 large garlic cloves, minced

4 sprigs thyme

1 bay leaf

5 tablespoons olive oil

Coarse salt and freshly ground white pepper

4 cups Fumet (page 296)

1 large carrot, diced

1 cup chopped plum tomatoes (or Pomì tomatoes)

2 sprigs tarragon

A handful of parsley stems

1 cup dry white wine

1 teaspoon white peppercorns

1½ cups frozen corn, rinsed under hot water to defrost

1 cup heavy cream

Cayenne

5 scallions, minced

Dispatch the lobsters by cutting through the heads with a heavy knife (see page 46). Pull off the tails and claws. Crack the claws with the back of your knife and put them aside. Split the bodies and discard the tomalley, sand sacs, and lungs. If you have female lobsters, spoon the roe out into a small bowl; add the 3 tablespoons cognac, cover, and refrigerate for later. Cut the bodies into small pieces.

Put half the onions, half the celery, half the shallots, half the garlic, and the thyme and bay leaf in a wide pot (large enough to hold the lobster tails and claws in a single layer). Drizzle on 2 tablespoons olive oil, cover the pot, and turn the heat to medium. Sweat the vegetables until the onion is just starting to soften, about 5 minutes. Add the tails and claws, season with salt and white pepper, and cover the pot again. Cook for 2 minutes. Pour in the fumet and turn the heat to high. Bring to a boil and boil for 2 minutes. Turn off the heat and let sit for 10 minutes.

Remove the lobster and let it cool. When it's cool, shell the lobster and chop the meat. Cover and refrigerate. Discard the thyme and bay leaf. Set the fumet and vegetables aside.

Heat a large heavy wide pot (enameled cast iron is best) over high heat. When the pot is good and hot, add the remaining 3 tablespoons olive oil and the chopped lobster bodies. Sauté, stirring constantly, until the shells turn bright red, about 2 minutes. Add the carrot and the remaining onions, celery, shallots, and garlic and sauté, stirring and scraping the bottom of the pot, for 1 minute.

Pull the pot off the heat and pour in the ⅓ cup cognac. Return to the heat and flame the cognac (either tip the pot—carefully—or use a long match to ignite it). When the flames die down, add the tomatoes, tarragon, and parsley stems and bring to a boil. As you're cooking, smash down on the lobster shells with a heavy wooden spoon or—even better—a potato masher to crack the shells. Add the wine, white peppercorns, and the fumet and vegetables and bring to a simmer. Cover, reduce the heat slightly, and simmer for 20 minutes. Turn off the heat and let cool for about 10 minutes.

Puree the base in batches—yes, shells and all—in the food processor, then work the puree through a fine sieve. For the silkiest bisque (and to make sure none of the solids have slipped past you), work the base through the sieve a second time. You can prepare the base early in the day or the day before. Store it, covered, in the refrigerator.

Bring the base to a simmer in a saucepan over medium heat. Add the roe and cognac if you have it and puree with an immersion blender (or puree the roe with some of the base in a regular blender and return to the pan).

Meanwhile, combine the corn and cream in a saucepan and bring to a simmer over medium heat.

Add the corn and cream to the base, along with the lobster meat, and season with cayenne. Check for salt. Bring back to a simmer, then serve, garnished with the scallions.

MANHATTAN CLAM CHOWDER

The flavors in this chowder—bacon, tomatoes, clams, even the dried herbs—are the ones I remember from growing up. Nothing was better than clam chowder on the beach on a windy day.

I love the real ocean flavor you get from big, meaty quahogs. Promise that you won't overcook them.

This chowder is great served the same day it is made, but it will be even better if you make the base a day ahead. *Serves 4 to 6*

ACCEPT SUBSTITUTES

Quahogs aren't always easy to find; you can substitute
4 dozen littleneck clams or 2 dozen topneck clams.

12 quahog or chowder clams, scrubbed

1 cup water

6 slices (about 4 ounces) bacon, chopped

1 tablespoon vegetable or olive oil

1 large onion, chopped

2 garlic cloves, minced

2 celery ribs, diced

2 carrots, diced

1 bay leaf

1 teaspoon dried thyme

1 teaspoon dried oregano

1 teaspoon dried basil

1 (14.5-ounce) can tomatoes (stewed tomatoes are nice here)

¾ cup bottled clam juice

¾ pound red-skinned potatoes, scrubbed and cut into ½-inch cubes

Coarse salt and freshly ground white pepper

Crushed red pepper (optional)

½ cup chopped fresh parsley

1 tablespoon fresh lemon juice

Put the clams in a single layer in a large pot or skillet and add the water. Cover and turn the heat as high as you can. Cook, shaking the pot once in a while, just until the clams open, about 10 minutes. Drain the clams in a strainer set over a bowl.

When the clams are cool enough to handle, remove the meat and chop it. Strain the clam broth through a fine sieve (leave the last tablespoon or two, with the grit in it, in the bowl). Put the chopped clams in a small bowl and cover with some of the broth. Refrigerate the clams and the remaining broth separately until you need them.

Put the bacon and oil in a large saucepan or stockpot over medium heat and cook until the bacon renders its fat (you want to release the smoky flavor of the bacon, but

Let me tell you something about clams: they don't all pop open at the same time, and some of them can be pretty persistent about keeping "clammed up." This is very much the case when you're steaming a lot of clams, like the four dozen for the New England chowder.

So keep your eye on the pan and remove the clams with tongs as they open. Transfer the opened clams to the colander set over the bowl, then put the lid back on and shake the pan again. Check in another minute, and keep removing clams as they open.

Then there are clams that never seem to open. Kitchen wisdom says to discard unopened clams, but I've never had a problem with them. These clams seem to be the ones with the strongest muscles, and if you look at them after they've steamed for a while, you'll see that they are actually just the smallest bit open. So I use a small knife to cut the muscle and drop the clam in with the rest.

you don't want to brown it). Add the onion and garlic, stir, cover, and cook for 5 minutes, or until the onion is starting to become translucent. Add the celery, carrots, bay leaf, and dried herbs. Stir, cover, and cook for another 5 minutes.

Pour the tomatoes into a bowl and crush them with your hands. Add to the pot, along with the bottled clam juice. Bring to a simmer, cover, and simmer for 10 minutes. (You're building flavor now.) Add the reserved clam broth and the potatoes and bring to a simmer. Cook until the potatoes are just tender, about 10 minutes.

Taste the base, then season with salt and white pepper—and a pinch of crushed red pepper, if you like. You can finish the chowder now or let the base cool, then refrigerate it overnight.

Remove the bay leaf and bring the base to a simmer if necessary. Add the chopped clams and turn off the heat—you want the clams to heat through but not cook any more, since that would make them tough. Stir in the parsley and lemon juice and serve.

VARIATIONS

You could up the clam quotient by adding 1½ pounds of Manila clams or cockles to the base before you add the chopped clams and simmering until they open.

Another option would be to add a pound or so of bay scallops (remove the tough bits) and simmer for just a minute before adding the chopped clams.

NEW ENGLAND CLAM CHOWDER

The carrot in this chowder isn't traditional, but I like the color and sweetness it adds. The wine isn't traditional either.

Traditional or not, this is one hearty chowder. It's a meal, not a dainty little first-course soup.

If you can, make the base early in the day, or even a day ahead, and finish the chowder right before serving.

Serves 6

ACCEPT SUBSTITUTES

Two dozen topneck clams will stand in for the littlenecks if that's all you can find.

1 cup water
48 littleneck clams, scrubbed
3 tablespoons unsalted butter
4 slices thick-cut bacon, chopped
1 large onion, minced
1 carrot, minced
2 celery ribs, minced
1 leek (white and light green parts), minced
2 tablespoons all-purpose flour
1 cup dry white wine

A handful of parsley stems, 4 sprigs thyme, and 1 bay leaf, tied together with kitchen string for an herb bouquet
½ pound red-skinned potatoes, scrubbed and diced
Freshly ground white pepper
2 cups heavy cream or half-and-half
¼ cup chopped fresh chives or parsley
1 tablespoon chopped fresh dill
Half a lemon

Bring the water to a boil in a wide deep skillet. Add the clams, cover immediately, and shake the pan. Steam until the clams open, about 5 minutes. Drain in a colander set over a bowl.

When the clams are cool enough to handle, pull them out of the shells, coarsely chop, and refrigerate, covered. Pour the liquid into a measuring cup—leaving the last tablespoon or so and any grit in the bowl—and add enough water to make 2 cups. Save this for later.

Put the butter and bacon into a stockpot over medium heat. Cook, stirring once in a while, until the bacon has rendered its fat, 2 to 3 minutes (you want to release the smoky flavor, but don't brown the bacon). Add the onion, carrot, and celery, stir, cover, and cook until the onion is translucent, about 5 minutes. Add the leek, stir, cover again, and cook until it is translucent, about 1 minute.

Stir in the flour and cook, stirring, for 2 minutes. Be sure to scrape the bottom of the pot. Stir in the wine, add the herb bouquet, and bring to a boil. Boil for 2 minutes, then add the reserved clam liquid and the potatoes. Season with white pepper and bring to a simmer, then reduce the heat and let the chowder simmer for 10 minutes. You can finish the chowder now, but it will be much better if you cool it down, cover, and refrigerate it for a few hours, or overnight.

Remove the herb bouquet and bring the base back to a simmer if necessary. Add the cream or half-and-half and bring back to a simmer. Stir in the clams, chives or parsley, and dill. Check the seasoning.

Stir in a few squirts of lemon juice and serve.

VARIATIONS

These are really more stews than chowders. If you find them too thick for your taste, thin them down with a little bottled clam juice.

- For Cod and Clam Chowder, combine ¾ pound cod, cut into ½-inch cubes, in a saucepan with the cream or half-and-half. Bring to a simmer before adding to the base and continuing with the recipe.

- For Corn and Clam Chowder, combine 2 cups corn kernels (frozen are fine) in a saucepan with the cream or half-and-half. Bring to a simmer before adding to the base and continuing with the recipe.

- For Cod, Corn, and Clam Chowder, combine ¾ pound cod, cut into ½-inch cubes, and 1½ cups corn kernels (frozen are fine) in a saucepan with the cream or half-and-half. Bring to a simmer before adding to the base and continuing with the recipe.

- For Rock Shrimp Chowder, substitute 1 pound rock shrimp for the clams. Replace the broth you would make if cooking the clams with 2 cups Shrimp Stock (page 323) or bottled clam juice.

MUSSEL CHOWDER

When I was a kid, we used to go to Sag Harbor, New York, and I always thought the air there smelled like mussels. There was a bracing edge to it, something clean and alluring. I wanted to capture that memory with a soup.

So, here's your introduction to Sag Harbor elegance. This chowder is silky, just rich enough, and the flavor is huge. The ingredient list may look long, but it's stuff you should have in the house, and you can have the chowder on the table in just about an hour.

Serve this with big, flaky biscuits.

Serves 8

FOR THE MUSSELS
2 tablespoons olive oil
2 tablespoons minced garlic
2 tablespoons minced shallots
    or onion
3 pounds mussels, scrubbed and
    debearded
2 cups dry white wine

FOR THE CHOWDER
6 tablespoons unsalted butter
2 cups finely chopped onions
2 cups finely chopped leeks (white
    and some light green parts)
1 cup finely chopped carrots
1 cup finely chopped celery
2 sprigs thyme, 1 bay leaf, and the
    green from 1 leek, tied together
    with kitchen string for an herb
    bouquet

Coarse salt and freshly ground black
    pepper
⅓ cup all-purpose flour
3 tablespoons Madras curry powder
    (or your favorite blend)
3 cups Quick Vegetable Stock (page
    476)
1 russet potato, peeled and cut into
    ⅓-inch dice (about 1½ cups)
2 large red-skinned potatoes, scrubbed
    and cut into ⅓-inch dice
1 cup heavy cream
Juice of 1 lemon (zest the lemon for
    garnish before juicing it)

FOR GARNISH
Grated zest of 1 lemon
¼ cup finely chopped fresh chives

FOR THE MUSSELS: Put the oil, garlic, and shallots or onion in a large deep skillet over medium-high heat. Cook for just a minute or two, until the shallots or onion are softened and the garlic fragrant—you definitely don't want to brown this. Crank the heat up to high, add the mussels and white wine, and cover the pan. Cook, giving the skillet a solid shake a few times, until the mussels open, 6 to 7 minutes.

Set a strainer over a large bowl and pour the mussels into the strainer. Save that beautiful liquid for the chowder.

FOR THE CHOWDER: Melt the butter in a stockpot over medium-low heat. Add the onions, leeks, carrot, celery, and herb bouquet and season with salt and black pepper (be careful with the salt; the mussel liquid will be salty). Cover and sweat the aromatics until they've softened, about 5 minutes. Take out the herb bouquet for a moment and stir in the flour and curry powder. Cook, stirring often, until flour/roux smells toasty, about 5 minutes.

Stir in the stock and the liquid from the mussels and bring to a simmer. Drop the herb bouquet back into the pot and cook for 5 minutes. Add the potatoes, kick the heat up to medium-high, and bring back to a simmer. Cut the heat back and simmer until the potatoes are just tender, about 15 minutes.

Meanwhile, pull the mussels from their shells. Toss the shells into the trash, reserve the mussels, and add any liquid and aromatics to the chowder.

Bring the cream to a boil in a saucepan over medium-high heat. Boil for a minute or so to reduce the cream slightly, then turn off the heat.

When the potatoes are tender, remove the herb bouquet. Stir in the mussels and cream, add the lemon juice, and taste for salt and pepper.

Ladle the chowder into wide soup plates, garnish with the lemon zest and chives, and serve.

CORN AND LOBSTER CHOWDER

Soups like this celebrate summer. They're so satisfying, and you can taste every ingredient in them.

Serves 4

2 tablespoons unsalted butter

1 onion, cut into medium dice

2 celery ribs, cut into medium dice

1 carrot, cut into fine dice

2 sprigs thyme

1 bay leaf

1 lobster (about 1½ pounds), prepared
   for pan-roasting (see page 47)

4 cups Fumet (page 296)

4 slices bacon, diced

Coarse salt

½ pound red-skinned potatoes,
   scrubbed and cut into ⅓-inch dice

1 cup corn kernels (frozen are fine;
   rinse under hot water to defrost)

1 cup heavy cream

1 tablespoon minced fresh chives

Put 1 tablespoon butter into a wide saucepan and add half the onion, half the celery, half the carrot, and the thyme sprigs and bay leaf. Cover and sweat the vegetables over medium heat for about 2 minutes; they should be barely softening. Add all the lobster pieces, cover, and sweat for another 2 minutes. Crank the heat up to high and pour in the fumet. Bring to a boil and boil for 1 minute. Cover, turn off the heat, and let sit for 10 minutes.

Remove the lobster pieces; keep the poaching liquid on the stove. Discard the lobster body. Let the tail and claws cool, then shell and chop the meat into bite-sized pieces.

Put the bacon and the remaining 1 tablespoon butter into a stockpot over medium heat. When the bacon starts to brown, add the remaining onion, celery, and carrot, season with salt, and turn the heat up to medium-high. Sauté, stirring often, until the vegetables start to soften, about 4 minutes. Add the poaching liquid (with all its solids) and the potatoes, bring to a simmer, and cook until the potatoes are just tender, about 10 minutes.

Put the corn and cream into a small saucepan. Bring to a boil over medium-high heat.

Stir the corn, cream, and lobster into the chowder. Remove the bay leaf and thyme. Serve hot, garnished with the chives.

POTATO LEEK STEW WITH SHRIMP AND HAKE

Think of this stew as an exercise in simplicity. It's comfort food in half an hour.

Serves 4

ACCEPT SUBSTITUTES

Hake isn't the easiest fish to find; you can substitute cod or scrod or any flaky fish.

4 tablespoons unsalted butter, cut into pieces

1 large onion, chopped

2 large leeks (white and light green parts), sliced

1 bay leaf

½ teaspoon fresh thyme leaves

Coarse salt and freshly ground white pepper

¾ pound Yukon Gold potatoes, scrubbed and cut into bite-sized pieces

1 cup chicken stock or Quick Vegetable Stock (page 476)

1 pound hake, silverskin removed and fish cut into large chunks

½ pound medium (31–35 count) shrimp, shelled

1 cup chopped scallions

1 cup heavy cream

1 bunch watercress (tough stems discarded), chopped

Heat a wide saucepan or stockpot over high heat. Add the butter and onion and cook, stirring, for 1 minute. Add the leeks, bay leaf, thyme, and salt and white pepper to taste and reduce the heat to medium. Cover and cook, stirring once or twice, until the leeks start to collapse, about 5 minutes. Add the potatoes and stock, cover, and cook until the potatoes are just tender, about 15 minutes.

Season the hake and shrimp with salt and white pepper. Add to the pot, along with the scallions and cream, and kick up the heat to medium-high. Cook for 10 minutes. Remove the bay leaf.

Divide the cress among four soup plates and spoon the stew on top. Serve hot.

OYSTER STEW

There is something completely satisfying about this simple lunchtime soup. Shucked oysters make preparing it a snap.   Serves 4 to 6

8 tablespoons (1 stick) unsalted butter

4 cups whole milk

1 cup heavy cream

Coarse salt and freshly ground white
 pepper

Tabasco sauce

1 pint shucked oysters, with their
 liquor

Oyster crackers

Melt the butter in a wide saucepan over medium heat. Add the milk and cream and bring to a simmer. Season well with salt and white pepper and Tabasco (remember, you're putting in the Tabasco so you can taste it, so don't be shy), then add the oysters and their liquor. Cook just until the edges of the oysters curl; they'll look like ruffled petticoats.

Serve hot, with plenty of oyster crackers.

SALMON "GRAVY"

I just couldn't help including this retro dish. My mother called it salmon gravy, but it's also called salmon wiggle. It's winter food, come-in-from-the-cold comfort.

Serves 4

ACCEPT SUBSTITUTES

The "classic" version would be made with canned salmon.
You could try that too. Or substitute char.

8 tablespoons (1 stick) unsalted butter

½ cup all-purpose flour

4 cups whole milk, heated

1 (1¼-pound) piece skinless wild salmon fillet

Coarse salt

2 cups frozen peas, rinsed under hot water to defrost

¼ cup chopped fresh dill

Juice of 1 lemon

Freshly ground white pepper

Toasted white bread for serving

Melt the butter in a large saucepan over medium-low heat. Stir in the flour and cook, stirring almost constantly, for about 10 minutes. You want to cook the roux until it smells nutty and toasty, without letting it brown.

Take the pan off the heat and whisk in the milk, then bring to a simmer, whisking often and sometimes switching to a spatula so you can get into the edges of the pan. Reduce the heat to low and simmer for about 8 minutes, until the sauce is very thick.

Meanwhile, cut the salmon into ½-inch slices and season with salt.

Add the salmon to the sauce and cook, stirring and breaking it up, for 5 minutes. Taste, checking for salt. Stir in the peas and cook for another 5 minutes. Stir in the dill, lemon juice, and a hefty dose of white pepper.

Serve over toast, with some more pepper if you want.

HOT-AND-SOUR SOUP

The flavors in this head-clearing soup—tamarind's earthy acidity combined with the brightness of lime and the edge of fish sauce—are more Thai than Chinese.

Your most difficult task may be finding the Asian ingredients, but it's well worth the effort. *Serves 4*

ACCEPT SUBSTITUTES

No substitutes for the shrimp, of course, but tilapia, tilefish, striped or sea bass, and sea scallops can all stand in for the catfish.

FOR THE FISH

1 pound medium (31–35) shrimp in the shell

2 tablespoons minced fresh ginger

1 tablespoon fish sauce

1 tablespoon homemade tamarind paste (see Note)

1 pound catfish fillets, cut into ¾-inch pieces

FOR THE BASE

4 stalks fresh lemongrass

1 teaspoon vegetable oil

1 tablespoon minced fresh ginger

1–2 red chiles, bottom half sliced open

5 cups Fumet (page 296)

1 teaspoon fish sauce

TO FINISH

Grated zest and juice of 1 lime

3 tomatoes, chopped

3 tablespoons chopped fresh cilantro

3 scallions, cut into thin slices

½ teaspoon chili paste (sambal oelek), or more to taste

Jasmine rice for serving

FOR THE FISH: Shell the shrimp, leaving the tails on. Reserve the shells for the soup base and refrigerate the shrimp.

Stir the ginger, fish sauce, and tamarind paste together in a small bowl. Add the catfish, stir to coat the fish evenly with the marinade, cover, and refrigerate. Marinate for 2 hours.

MEANWHILE, MAKE THE BASE: Strip the tough outer leaves off 1 stalk of lemongrass and cut off the top. Smash the tender core with the handle of a heavy knife, then mince it; reserve 2 tablespoons minced lemongrass to finish the soup. Chop the remaining lemongrass, including everything you stripped from the first stalk.

Heat a stockpot over medium-high heat. When the pot's hot, add the oil and chopped lemongrass and sauté for 1 minute. Add the shrimp shells, ginger, and chiles and sauté, stirring, until the shells turn pink, about 1 minute. Add the fumet and fish sauce and bring to a boil. Turn off the heat, cover the pot, and let the base rest for 1 hour.

Line a strainer with cheesecloth and set it over a bowl. Strain the base, then lift up the cheesecloth and squeeze to get all the liquid out of the solids. Wipe out the pot and return the base to it.

TO FINISH: Add the reserved 2 tablespoons minced lemongrass to the soup base, along with the lime zest, and bring to a boil over high heat. Add the tomatoes and bring back to a boil. Add the catfish (and any juices in the bowl), shrimp, cilantro, scallions, and chili paste. Bring to an active simmer, then turn off the heat. Let the soup sit for 6 to 7 minutes, until the seafood is cooked through.

Stir the lime juice into the soup.

Spoon some rice into four soup bowls and ladle the soup around it.

NOTE: You can find commercial tamarind paste in many Asian and specialty markets, but it's often pretty sour. Making your own is better. Cut up a 2-inch hunk of brick tamarind, put it in a heatproof bowl, and cover it with boiling water. When it's cool, work it through a strainer, water and all. Most of the paste will stick to the outside of the strainer, so be sure to scrape it off. Discard the tough bits.

Both brick tamarind and tamarind paste are available online from www.kalustyans .com.

CREAMY FENNEL SOUP WITH SEARED SALMON AND CITRUS RAGÙ

Here's another riff on my favorite marriage of flavors: fennel and citrus. In this soup, rich salmon is countered by clean fennel, with citrus and oil working a balancing act.   Serves 4

ACCEPT SUBSTITUTES

Try this with char.

FOR THE CITRUS RAGÙ
⅓ cup olive oil
1 grapefruit, peeled and segmented
  (see page 474)
1 orange, peeled and segmented
1 lemon, peeled and segmented
1 lime, peeled and segmented

FOR THE SOUP
1 tablespoon vegetable oil
1 large fennel bulb (about 1 pound),
  trimmed (reserve the fronds for
  garnish) and chopped
1 small yellow-fleshed potato,
  scrubbed and cut into thin slices
1 shallot, cut into thin slices
1 garlic clove, cut into thin slices
2 tablespoons fennel seeds, toasted
  and tied in cheesecloth

Coarse salt and freshly ground white
  pepper
2 cups Quick Vegetable Stock (page
  476) or chicken stock
1 cup heavy cream
Half a lemon

FOR THE FISH
4 (3-ounce) pieces skinless wild salmon
  fillet
Coarse salt and freshly ground white
  pepper
½ teaspoon vegetable oil
2 tablespoons chopped reserved fennel
  fronds
Coarse sea salt

FOR THE RAGÙ: Pour the oil into a small nonreactive saucepan and add the citrus segments. Turn the heat to the lowest setting and warm the citrus until the juices—which will be released as you warm the segments—and oil just barely come to a simmer. Remove from the heat and give the ragù a whisk to break up the segments. This can sit on the counter for a few hours.

FOR THE SOUP: Heat a medium saucepan over medium-low heat. When the pan's hot, add the oil, fennel, potato, shallot, garlic, and fennel seeds. Season with salt and white pepper, then cover the pot and sweat the vegetables until tender, about 15 minutes. Stir every once in a while, and monitor the heat; you don't want the vegetables to brown.

Add the stock and bring back to an easy simmer. Cover and simmer for 10 minutes.

Add the cream and bring back to a simmer, then cover and remove from the heat. Let the soup sit for 20 minutes or so for the flavors to mellow.

Remove the fennel seeds. Puree the soup in a blender or food processor until very smooth. Strain the soup through a fine sieve—you want this silky—into a clean saucepan. Add a squirt of lemon juice and check for salt and pepper. Keep the soup hot, but not simmering.

FOR THE FISH: Season the salmon with salt and pepper. Heat the oil in a nonstick skillet over high heat. When the pan's good and hot, add the salmon skinned side up and cook for 2 minutes, to make a nice brown crust. Turn and sear the fish for 30 seconds (I like the fish rare for this dish).

To serve, place the fish in four soup plates or bowls, browned side up. Spoon a tablespoon or so of the citrus ragù on top of each fillet. Ladle the soup around the fish and garnish with the fennel fronds and sea salt.

BOUILLABAISSE FOR THE AMERICAN KITCHEN

Most of the fish that make this fragrant Mediterranean soup so distinctive just aren't available here, but that's no reason not to make something fantastic. My version uses fish and shellfish that are commonly available, and it's redolent of garlic, fennel, and saffron. (The photo is on page 194.)

I'm giving you ingredients for a fumet that really ups the flavor quotient. Making the fumet and the soup base the day before also plays a part in intensifying the flavor—so plan ahead.

Ask your fishmonger to split the fish heads for the fumet.   Serves 4 to 6

ACCEPT SUBSTITUTES

This is like a paella—you can add what you want. So experiment. Sturgeon would be delicious. So would skinless dorade. There's no need to marinate dorade; add it with the mussels and expect it to fall apart. And if you can find rouget (red mullet), use the bones for the fumet and add the fillets (skin on) with the mussels.

FOR THE FUMET
1 tablespoon olive oil
2 whole garlic heads, halved through
    the equator
Green parts of 2 leeks, chopped
Tops and outer sections of 2 fennel
    bulbs, chopped
1 large onion, cut into thin slices
3–4 sprigs thyme
2 teaspoons fennel seeds, toasted
1 bay leaf
Big pinch of saffron threads
4 pounds fish frames and heads (from
    snapper and black sea bass if
    possible)

Coarse salt
Shells from the shrimp (see below)
About 8 cups water
Stems from 1 bunch parsley

FOR THE BASE
⅓ cup olive oil
3 cups chopped onions
3 cups chopped fennel
½ cup chopped garlic
White parts of 2 leeks, chopped
½ teaspoon saffron threads
1 (14.5-ounce) can tomatoes
Coarse salt
½ cup dry vermouth
½ cup Pernod

FOR THE FISH AND SHELLFISH

1 tablespoon olive oil

1 tablespoon dry vermouth

1 teaspoon chopped garlic

Pinch of saffron threads

½ pound sea scallops, tough bits removed

½ pound large (21–30 count) shrimp, shelled

1 pound halibut fillet, cut into chunks

12 littleneck clams, scrubbed

1 pound mussels, scrubbed and debearded

FOR SERVING

2–3 tablespoons chopped fresh parsley

Croutons (see page 475)

Rouille (page 414)

FOR THE FUMET: Spoon the oil into a wide stockpot (you want a lot of surface area for fumet) and layer in the garlic, leek greens, fennel, onion, thyme, fennel seeds, bay leaf, and saffron. Cover, turn the heat to medium-high, and sweat the vegetables for 10 minutes.

Meanwhile, take out your heaviest knife and chop into the spines of the fish frames on both sides at about 2-inch intervals. You're just cracking the bones open, not trying to cut the frames into pieces. Wash the heads and frames thoroughly under cold water to get rid of the blood.

Season the frames and heads with salt and set them on top of the vegetables. Cover the pot and sweat for another 20 minutes, or until the bones are just opaque.

Add the shrimp shells and barely cover the solids with water; it will take about 8 cups. Add the parsley stems, cover, reduce the heat to medium-low, and bring to a simmer. Turn off the heat and let the fumet sit for 1 hour.

Strain the fumet into a clean pot and reduce it over medium-high heat to 6 cups. This will be enough for 2 batches of bouillabaisse. Let cool, then freeze half of the fumet for another time.

FOR THE BASE: Place a stockpot over medium-high heat. When the pot's hot, add the olive oil, onions, and fennel. Sauté until the onions soften, about 7 minutes. Add the garlic and leeks, crumble in the saffron, and reduce the heat to medium. Cook, stirring often, for 2 minutes.

Reserve 1 of the canned tomatoes for the marinade. Crush the remaining tomatoes with your hands and add them, and their juices, to the pot. Season with salt and bring to an active simmer. Cook for about 10 minutes, until the tomatoes have thickened.

Pour in the vermouth and Pernod and bring to a simmer. Cook for about 2 minutes, to lose the alcohol taste. Add 3 cups fumet and bring to a simmer. Remove from the heat and let cool, then cover and refrigerate overnight.

FOR THE FISH AND SHELLFISH: Cut the reserved tomato into small bits and put it in a medium bowl with the oil, vermouth, and garlic. Crumble in the saffron and stir. Add the scallops, shrimp, and halibut and stir well to coat with the marinade. Cover and refrigerate for 4 to 6 hours.

To finish, bring the soup base to a boil over medium-high heat. Stir in the clams and the scallops, shrimp, and halibut, along with any juices in the bowl, cover, and cook for 3 minutes. Add the mussels and bring back to a boil, then cover and turn off the heat. Let the soup sit for a few minutes, until the mussels open.

Divide the soup among soup plates, garnish with the parsley, and serve right away with the croutons spread with rouille.

CIOPPINO

There are two schools of thought when it comes to the wine that goes into this Italian-American seafood stew: some people say it should be red, others say it's got to be white. I'm not going to get involved in the dispute. I use white, but you should let your taste be your guide. The other thing to remember is that cioppino is a stew. No dainty thin soup here — this is a hearty main course. And it will be even better if you make the base the day before.

The pasta is my addition.   Serves 6

FOR THE BASE
¼ cup olive oil
2 onions, chopped
2 celery ribs, chopped
A handful of parsley stalks, 3–4 thyme
    sprigs, 1 small bay leaf, 1 teaspoon
    dried oregano, and 1 teaspoon
    white peppercorns, tied in a square
    of cheesecloth for an herb bouquet
5–6 garlic cloves, chopped
1 cup chopped leeks, white and light
    green parts
¾ pound mushrooms, sliced
Coarse salt and freshly ground white
    pepper
1 cup dry white wine
1 cup chopped canned tomatoes
    (Pomì preferred)
4 cups Fumet (page 296)

FOR THE SHELLFISH
12 littleneck clams, scrubbed
½ pound sea scallops, tough bits
    removed
½ pound medium (31–35 count)
    shrimp, shelled, tails left on, and
    deveined
1 pound mussels, scrubbed and
    debearded
1 pound lump crabmeat, picked over
½ cup chopped fresh parsley

FOR SERVING
1 pound linguine

FOR THE BASE: Heat a large heavy pot over medium-high heat. When the pot's hot, pour in the oil and add the onions, celery, and herb bouquet. Sauté, stirring often, until the onions start to soften, about 5 minutes. Add the garlic and leeks and sauté until the garlic is fragrant, about 30 seconds. Add the mushrooms, season with salt and white pepper, and sauté until the mushrooms have softened and are starting to release their juices, 3 to 4 minutes. Pour in the wine and bring to a boil. Boil for 2 minutes, to cook off most of the alcohol.

Add the tomatoes and fumet and bring to a boil. Reduce the heat and simmer for 15 minutes. Turn off the heat and let the base rest for 30 minutes to 1 hour before proceeding. The cioppino will be even better if you make the base a day ahead and refrigerate it. Either way, take the bouquet out after it's cooled.

FOR THE SHELLFISH: Bring the base back to an active simmer over medium-high heat. Add the clams and simmer for 2 minutes. Add the scallops and shrimp, bring back to a simmer, and cook for 1 minute. Stir in the mussels and cook until the mussels open, another minute or so. Stir in the crabmeat and parsley.

Meanwhile, put a large pot of salted water up to boil when you start bringing the base back to a simmer. Cook the linguine until al dente.

Drain the pasta and divide among six soup plates. Ladle the cioppino on top and serve right away.

VARIATION

Serve the cioppino over Croutons (page 475) instead of over linguine.

SCALLOP CIOPPINO

Because this calls for clam juice instead of fumet, I think of it more as a throw-together dish. But as with traditional cioppino, you can make the base a day before.

Serves 6

ACCEPT SUBSTITUTES

This is one dish where frozen scallops can be acceptable.
If you'd like, substitute clams for some of the scallops, or just add some clams.
Use the tiniest ones you can find, though—Manila clams or cockles.

FOR THE CROUTONS
Olive oil
1 baguette or loaf of Italian bread, cut into 1-inch slices
1 large garlic clove, cut in half

FOR THE CIOPPINO
⅔ cup olive oil
2 large onions, cut into medium dice
6 garlic cloves, minced
4 small bell peppers (use a mix of red, yellow, and green peppers), cut into ½-inch dice
2 teaspoons dried oregano
2 jalapeño chiles, minced (leave the seeds in)

¼ cup tomato paste
1 cup dry white wine
Coarse salt and freshly ground white pepper
2 (8-ounce) bottles clam juice
1 (28-ounce) can diced tomatoes (see Note)
2 pounds sea scallops, tough bits removed
⅔ cup chopped fresh parsley
⅔ cup chopped fresh basil

FOR SERVING
Cilantro Aïoli (page 419)

FOR THE CROUTONS: Heat the oven to 200 degrees.

Heat a nonstick skillet over high heat. Add about 1 tablespoon olive oil and as many slices of bread as will fit comfortably. Sauté the bread until it's a rich brown, about 2 minutes. Turn the slices and sauté for another minute. Set the slices on a baking sheet and continue browning the bread, adding more oil as needed.

Slide the baking sheet into the oven and bake until the croutons are dry. This will take 15 to 20 minutes, and you should turn the slices over about halfway through.

Rub the croutons with the cut sides of the garlic cloves and let them cool completely. You can make these early in the day. Store them in an airtight container.

FOR THE CIOPPINO: Heat a large stockpot over high heat. Add the olive oil and onions and sauté, stirring often, until the onions are becoming translucent, about 3 minutes. Add the garlic and sauté for 1 minute. Add the bell peppers and crumble in the oregano. Sauté for 2 minutes. Add the jalapeños and tomato paste and sauté, stirring often, for another 2 minutes, or until the peppers are almost tender and the tomato paste has turned brick red. Take care not to burn the paste.

Pour in the wine, bring it to a boil, and reduce until the wine is syrupy, about 5 minutes. Season with salt (carefully, because the clam juice will be salty) and white pepper (a lot).

Add the clam juice and tomatoes and bring to a boil. Reduce the heat so the base will simmer actively and cook for 30 minutes to concentrate the flavors. You can make the cioppino base in advance. Let it cool, then cover and refrigerate. Bring it back to an active simmer when you're ready to serve.

Add the scallops and herbs to the base, return to an active simmer, and cook for 3 to 4 minutes, until the scallops are barely cooked through (they will continue to cook from the heat of the stew). You can take one out and cut it in half to check.

To serve, put a couple of croutons in each soup dish. Ladle on the stew and pass the aïoli for those who want to stir in a spoonful or two.

NOTE: Diced tomatoes with different flavorings or preparations are becoming more widely available. If you can find fire-roasted tomatoes or diced tomatoes with garlic and onion, by all means use them here.

SHRIMP AND BRANZINO STEW, CARIBBEAN-STYLE

This is a very simple stew to pull together, but the stock is probably more important than any other ingredient, so please do make your own if you have the time.

The stew's great for a family dinner, but it's classy enough to serve in the good china for company. It's easily doubled. (The photo is on page 195.)   Serves 4

ACCEPT SUBSTITUTES
Try catfish or tilapia.

3 small garlic cloves, chopped, plus
    4 large garlic cloves, cut into very
    thin slices
2 serrano chiles, chopped (with seeds)
1 cup fresh cilantro (small stems are
    fine)
2 tablespoons fresh lime juice
2 tablespoons vegetable oil
Coarse salt
1 pound medium (31–35) shrimp,
    shelled and deveined
¼ cup olive oil
2–3 celery ribs (pick stalks from the
    heart, with leaves), chopped

1 onion, chopped
1½ bell peppers (a mix of colors is
    nice), chopped
¾ pound plum tomatoes, chopped
4 allspice berries
Freshly ground white pepper
4 cups Fumet (page 296) or Shrimp
    Stock (page 323)
¾ pound branzino fillet, cut into cubes

FOR SERVING
White rice

Combine the chopped garlic, chiles, cilantro, lime juice, vegetable oil, and a good pinch of salt in a small food processor. Pulse and process, scraping down the sides as you need to, until you've made a smooth paste.

Spoon 2 tablespoons of the paste into a small bowl and add the shrimp. Toss to coat the shrimp well, cover, and refrigerate for 1 to 2 hours. Scrape out the rest of the paste into a small bowl, cover, and refrigerate it until you're ready to serve the stew.

Heat a large pot over high heat. Add the oil, celery, and onion and cook, stirring often, for 2 minutes. Add the bell peppers and cook for another 5 minutes, stirring often. Add the sliced garlic, tomatoes, and allspice and season with salt and white pepper. Cook for another 3 minutes. Reduce the heat to medium-high, add the fumet or stock, and bring to a boil. You can prepare the stew up to this point in advance. Set aside for up to 1 hour, or cover and refrigerate overnight. When you're ready to serve it, bring it back to a boil.

Add the shrimp and fish to the stew and bring to a simmer. Reduce the heat and simmer for 5 minutes.

To serve, ladle the stew into soup plates and add a spoonful of the cilantro paste to each. Pass the rice and the rest of the paste at the table.

SHRIMP STOCK

Make this when you're peeling shrimp for a dish, and freeze the stock so you have it on hand. Then you're ready for risotto, or shrimp creole, or a quick improvisational soup. Or freeze the shrimp shells in plastic bags and make the stock later. Be sure you label the bags so you know how many shells you have when you're ready to use them. There's no need to defrost the shells; they can go into the pot right out of the freezer.

I'm giving proportions for small and big batches here.

SMALL BATCH
(MAKES ABOUT 2 CUPS)
2 teaspoons olive oil
½ cup thinly sliced onion
¼ cup thinly sliced celery
Shells from 1 pound shrimp
1 small bay leaf
½ cup dry white wine
2 cups water

BIG BATCH
(MAKES ABOUT 4 CUPS)
1 tablespoon olive oil
1 cup thinly sliced onion
½ cup thinly sliced celery
Shells from 2 pounds shrimp
1 bay leaf
1 cup dry white wine
4 cups water

Heat a saucepan over medium-high heat. When the pan's hot, add the oil, onion, and celery. Sauté, stirring, for 2 to 3 minutes, until the onion starts to soften. Add the shrimp shells and sauté, stirring constantly, for another minute or two, until all the shells turn pink. Add the bay leaf, wine, and water and bring to a boil. Reduce the heat and simmer the stock—just lazy bubbles—for 30 minutes.

Turn off the heat and let the stock sit for 30 minutes for the flavor to deepen.

Line a strainer with cheesecloth, set the strainer over a bowl, and pour in the stock. Lift up the corners of the cheesecloth and squeeze to make sure you extract all the liquid from the solids.

You can use the stock right away or freeze it for later. It will keep for about 3 days in the refrigerator and 3 months in the freezer.

SHRIMP GUMBO

If you've ever read a Southern cookbook or a good recipe for gumbo, then you know the real secret is the roux. Don't expect shortcuts, and don't think you can rush the process. A good dark roux is going to take at least an hour of constant stirring, but the rewards and depth of flavor are amazing. Plan on making gumbo when you've got a friend or two in the kitchen with you. You can set them up stirring the roux while you prep the rest of the ingredients.

I've written this recipe using a shrimp stock, which you make while the roux cooks, but if you've got fish stock in the freezer, by all means use that instead. You'll need 4 cups.

Serves 6

FOR THE STOCK
Shells from the shrimp (see below)
1 cup sliced onion
½ cup sliced celery
5½ cups water
1 bay leaf

FOR THE ROUX
4 tablespoons unsalted butter
½ cup all-purpose flour

FOR THE GUMBO
5 tablespoons vegetable oil
½ pound okra, trimmed and cut into
    ½-inch pieces
Coarse salt and freshly ground white
    pepper
6–8 ounces tasso or andouille,
    chopped (see Note)

1½ cups chopped onions
1 cup chopped celery
1 cup chopped bell peppers (a mixture
    of red and green is nice)
2 tablespoons chopped garlic
2 tablespoons chopped jalapeño chiles
    (with seeds)
1 cup canned tomatoes, crushed with
    your hands
1 teaspoon dried oregano
2 pounds extra-large (16–20 count)
    shrimp, shelled, shells reserved

FOR SERVING
White rice
Tabasco sauce

FOR THE STOCK: Heat a medium saucepan over high heat. When the pan's good and hot, add the shrimp shells and cook, stirring often, for a minute or two, until the shells have turned pink and have started to stick all over the bottom of the pan. Add the onion, celery, and water and stir to deglaze the pan. Add the bay leaf and bring to a simmer. Reduce the heat and simmer for 20 minutes. Turn off the heat and let the stock sit on the stove until you need it. It will continue to develop flavor.

MEANWHILE, FOR THE ROUX: Melt the butter in a large wide saucepan over medium heat. Stir in the flour. This will be a tight mixture, with the consistency of wet sand. Reduce the heat to medium-low and cook, stirring and scraping the bottom and sides of the pan, until the roux is a rich mahogany color. This will take at least 1 hour, perhaps 1½ hours. As the roux cooks, it will appear to melt, becoming more liquid, and it should brown slowly. Keep your eye on the heat and your nose alert. If it looks or smells as if the roux is cooking too quickly, lower the heat immediately. There is no way to fix a roux that burns. When the roux reaches that beautiful mahogany color, take it off the heat, but continue to stir until the pan cools down, so the roux doesn't burn.

Strain the shrimp stock, pressing down hard on the solids to get all the stock out (there's a lot that gets captured in the shells). Measure. You want 4 cups; if you're shy, add some water.

FOR THE GUMBO: Heat a large skillet over medium-high heat. When the skillet's hot, add 2 tablespoons vegetable oil and the okra. Season with salt and white pepper. Cook, stirring often, until the okra is browned and no longer slimy, about 5 minutes. Transfer the okra to a bowl with a slotted spoon, leaving as much oil in the skillet as possible.

Add the tasso or andouille and 2 tablespoons oil to the pan and cook, stirring often, until the meat is browned. Transfer with a slotted spoon to the bowl with the okra.

Add the remaining 1 tablespoon oil to the skillet along with the onions, celery, and bell peppers. Cook, stirring often, until the vegetables have started to soften, about 6 minutes. Add the garlic and jalapeños and cook for another 2 minutes. Add the tomatoes and oregano and cook for another 2 minutes, or until the vegetables are tender.

Return the roux to medium heat, and when it's hot, scrape in the vegetables, as well as the okra and tasso or andouille. (If you've got someone helping you, you can have the vegetables cooked and ready to add when the roux is finished.) Cook, stirring, for about 1 minute, then stir in the shrimp stock. Stir very well to dissolve the roux, and bring to a simmer. Reduce the heat to low and simmer gently for 1½ hours, stirring and scraping the bottom of the pan often. Taste for salt.

Turn the heat up to medium. Season the shrimp with salt and stir them into the gumbo. Cook for about 10 minutes, until they are cooked through.

Serve in bowls, over rice. Pass the Tabasco.

VARIATIONS

Should I call these variations or ways of gilding the lily?

Add 1 pound of lump crabmeat, picked over, with the shrimp.

Add 1 pound of fish fillets—sole, turbot, grouper—cut into chunks with the shrimp.

NOTE: Tasso and andouille are both classic Cajun ingredients. Tasso is a lean strip of marinated pork that's smoked; andouille is a spicy smoked sausage. You can get both online from sources like www.cajungrocer.com.

SHRIMP CHILI

Chili is too good to be reserved just for meat. You could use any seafood, but I think this simple chili with beans is best with shrimp.

You can make the base for the chili a day ahead.   Serves 4

FOR THE BASE

3 tablespoons peanut or vegetable oil

2 cups chopped onions

2 cups chopped bell peppers (red and green)

3 tablespoons chopped garlic

2 large jalapeño chiles, seeded and minced

2 tablespoons chili powder

1 tablespoon ground toasted cumin seeds

1 (15-ounce) can red kidney beans, rinsed and drained

1 (14.5-ounce) can diced tomatoes packed in juice

½ cup dark beer (I like Negra Modelo)

1 tablespoon minced chipotle in adobo (optional)

1 bay leaf (optional)

Coarse salt and freshly ground black pepper

FOR THE SHRIMP

1 pound medium (31–35) shrimp, shelled

2 tablespoons adobo sauce (from the chipotle can)

FOR SERVING

Fried tortilla strips (see page 330)

Minced white onion

Chopped fresh cilantro

Sour cream

Shredded sharp cheddar

Lime wedges

FOR THE BASE: Heat a wide saucepan over medium-high heat. When the pan's hot, add the oil, onions, and bell peppers. Sauté, stirring often, until the onions are translucent, about 3 minutes. Add the garlic and cook for 1 minute. Add the jalapeños, chili powder, and cumin and sauté, stirring, for 2 minutes. Add the beans, tomatoes, and beer. Add the chipotle and bay leaf if you're using them, and season with salt and black pepper. Bring to a simmer, reduce the heat to medium-low, and cook the base at an active simmer for 15 minutes. Check for salt and pepper. You can prepare the base hours or even a day ahead; bring back to a simmer before adding the shrimp.

MEANWHILE, FOR THE SHRIMP: Once you've started making the base, cut the shrimp into nuggets and toss with the adobo sauce. Refrigerate until just before you are ready to serve.

Stir the shrimp into the base and cook over medium-high heat until it is cooked through. It will take about 1½ minutes once you have a simmer again.

To serve, set out bowls of all the garnishes. Spoon the chili into bowls and serve it hot.

LOBSTER GAZPACHO

What we've got here is my purely American adaptation of this cool Spanish soup. (The photo is on page 195.)

Make the lobster stock in the morning or the day before. Serves 4 to 6

ACCEPT SUBSTITUTES

Try this with shrimp too — see the variation.

FOR THE STOCK
1 lobster (about 1½ pounds)
1 onion, cut into thin slices
2 celery ribs, cut into thin slices
1 bay leaf
1 tablespoon olive oil
Coarse salt
½ cup dry white wine
1½ cups water

½ green bell pepper, cut into chunks
1 small onion, cut into chunks
1 serrano chile, minced
2 small garlic cloves, chopped
3–4 tablespoons chopped fresh cilantro
4 ice cubes
⅓ cup red wine vinegar
¼ cup ketchup
Coarse sea salt

FOR THE GAZPACHO
1 cucumber, peeled, seeded, and
    chopped
¾ pound plum tomatoes, cut into
    chunks
½ red bell pepper, cut into chunks

FOR THE GARNISH
2–3 corn tortillas
Vegetable oil
Coarse sea salt
Half a cucumber, peeled, seeded, and
    cut into small dice

FOR THE STOCK: Dispatch the lobster by cutting through the head with a heavy knife (see page 46). Pull off the tail and claws. Split the body and discard the tomalley, roe (if you have a female lobster), sand sac, and lungs. Cut the body into small pieces. Split the tail and remove the vein. Crack the claws with the back of a heavy chef's knife — you want those juices to come out into the stock.

Put the onion, celery, and bay leaf into a wide pot. Drizzle with the oil and set the lobster pieces and shells on top. Season with salt, cover, and sweat the vegetables over medium heat for 10 minutes. Pour in the wine and water, cover, and bring to a simmer — this should take about 10 minutes. Turn off the heat and let the stock sit for 10 minutes.

Remove the lobster tail and claws and refrigerate them. Mash the solids with a potato masher, cover the pot, and let the stock sit for an hour or so. (You could strain the stock right away, but better flavor awaits.)

Strain the stock, pushing down on the solids to make sure you get all that flavor. Cover and refrigerate.

FOR THE GAZPACHO: Combine the cucumber, tomatoes, bell peppers, onion, serrano, garlic, cilantro, and ice cubes in a food processor and pulse to make a chunky soup with recognizable pieces of vegetables. Transfer to a bowl and stir in the vinegar, ketchup, and stock. Taste for salt, then cover and refrigerate for at least 1 hour, until well chilled.

FOR THE GARNISH: Cut the tortillas in half, stack them, and cut into thin strips.

Heat about ½ inch of vegetable oil in a small skillet over medium-high heat until very hot. Check by dropping in a tortilla strip: if it sizzles instantly, the oil is ready. Fry the tortilla strips in batches until golden. Remove with a slotted spoon, drain on paper towels, and sprinkle with salt. You can make these an hour or so in advance.

Shell the lobster tail and claws and chop the meat.

To serve, divide the lobster meat among the soup bowls. Ladle in the soup, and pile some diced cucumber and fried tortillas in the center.

VARIATION

Shrimp is a lot easier to find in the market — and cheaper — and it makes a great gazpacho.

FOR THE STOCK: Start by shelling 1 pound large (21–30) or extra-large (16–20) shrimp. Save the shells and refrigerate the shrimp.

Heat a medium saucepan over medium-high heat. When the pan's hot, add 2 tablespoons olive oil, ½ cup thinly sliced onion, and ¼ cup thinly sliced celery. Sauté, stirring, for 2 to 3 minutes, until the onion starts to soften. Add the shrimp shells and sauté, stirring constantly, for another minute or two, until all the shells turn pink. Add 1 bay leaf, ½ cup dry white wine, and 2 cups water and bring to a boil. Reduce the heat and simmer the stock — just lazy bubbles — for 25 minutes.

Add the shrimp to the pan, pushing them down to submerge them in the stock. Cover and simmer for 5 minutes. Turn off the heat and pick out the shrimp. Cool to room temperature, then cover and refrigerate. Let the stock sit for 30 minutes for the flavors to deepen.

Line a strainer with cheesecloth. Set the strainer over a bowl and pour in the stock. Lift up the corners of the cheesecloth and squeeze to make sure you extract all the liquid from the solids. Cool, cover, and refrigerate.

Proceed with making the gazpacho. Divide the shrimp among the bowls before adding the soup.

SALADS, CEVICHES, AND GRAVLAX

CLASSIC AMERICAN TUNA SALAD

Here's the deal: you don't want oil-packed tuna for this salad, because it muddies the flavor, but more often than not, those cans of tuna packed in water taste like cardboard. My solution? Poach a piece of tuna at home.

This makes enough for 2 very hearty sandwiches—or 3, if you're skimpy. It makes a great tuna melt too. I'm an open-faced tuna-melt guy. Pile the tuna onto toasted rye, top with sliced Swiss or cheddar, and pop it under the broiler until the cheese is bubbling and starting to brown.   Serves 2

ACCEPT SUBSTITUTES

If you must, use canned tuna. Or try it with canned salmon.

2 tablespoons minced red onion

2 heaping tablespoons minced celery

3 tablespoons mayonnaise

1 teaspoon Dijon mustard

1 teaspoon chopped fresh dill

6 ounces poached tuna (see box on page 336)

Coarse salt and freshly ground white pepper

FOR SERVING

Sliced dill pickles

2 potato rolls (I like Martin's) or hamburger buns, split and toasted

Potato chips

Mix the onion, celery, mayonnaise, mustard, and dill together in a bowl. Break up the tuna into pretty small flakes with your fingers and add it to the bowl, along with some salt and white pepper. Stir it up, and check the seasoning.

To serve, put a layer of dill pickle slices on the bottom of the rolls. Spoon the tuna salad on top of the pickles, then pile on a handful of potato chips. Set the tops of the rolls on the chips and press down, so you crush the chips into the tuna.

Slice in half. Or not.

TUNA SALAD WITH PICKLED VEGETABLES

Here iceberg lettuce is a crunchy medium to carry the richness of the tuna and the tartness of the vegetables. *Serves 6 as an appetizer*

1 head iceberg lettuce, cored
   and shredded
¼ cup olive oil
2 tablespoons red wine vinegar
Coarse salt and freshly ground white
   pepper

Dried oregano
Tuna (or Salmon) Preserved in Oil
   (page 98 or 99)
Mixed Pickled Vegetables (page 401)

Toss the lettuce with the oil and vinegar in a large bowl. Season with salt and white pepper and crumble in a pinch or two of oregano. Toss again. Break the fish into pieces and toss with the salad.

Divide the salad among six salad plates. Cut the pickled vegetables into bite-sized pieces and garnish the plates, making sure each serving gets carrots and beets.

NIÇOISE SALAD

Here's your opportunity to showcase the tuna you've poached in oil or water.

I've added my own twists to this composed salad. Rather than putting a few anchovy fillets on the plate, I make a warm, garlicky, anchovy vinaigrette, which does great things in your mouth. And I include some pickled onions in the mix. They're a fantastic palate cleanser, just like the pickled ginger you eat with sushi.

The vinaigrette will be at its absolute best if you make it with the oil from Tuna Preserved in Oil (page 98), but you can certainly use your best extra virgin olive oil. As for the other ingredients, use enough to suit your own taste.   Serves up to 6

FOR THE VINAIGRETTE
½ cup extra virgin olive oil
   (see headnote)
¼ cup minced garlic
16 anchovy fillets, chopped
2 tablespoons sherry vinegar

FOR THE SALAD
Mixed greens
Fresh parsley leaves
Boiled creamer or red-skinned
   potatoes, peeled and sliced, at room
   temperature

Chopped tomatoes (ripe summer ones)
   or halved grape tomatoes
Hard-cooked eggs, sliced or quartered
Green beans, blanched until crisp-
   tender and refreshed under cold
   running water
Pickled Onions (page 400)
Poached tuna (see box), Tuna
   Preserved in Oil (page 98), or canned
   tuna in olive oil

POACHED TUNA

You can't beat the fresh ocean flavor of albacore you've poached at home. I call for albacore because it's the most economical, but you could use any tuna.

Start with a 6-ounce piece of albacore and a small skillet or saucepan that's just wide enough to hold the fish. Pour about 1 inch of water into the pan—enough to just cover the fish—and salt it

well. Add the fish and bring the water to a simmer over medium-high heat. Once you've got the water simmering, take the pan off the heat and let the tuna cool in the water for 30 minutes. That's it—it's that simple.

Lift the tuna out with a slotted spoon and pat it dry with paper towels.

FOR THE VINAIGRETTE: Heat a sauté pan over medium-high heat. When the pan is hot, add the oil and garlic and sauté until the garlic is fragrant and just starting to brown, about 1½ minutes. Add the anchovies and sauté, stirring, until the anchovies begin to melt in the oil, about 30 seconds.

Take the pan off the heat and add the vinegar. Stir or whisk, and use as soon as you assemble the salad. Or set the pan on the back of the stove for an hour or so and reheat the vinaigrette before serving.

FOR THE SALAD: Pile a handful of greens in the center of each plate and scatter some parsley leaves on top. Surround with a few slices of potato, a mound of tomatoes, an egg, some green beans, and a small mound of pickled onions. Put a good-sized hunk of tuna on top of the greens.

Drizzle the salad (except for the onions) with the warm dressing.

SICILIAN TUNA SALAD SANDWICH

The first time I made this, I was on a bike trip on the Aeolian island of Lipari. The combination of flavors captures that feeling of the sun and the coast of those islands near Sicily.

This is one big-ass sandwich. Make it for 2 only when you've got some big appetites. You could also halve the salad recipe and use it to top about 24 crostini.

If all you can find are sun-dried tomatoes packed in oil, skip the soaking step. Use the oil from the tomatoes for brushing the bread.   Serves 2 to 4

3 sun-dried tomatoes (6 halves)
1 (10- to 12-ounce) loaf semolina
    bread
Olive oil
2 (6-ounce) cans tuna packed in
    olive oil

10 ounces baby spinach
2 tablespoons drained capers
Coarse salt and freshly ground white
    pepper
2 large hard-cooked eggs

Put the tomatoes in a small bowl and cover them with hot water. Let them reconstitute for about 15 minutes. Drain, blot the tomatoes dry on paper towels, and cut into thin matchsticks.

Split the bread in half lengthwise and pull out some of the soft insides. Drizzle or brush some olive oil on the cut sides of the bread.

Heat a large skillet over high heat. Once you've got the pan hot, add the tuna, the oil from the cans, and the tomatoes. Cook, stirring and breaking up the tuna, for about 2 minutes, until the tuna is hot. Add the spinach and cook, tossing and stirring, for 1 to 2 minutes, until it is wilted. Stir in the capers and season with salt and white pepper — be careful with the salt.

Pile the hot tuna salad onto the bottom half of the bread. Slice the eggs and lay them down on the tuna. Top with the other half of the bread and press down firmly. Push any of the salad that squishes out back into the sandwich, and let the sandwich sit for about 5 minutes.

Cut into pieces and serve.

LOUIS SALAD

I bet you're wondering why this isn't called by its traditional name, Crab Louis. Well, this salad is just too good to be limited. As you'll see, you can make a Louis salad with lobster, with shrimp, with poached tuna (yum), with poached salmon, and, yes, with crabmeat. (The photo is on page 147.)

Think of the dressing as a West Coast version of Thousand Island. The recipe makes enough dressing for 4, but it keeps for weeks in the refrigerator, so you may want to double or triple it and have on hand.   Serves 4 as a first course

FOR THE LOUIS DRESSING
1 cup mayonnaise
2 tablespoons chili sauce
2 tablespoons heavy cream
1 teaspoon fresh lemon juice
Tabasco sauce
Worcestershire sauce
2 tablespoons minced cornichons or
    dill pickle

FOR THE SALAD
4 handfuls mixed greens
Boiled lobster (page 118), poached
    shrimp (see page 84), poached tuna
    (page 336), poached salmon (page
    99), or jumbo lump crabmeat
2 avocados, peeled, pitted, and sliced
4 large hard-cooked eggs, sliced or
    quartered
Chopped tomatoes (ripe summer ones
    or grape tomatoes)

FOR THE LOUIS DRESSING: Combine the mayonnaise, chili sauce, heavy cream, and lemon juice in a bowl. Add 4 dashes of Tabasco and 3 dashes of Worcestershire and whisk until smooth. Stir in the pickle.

Refrigerate the dressing for at least an hour before serving, or make it way in advance.

FOR THE SALAD: Pile some greens on each plate. Top with a generous mound of seafood, and arrange the avocado, egg, and tomatoes around. Serve the dressing on the side.

NOTE: If you want to gild the lily, top the seafood with a spoonful of paddlefish caviar or salmon roe.

LOBSTER AND POTATO SALAD

Serve this on a bed of lettuce for a casual lunch or put it to the side of a piece of grilled fish for a wonderful dinner. (The photo is on page 199.)

Cook the potatoes well in advance, so they have time to cool. You can even make the potatoes and lobsters the day before, if you want. And please make sure to give the flavors time to develop and meld in the refrigerator before serving.

Serves 4 to 6

ACCEPT SUBSTITUTES

You could make do with shrimp and be happy,
and you could even make this salad with steamed salmon.

FOR THE SALAD

1 cup frozen petite peas

1 cup frozen corn

2 (1½-pound) lobsters, boiled (page 118) and chilled

1½ pounds white or red-skinned potatoes, boiled, peeled, and sliced

¾ cup finely diced celery (go for the tender inner ribs)

½ cup thinly sliced scallions

1 (3.75-ounce) can smoked oysters

FOR THE DRESSING

¾ cup mayonnaise

2 tablespoons sour cream

1 tablespoon Dijon mustard

4 teaspoons champagne vinegar

2 tablespoons minced shallots

3 large hard-cooked eggs, coarsely chopped

Coarse salt and freshly ground white pepper

FOR THE SALAD: Put the peas and corn in a strainer and run hot water over them to defrost. Drain well.

Remove the lobster meat from the shells and cut it into large chunks.

Combine the peas, corn, lobster, potatoes, celery, scallions, and oysters in a bowl. Toss.

FOR THE DRESSING: Whisk the mayonnaise, sour cream, mustard, vinegar, and shallots together until smooth. Stir in the eggs. Season with salt and white pepper.

Scrape the dressing into the bowl with the salad and stir very well. Cover and refrigerate for at least 1 hour before serving.

CITRUS ROAST LOBSTER SALAD

Crunchy salad and an Asian-style dressing combine with cool roast lobster. No mayonnaise here. This is a great lunch or a dinner for a warm summer night.

Serves 4

FOR THE DRESSING

2 small garlic cloves, minced
1 serrano chile, seeded and minced
1 small red onion, cut into very thin
   half-moons
2 tablespoons sugar
¼ cup rice vinegar
¼ cup fish sauce
1 tablespoon fresh lemon juice
1 tablespoon fresh lime juice
6 tablespoons vegetable oil

FOR THE SALAD

3 cucumbers, peeled, seeded, and
   cut into half-moons
3 carrots, cut into matchsticks
1 jicama, cut into matchsticks
1 bunch frisée, torn into bite-sized
   pieces
Citrus Roast Lobster (page 210),
   at room temperature
2 oranges, peeled and cut into
   segments (see page 474)
1 grapefruit, peeled and cut into
   segments

FOR THE DRESSING: Combine all the ingredients in a jar and shake well.

FOR THE SALAD: Combine the cucumbers, carrots, jicama, and frisée in a large bowl. Drizzle on a few tablespoons of the dressing, to taste, and toss.

Divide the salad among four large plates, piling it in the center. Surround with the lobster pieces and drizzle some more dressing around the edges of the plates. Garnish with the orange and grapefruit segments.

Store leftover dressing in the refrigerator.

SAUMON AU FRISÉE

Here's my spin on a classic from the French kitchen. No lardons—I've substituted smoked fish for the usual bacon. It's a great lunch, particularly when you want to impress. (The photo is on page 200.)

Make the potatoes early in the day. Serves 4

ACCEPT SUBSTITUTES

Any smoked fish will work. Try this salad with Smoked Sturgeon (page 184).

FOR THE POTATOES
2 tablespoons olive oil
1 large onion, quartered and cut into
    very thin slices
¾ pound creamer or red-skinned
    potatoes, scrubbed and cut into
    very thin slices (use a mandoline or
    vegetable slicer if you have one)
Coarse salt and freshly ground white
    pepper
½ teaspoon fresh thyme leaves
½ cup chicken stock

FOR THE VINAIGRETTE
2 tablespoons whole-grain mustard
2 tablespoons sherry vinegar
Coarse salt and freshly ground white
    pepper
⅓ cup olive oil

1 large head frisée (you can substitute
    chicory or curly endive)
1–2 tablespoons fresh tarragon leaves
About ½ pound sliced smoked salmon
4 large eggs, poached (see page 97)

FOR THE POTATOES: Heat a skillet over medium-high heat. When the pan's hot, add the oil and onion. Sauté, stirring, for 2 minutes, or until the onion is starting to become translucent. Add the potatoes, salt and white pepper to taste, and the thyme. Cook, stirring once in a while but trying not to break up the potatoes, for 4 minutes. Spread the potatoes out evenly in the pan and pour in the chicken stock; the potatoes should be barely covered. Reduce the heat so the stock simmers, cover the pan, and cook until the potatoes are just tender, about 10 minutes. Cool to room temperature.

FOR THE VINAIGRETTE: Whisk the mustard, vinegar, and salt and pepper to taste together in a small bowl. Whisk in the oil in a steady stream to make an emulsion.

Shave any dark green parts of the frisée leaves off with a chef's knife. Separate all the tender pale leaves, wash well, and spin dry.

Toss the frisée with the tarragon and most of the vinaigrette (hold back about 4 teaspoons).

Divide the potatoes among four plates. Top with the frisée and slices of smoked salmon. Place an egg on top of the smoked salmon on each salad and drizzle the eggs with the remaining vinaigrette.

KEY WEST CEVICHE WITH GROUPER

Oregano is the surprise flavor here. This "big brother" of the mint family has a masculine, almost aggressive flavor, and it sets the ceviche apart. I came up with this combination when I worked at the Ocean Room in Key West.

Serves 4 as an appetizer

ACCEPT SUBSTITUTES

Try this with quartered sea scallops.

1 cup minced onion, plus 1 cup thinly
    sliced onion
1 tablespoon minced garlic
½ teaspoon grated lemon zest
¼ teaspoon grated lime zest
½ cup fresh lemon juice
¼ cup fresh lime juice
3 tablespoons olive oil

2 tablespoons sugar
1 teaspoon dried oregano, crumbled
½ teaspoon ground toasted coriander
Coarse salt and freshly ground white
    pepper
1 pound grouper fillet, cut into ½-inch
    pieces
¼ cup chopped fresh parsley

ABOUT CEVICHE

I think of ceviches almost as citrus cocktails. The fish is "cooked" in the acid from the citrus juice, so you see none of the changes in flavor that are associated with heat. No smokiness from grilling, no caramelization—just clean ocean flavor. Paired with spice and heat from chiles and crunch from ingredients like carrots or pomegranate seeds, ceviches are light and fresh.

Serve them with cocktails or as a first course. You could be fancy and pile them into martini glasses, or just spoon them into small bowls. Some fresh tortilla chips on the side are always welcome.

These ceviches should cure for at least 2 hours in the refrigerator.

Combine the minced onion, garlic, lemon and lime zests, juices, olive oil, sugar, oregano, and coriander in a bowl. Stir to mix well. Season with salt and white pepper.

Season the fish with salt and let sit at room temperature for 5 minutes.

Add the fish to the ceviche base and stir, making sure all the fish is covered by the liquid. Cover and refrigerate for at least 2 hours, stirring occasionally.

Right before serving, stir in the sliced onion and parsley.

GRAPEFRUIT-POMEGRANATE CEVICHE WITH BLACK SEA BASS

The balance here is between the sweetness of pomegranate juice and the bracing acidity of grapefruit zest and juice. Pomegranate seeds add crunch. Jalapeño adds a bit of heat.   Serves 4 as an appetizer

ACCEPT SUBSTITUTES

This is pretty good with sea scallops too. Quarter them before adding to the base. Char works as well.

1 teaspoon grated grapefruit zest
1 teaspoon grated lime zest
½ cup fresh grapefruit juice
¼ cup pomegranate juice
1 tablespoon diced jalapeño chile
   (with seeds)
1 teaspoon ground toasted coriander
1 pound black sea bass fillet, cut into
   ½-inch pieces
Coarse salt

TO FINISH
1 grapefruit, peeled and cut into
   segments (see page 474)
Seeds from 1 pomegranate
Fresh cilantro leaves
Sliced scallions

Combine the zests, juices, jalapeño, and coriander in a bowl. Stir to mix well.

Season the fish with salt and let sit at room temperature for 5 minutes.

Add the fish to the ceviche base and stir, making sure all the fish is covered by liquid. Cover and refrigerate for at least 2 hours, stirring occasionally.

To serve, stir in the grapefruit segments, pomegranate seeds, and cilantro and scallions to taste.

TEQUILA FENNEL CEVICHE WITH MACKEREL

Tequila blends naturally with the lime and lemon juices and helps bring a creaminess to the mackerel. Diced fennel adds crunch, which is always welcome.

Serves 4 as an appetizer

ACCEPT SUBSTITUTES

This ceviche also works very well with char, squid, or shrimp.

1 cup thinly sliced red onion
½ cup thinly sliced red bell pepper
½ cup diced fennel
½ cup chopped scallions
¼ cup chopped fresh cilantro
1 tablespoon minced serrano chile (with seeds)

½ cup fresh lime juice
¼ cup fresh lemon juice
¼ cup tequila
¼ cup olive oil
1 pound mackerel fillet (Boston or Spanish), cut into ½-inch pieces
Coarse salt

Combine the onion, bell pepper, fennel, scallions, cilantro, chile, lime and lemon juices, tequila, and olive oil in a bowl. Stir to mix well.

Season the fish with salt and let sit at room temperature for 5 minutes.

Add the fish to the ceviche base and stir, making sure all the fish is covered by liquid. Cover and refrigerate for at least 2 hours, stirring occasionally, before serving.

MANGO MOJO CEVICHE WITH SQUID

The orangey-piney tropical mango nectar offers a fine contrast to the flavor of squid. And don't listen to what anyone else tells you: it's pronounced "mo ho."

Serves 4 as an appetizer

ACCEPT SUBSTITUTES

Try this ceviche with sea scallops (remove the tough bits and quarter them) or black sea bass (cut into ½-inch pieces). Salt either and let sit for 5 minutes before adding to the base.

1 cup thinly sliced red onion
½ cup chopped scallions
⅓ cup chopped tomatoes (see Note)
1 tablespoon thinly sliced garlic
1 tablespoon chopped fresh cilantro
1 teaspoon grated lime zest
1 cup mango nectar

⅓ cup fresh lime juice
Coarse salt and freshly ground white pepper
1 pound cleaned squid (see page 43; bodies only), cut into ⅓-inch rings, blanched (see box), and chilled

Combine the onion, scallions, tomatoes, garlic, cilantro, lime zest, mango nectar, and lime juice in a bowl. Stir to mix well and season with salt and white pepper.

Add the squid to the ceviche base and stir, making sure all the rings are covered by liquid. Cover and refrigerate for at least 2 hours, stirring occasionally, before serving.

NOTE: Take a tip from a chef. If tomatoes are out of season, use Pomì chopped tomatoes in this recipe. (Or make it easy on yourself and use them whenever you make this.) They're the ones in a box, and you can find them at most grocery stores.

ABOUT SQUID FOR CEVICHE

Snow-white rings of squid in a tangy ceviche base can be both beautiful and delicious, but I think the squid tastes best when it's been helped along in the "cooking" process by a flash-blanch.

Bring a large saucepan of water to a boil. Add the squid, give it a stir, and drain immediately; it should be in the water for no more than 3 seconds. Spread the rings out on a plate or baking sheet and chill completely before adding them to the base.

No doubt you'll notice that I call just for squid bodies in the ceviche recipes. Much as I love tentacles, I don't like them in ceviche.

PINEAPPLE-CARROT CEVICHE WITH SEA SCALLOPS

This ceviche is truly clean and bright. Pineapple is the main "cooking" acid at work, ably assisted by lime and orange. Acidic as it is, though, pineapple has a natural sweetness. So I reinforce it with the sweetness of shredded carrot, which also adds color and crunch. (The photo is on page 148.)   Serves 4 as an appetizer

ACCEPT SUBSTITUTES

Try this with grouper, black sea bass, char, or squid (see page 347).
Cut the fish into ½-inch pieces, season with salt,
and let them sit for 5 minutes before adding to the base.

1 cup diced fresh pineapple
1 cup shredded carrots
1 teaspoon grated lime zest
1 teaspoon grated orange zest
1 teaspoon minced habanero chile
¾ cup pineapple juice

⅓ cup fresh lime juice
⅓ cup fresh orange juice
Coarse salt
1 pound sea scallops, tough bits
    removed, cut into quarters

Combine the pineapple, carrots, zests, chile, and the three juices in a nonreactive bowl. Stir to mix well. Season with salt.

Season the scallops with salt and let sit at room temperature for 5 minutes.

Add the scallops to the ceviche base and stir, making sure all the scallops are covered by liquid. Cover and refrigerate for at least 2 hours, stirring occasionally, before serving.

PINEAPPLE RUM CEVICHE WITH SHRIMP

The inspiration for this spicy shrimp ceviche cocktail—which packs a nice bit of heat—was planter's punch. The ceviche is just what you want for a hot, lazy summer afternoon. It will call up memories of ocean breezes.

If you want, garnish it with some shredded unsweetened coconut.

Serves 4 as an appetizer

ACCEPT SUBSTITUTES

This ceviche base is also delicious with mackerel, char, scallops, and squid (see page 347). The fish should be cut into ½-inch pieces, the scallops into quarters; season with salt and let sit for 5 minutes before adding to the base.

1 cup thinly sliced onion
½ cup thinly sliced red bell pepper
½ cup chopped scallions
¼ cup chopped fresh cilantro
1 tablespoon minced serrano chile
   (with seeds)
½ teaspoon grated lime zest

1 cup fresh lime juice (5–7 limes)
1 cup pineapple juice
¼ cup olive oil
¼ cup golden rum
Coarse salt
1 pound large (21–30) shrimp, shelled
   and blanched (see box)

Combine the onion, bell pepper, scallions, cilantro, chile, lime zest and juice, pineapple juice, olive oil, and rum in a nonreactive bowl. Stir to mix well. Season with salt.

Add the shrimp to the ceviche base and stir, making sure all the shrimp are covered by liquid. Cover and refrigerate for at least 2 hours, stirring occasionally, before serving.

ABOUT SHRIMP FOR CEVICHE

Shrimp need a quick blanch to firm them up before starting the "cooking" process.

Bring a large saucepan of water to a boil over high heat. Add the shrimp and stir. Cook for 2 minutes, timing from the moment you add the shrimp, and drain. Spread out on a plate or baking sheet and chill completely before adding to the ceviche base.

SPICY GINGER-LIME CEVICHE WITH BLACK SEA BASS

Here's a ceviche with an Asian twist.

The specialty ingredients are available at Asian and specialty markets and in the Asian section of most grocery stores.

Serves 4 as an appetizer

ACCEPT SUBSTITUTES

This base is delicious paired with scallops, char, and salmon;
remove the tough bits from the scallops and cut them into quarters.
I like this made with squid too (see page 347).

1 teaspoon grated lime zest
½ cup fresh lime juice
2 tablespoons hoisin sauce
2 tablespoons fish sauce
2 tablespoons chili paste (sambal oelek)
2 tablespoons grated fresh ginger (use a Microplane)

1 pound black sea bass fillet, cut into ½-inch pieces
Coarse salt
½ cup very thinly sliced red bell pepper
¼ cup chopped scallions
2 tablespoons chopped fresh cilantro

Combine the lime zest and juice, hoisin sauce, fish sauce, chili paste, and ginger in a bowl. Stir to combine well.

Season the fish with salt and let sit at room temperature for 5 minutes.

Add the fish to the ceviche base and stir, making sure all the fish is covered by liquid. Cover and refrigerate for at least 2 hours, stirring occasionally. Just before serving, stir in the bell pepper, scallions, and cilantro.

SARDINES (OR ANCHOVIES) IN VINEGAR (BOQUERONES)

Most likely you've seen something called "white anchovies" on restaurant menus, maybe served as a tapa or as part of a salad. That's what these are. Be sure to use the freshest fish. I like eating them as part of a salad, maybe with string beans and ripe tomatoes. But you could also eat them out in the sun, on croutons (see page 475).

Sardines (or anchovies), butterflied (see box)

Coarse salt

White vinegar

Olive or vegetable oil

Lay the sardines in a single layer, skin side down, in a baking dish. Sprinkle with salt, coating the fish lightly but thoroughly. Let the fish sit for 5 minutes, then pour in enough white vinegar to cover. Let the fish cure in the vinegar for 30 minutes.

Remove the sardines from the vinegar and blot them dry on paper towels.

Layer the fish in a clean plastic container and cover with olive oil. Cover and refrigerate until cold; the boquerones will keep for about a week.

BUTTERFLYING SARDINES (OR ANCHOVIES)

Scale the fish with your fingers under cold running water, working from the tail to the head. Be gentle—the skin is delicate.

Stand the fish on its belly on a cutting board and make a cut right behind the front fins and through the spine. Hold the body of the fish in one hand and the head in the other. Bend the head down toward the belly, pulling it off. Most of the guts will come out as you do this.

Push your index finger into the cavity you've made at the head end and open the fish up along its belly. Remove the remaining guts and rinse.

With the fish on its back, work your index finger under the spine at the head end. When your finger is in to the first knuckle, slide in your middle finger too. This will lift the small bones from the flesh. Continue working your fingers under the bones until you reach the tail. Pinch off the spine at the tail.

Lay the fish flat on your working surface and trim the edges. Pat down any ragged flesh.

ESCABECHE

This technique of preserving fish has roots in Spain, Provence, and Italy. The fish is fried before being pickled in an acid, which here is vinegar. Lots of onion is traditional; crunchy celery root is my addition. If you can't find celery root, substitute celery.

Think of escabeche as picnic food. Serve it at room temperature with some great bread.

Serves 4

ACCEPT SUBSTITUTES

Bluefish, anchovies, and sardines are all good.

1 pound mackerel fillets, skin on, cut in half

Coarse salt and freshly ground white pepper

All-purpose flour or Wondra flour, for dusting

¾ cup olive oil

2 scallions, cut into thin slices on the diagonal

2 tablespoons chopped fresh parsley

1 large onion, cut into very thin slices

3 garlic cloves, minced

2 sprigs thyme

1 bay leaf

1 red bell pepper, cut into very thin slices

1 small serrano chile, cut into very thin slices (don't seed it)

Grated zest of 1 lemon

1 teaspoon cumin seeds

½ cup white wine vinegar

½ cup water

Half a celery root, peeled, cut into thin sticks, and tossed with the juice of ½ lemon

Season the fish with salt and pepper. Be generous with the salt; it's part of the cure. Dust with flour, patting off the excess.

Heat ¼ cup oil in a large skillet over medium-high heat. When the oil shimmers, add the fish, skin side down, and press on it with the back of a spatula. (Work in batches if necessary, so you don't crowd the pan.) Fry for 2 to 2½ minutes, until the skin has blistered and turned the palest gold. Turn over and fry for another 30 seconds. Transfer the fish to a nonreactive container (an 8-inch square Pyrex baking dish is good here), leaving the oil in the skillet. Scatter the scallions and parsley over the fish.

Add ¼ cup olive oil, along with the onion, garlic, thyme, and bay leaf, to the skillet. Sauté for 1 minute, stirring. Add the bell pepper, chile, lemon zest, and cumin and sauté for another minute. Reduce the heat to medium and pour in the vinegar and water. When the liquid comes to a simmer, add the celery root. Bring back to a simmer and cook for 4 minutes. (You don't want this to reduce.)

Spoon the vegetables over the fish and pour in all the liquid from the skillet. Drizzle with the remaining ¼ cup oil and tamp the fish down with the back of a spatula to make sure it's covered with liquid. Cover with plastic and refrigerate for 24 hours before serving.

CORIANDER-DILL GRAVLAX

The classic dry cure here (rather than the wet cure of the Fennel-Onion Gravlax on page 356) gives the salmon a nice hit of dill flavor, perfumed with coriander.

Serves 8 as an appetizer, with leftovers

ACCEPT SUBSTITUTES

You can make gravlax with any wild salmon.

1 cup coarse salt
¾ cup sugar
⅓ cup packed chopped fresh dill

2 tablespoons toasted coriander seeds, ground in a spice grinder
1 (3-pound) piece wild king salmon fillet (in one piece and cut from the head end), pinbones removed

ABOUT SERVING GRAVLAX

Gravlax can make it into your mouth just about any time of the day. Have it as an appetizer, or dinner, or the centerpiece of a late breakfast.

- Butter slices of black bread and top with sliced gravlax. Drizzle with honey mustard sauce (page 355) and garnish with dill.

- Pair sliced gravlax with boiled potatoes and a cucumber salad. Pass the honey mustard sauce.

- Toast English muffins or sliced bagels and make a platter with gravlax, butter, cream cheese, sliced tomatoes, minced shallots or red onions, and fresh basil leaves.

- Make one of the cucumber salads (page 458 or 459), but cut the cucumbers into small spears instead of slices. Wrap the pickled cucumbers in slices of gravlax and serve over a salad.

- Toast slices of brioche, cut into fingers, and top with gravlax and orange cream (see page 357).

- Serve slices of gravlax on a plate, with orange cream or honey mustard sauce.

When you visit delis or classic appetizer shops like Russ and Daughters in New York City, you'll see the counter guys cutting beautifully thin slices, on an angle, right down to but not through the skin of lox or gravlax. If you have a long sharp knife, you can do this too, but I find it easier just to make thin slices straight down and then trim the skin off the slices.

Mix the salt, sugar, dill, and coriander in a bowl.

Cut a strip of plastic wrap a little more than twice the length of the salmon and set it on a baking sheet. Cut another strip of plastic, this time a little more than twice the width of the salmon, and set it crosswise on the center of the first piece. Spread about one third of the salt cure across the center of the plastic and set the salmon on top of it. Cover the salmon with the rest of the cure and wrap the plastic snugly around the fish.

Set another baking sheet on top and weight the fish (a couple of cans of tomatoes work well). Refrigerate for 36 hours. The salmon will exude lots of juice; you can pour it off halfway through the cure if you want.

Scrape off the solids and rinse the salmon. Dry it well with paper towels. You can serve it now (see box on opposite page), or store it wrapped tightly in plastic. It will keep for about a week.

HONEY MUSTARD SAUCE FOR GRAVLAX

Sweet and tangy, this sauce is ideal with gravlax, particularly the version with the coriander-dill cure.

Makes about ⅔ cup

2 tablespoons honey

2 tablespoons whole-grain mustard

1 tablespoon Dijon mustard

2 tablespoons red wine vinegar

1 tablespoon chopped fresh dill

Coarse salt and freshly ground white pepper

6 tablespoons vegetable oil

Whisk together the honey, mustards, vinegar, dill, and salt and white pepper to taste in a small bowl. Whisk in the oil in a steady stream. Check for salt and pepper.

The sauce will keep for a week in the refrigerator.

FENNEL-ONION GRAVLAX

This is a long, slow cure, and the salmon needs a day of rest before serving, so advance planning is a must. But the reward is a creamy consistency different from that of most gravlax, with the clean taste of fennel permeating the fish. (The photo is on page 149.)   Serves 8 as an appetizer, with leftovers

ACCEPT SUBSTITUTES

Make this with any wild salmon.

2 large red onions, chopped
1 large fennel bulb, trimmed and
    chopped, plus ½ cup chopped
    fennel fronds
1 cup coarse salt
¾ cup sugar
½ cup Pernod

½ cup water
1 (3-pound) piece wild king salmon
    fillet (in one piece and cut from the
    head end), skinless, pinbones
    removed
¼ cup chopped fresh dill
2 tablespoons fennel seeds, toasted and
    coarsely ground

Put the onions, chopped fennel (not the fronds), salt, and sugar into a food processor and pulse to make a coarse puree. Add the Pernod and water and pulse a few times, then process to make a smooth slush.

Pour half the cure into a 2½-quart baking dish or plastic container. Set the fish on top and pour in the rest of the cure. Cover with plastic wrap, pressing it down on the surface, or with the lid, if the container has one, and refrigerate for 3 days, turning the salmon over in the cure once or twice.

Remove the fish from the cure and rinse it under cool water. Pat it dry, wrap it snugly in plastic wrap, and refrigerate for another 24 hours.

Mix the fennel fronds, dill, and fennel seeds together in a small bowl. Spread over the top of the salmon, pressing down to make an even coating. You can serve the gravlax now or later (see page 354). It will keep, tightly wrapped in plastic, for about a week.

ORANGE CREAM FOR GRAVLAX

Serve this simple sauce with Fennel-Onion Gravlax and fingers of toasted brioche.   Makes about ¾ cup

½ cup crème fraîche

1 tablespoon grated orange zest

3 tablespoons fresh orange juice

Coarse salt

Whip the crème fraîche until stiff. Add the orange zest and juice and whip again until stiff. Beat in a pinch of salt and serve.

FISH CAKES AND BURGERS

SHRIMP AND TILAPIA BURGERS

This is a burger with tooth. It's juicy and a little bit chewy too. What I've done here is make a quick shrimp mousse as a binder for the tilapia. Don't worry about making the mousse — you're not going to believe how easy and fast it actually is. The little bit of ginger is a great accent flavor for the tilapia. (The photo is on page 197.)

This recipe is easily doubled.   Serves 4

½ pound tilapia fillets
½ pound medium (31–35 count)
   shrimp in the shell
½ teaspoon minced garlic
½ teaspoon grated fresh ginger, or
   more to taste
2 teaspoons soy sauce
Coarse salt
1 large egg white, beaten until frothy
⅓ cup heavy cream

3 scallions, chopped
Freshly ground white pepper
Vegetable oil for sautéing

FOR SERVING
Grilled flatbread or pita breads
Chipotle Sauce (page 425)
Leaf lettuce
Sliced ripe tomatoes

The key to a successful fish mousse is keeping everything cold, so put the bowl and steel blade from your processor into the freezer while you prep the ingredients. And put the tilapia in the freezer while you prep the shrimp so it will be easier to dice.

Shell the shrimp, devein them if you can see the veins, and coarsely chop the shrimp. Put in a small bowl and pop it into the freezer for 10 to 15 minutes.

Sharpen your knife and slice the tilapia into ⅓-inch strips. Then cut the strips into ⅓-inch dice, place in a bowl, and refrigerate.

Fill a bowl with ice and some water. Set a smaller stainless steel bowl on the ice. Check the shrimp. If it feels firm and partially frozen, you're ready to go.

Set up the processor. Add the shrimp, garlic, ginger, soy, a pinch of salt, and 1 tablespoon of the egg white. Pulse to chop the shrimp well. It is chopped enough when it starts to gather in a ball on the blade. Now, with the processor running, gradually pour in the cream.

Scrape the mousse out into the bowl set over ice, add the scallions and some white pepper, and fold well. If you've got any questions about your seasoning, now's the time to find out. Heat a small skillet over medium heat and coat it with a film of oil. Cook a teaspoon or so of the mousse until it's golden on both sides, then give it a taste. Want more pepper or more ginger? Add it.

Season the tilapia with a pinch of salt and fold it into the mousse. Wet your hands so the mixture won't stick to them, and form 4 burgers. You can prep the burgers up to 2 hours in advance and refrigerate them. Any longer, and the ginger will start to break down the mousse and the burgers will be grainy.

Heat a large skillet over medium heat. Pour in a film of vegetable oil and heat until it shimmers. Add the burgers and cook until golden (not brown), about 2 minutes a side, and firm (like the flesh at the base of your thumb).

To serve, slather each flatbread or pita bread with some chipotle sauce. Add a burger, some lettuce, and a thick slice of tomato.

LEFTOVERS

I love these cold too. Make a sandwich on white bread with some ballpark mustard for a real treat. It's like the best fish bologna you've ever eaten.

THAI-STYLE CATFISH BURGERS

Here's an improv on the Shrimp and Tilapia Burgers (page 360), with an accent on Thai flavors.

You can use your Microplane zester when you're prepping the garlic and ginger for more intense flavor.

Serves 4

ACCEPT SUBSTITUTES

Flounder, tilapia

½ pound medium (31–35 count) shrimp, shelled and coarsely chopped
1 tablespoon minced shallot
1–2 red chiles, minced (with seeds)
1 teaspoon grated lime zest
1 teaspoon sugar
¾ teaspoon minced or grated fresh ginger
½ teaspoon minced or grated garlic
2 teaspoons fish sauce
About 2 teaspoons vegetable oil
1 large egg white, beaten until frothy
Coarse salt

1 pound catfish fillets, chilled in the freezer for about 20 minutes
2 scallions, chopped
2 tablespoons chopped fresh cilantro

FOR SERVING
Tender lettuce leaves (red or green leaf, Boston, Bibb)
Fresh basil, mint, and cilantro leaves, cut into thin strips
OR
Toasted pita breads
Cilantro Aïoli (page 419)
Tender lettuce leaves

Have ready a bowl filled with ice and some water. Set another bowl on the ice.

Combine the shrimp, shallot, chiles, zest, sugar, ginger, garlic, fish sauce, 1 teaspoon vegetable oil, and 1 tablespoon of the egg white in a food processor. Season lightly with salt—be careful here, the fish sauce is salty. Pulse and process until you have a thick, smooth paste. Scrape the paste out into the bowl set over ice and spread it thin, so it will chill quickly.

Trim out the center (bloodline) of the catfish fillets (see page 37), then cut the fillets into ⅓-inch dice. This process should go pretty quickly as long as your knife is very sharp. You do keep your knives sharp, right?

Add the catfish, scallions, and cilantro to the shrimp paste and fold together thoroughly.

Heat 1 teaspoon or so of vegetable oil in a large nonstick skillet over medium heat. You can, if you want, use a Foreman grill (see page 136) for these burgers. They will cook in about 3 minutes, but they won't be as nicely browned as when they're cooked in the skillet.

Meanwhile, shape the fish into 4 patties. This will be a lot easier to do if you wet or oil your hands first. Cook the burgers until golden brown, about 5 minutes a side. Give them a poke: they should be firm and springy.

To serve, you can put the burgers out on a platter with the lettuce leaves and a bowl of herbs. Then put a burger in a cup of lettuce leaves, add a big pinch of herbs, and wrap it up. Or you can make sandwiches with the pita, aïoli, and lettuce.

JALAPEÑO SALMON BURGERS

These are good and spicy, but if you really like heat, use serranos or another chile with a bigger kick.   Serves 4

ACCEPT SUBSTITUTES

Char, red rainbow trout (add another tablespoon
of sour cream), mackerel

1 pound skinless wild salmon fillet,
  chilled in the freezer for 1½ hours
½ cup chopped scallions
¼ cup minced red bell pepper
2 tablespoons minced jalapeño chile
2 tablespoons sour cream
2 teaspoons Tabasco sauce
Coarse salt and freshly ground white
  pepper
1 large egg white, beaten to soft peaks
1 teaspoon vegetable oil

FOR SERVING
4 pita breads
Olive oil
2 avocados
Juice of 2 limes
Coarse salt

Heat the oven to 400 degrees.

Take the salmon out of the freezer and cut it into ⅓-inch dice. Sorry, but the food processor won't work for this; you'll just make mush.

Put the salmon in a medium bowl with the scallions, bell pepper, jalapeño, sour cream, and Tabasco. Season well with salt and white pepper and fold together with a rubber spatula. Add the beaten egg white and fold it in gently but thoroughly. The burger mixture will be pretty loose.

Heat the vegetable oil in a large ovenproof nonstick skillet over medium-high heat while you form the fish into 4 burgers. The easiest way to do this is on a plate; divide the mix into quarters and shape into burgers with the rubber spatula or moistened hands.

Slide the burgers into the skillet. Reshape them with the spatula if you need to, and cook for 1 minute, to set the bottoms.

Slip the skillet into the oven and bake for 2 to 3 minutes, until the tops are opaque and milky. Let the burgers rest in the skillet for 5 minutes.

Meanwhile, split the pitas and brush the insides with olive oil. Grill the pitas — on a stovetop grill or in a Foreman grill (see page 136) — until hot and toasted.

Peel, pit, and chop the avocados. Coarsely mash with the lime juice and a big pinch of salt.

To serve, put each burger on a pita half, divide the avocado among the burgers, and top with the remaining pita halves.

SALMON BURGERS
WITH GREEN TARTAR SAUCE

The tartar sauce for this elegant, refined burger is best when you make it a day ahead. It's easier to dice the fish if you've firmed it up in the freezer first.   Serves 4

ACCEPT SUBSTITUTES

Char and rainbow trout make great burgers.
You can also try bluefish, striped bass, or swordfish.

4 pita breads
Olive oil
1½ pounds skinless wild salmon fillet, chilled in the freezer for 20 to 30 minutes
½ cup diced red bell pepper
½ cup diced green bell pepper
¼ cup chopped scallions
¼ cup heavy cream
2 teaspoons Tabasco sauce
2 teaspoons salt

Freshly ground white pepper
1 large egg white, whipped to soft peaks
1 tablespoon canola oil
2 teaspoons unsalted butter

FOR SERVING
1 ripe beefsteak tomato, cored and cut into 4 thick slices
Green Tartar Sauce (page 417)
A handful of tender salad greens

Heat the broiler. Using a pastry brush or your fingers, coat each side of the pita breads with a thin layer of olive oil. Place on the broiler rack and broil for about 2 minutes, until brown. Turn and broil for another 2 minutes. Wrap in a kitchen towel.

Sharpen your knife and cut the salmon into a fine dice. Place the salmon in a medium bowl. Add the bell peppers, scallions, and cream and combine gently with your hands. Season with the Tabasco, salt, and white pepper. Gently fold in ¼ cup of the beaten egg white. Form into 4 patties.

Heat the canola oil in a large nonstick skillet over medium-high heat. When the oil is shimmering, add the burgers. Lower the heat to medium and put ½ teaspoon butter next to each burger. Cook for 3 minutes, then flip until browned. Cook for another 2 minutes, or until nicely browned on the second side.

Split the pita breads open. Set each burger on one pita half and top with a slab of tomato, a dollop of tartar sauce, some of the greens, and the other pita half.

TUNA BURGERS
WITH HARISSA MAYONNAISE

Tuna burgers deliver all the juicy satisfaction and richness of a hamburger. (The photo is on page 196.)

You do need to dice the tuna by hand; a food processor or grinder is going to make glue.   Serves 4

FOR THE HARISSA MAYONNAISE
¼ cup mayonnaise
1 teaspoon harissa (page 443 or store-
   bought), or more to taste
1 teaspoon grated lemon zest
2 teaspoons fresh lemon juice

FOR THE BURGERS
1 pound tuna, chilled in the freezer
   for 15 minutes

2 tablespoons chopped fresh chives
1 tablespoon chopped fresh dill
Coarse salt
Vegetable oil

FOR SERVING
Toasted potato rolls or hamburger
   rolls
Mom's Cucumber Salad (page 459; see
   Note)

FOR THE HARISSA MAYONNAISE: Stir the mayonnaise, harissa, lemon zest, and juice together in a small bowl.

FOR THE BURGERS: Cut the tuna into ¼-inch dice, then chop it, to get a tiny dice. Put the tuna into a bowl and add the chives, dill, 4 teaspoons of the harissa mayonnaise, and salt to taste. Mix it all up with your hands, then moisten your hands and form 4 burgers.

Heat a little vegetable oil in a large nonstick skillet over medium-high heat. When the pan is hot, reduce the heat to medium, put the burgers in the pan, and cook for 2 minutes to brown the first side. Turn the burgers over and cook for another 2 minutes for medium-rare.

To serve, spread the rolls with harissa mayonnaise. Add the burgers and pile on some cucumber salad.

NOTE: You can also make a very quick cucumber relish by peeling, seeding, and dicing a cucumber, tossing it with salt, and pouring in about ⅓ cup white vinegar; let it sit while you make the burgers.

"BRANDADE" CAKES

Classic brandade is made with salt cod, but I started playing with the dish, adapting it to use up the scraps of fish I'd have in the walk-in refrigerator in my restaurants.

You've got options for serving these. They can be a main course for 4 or a generous appetizer for 8, or you can make tiny cakes and pass them, with a few drops of the vinaigrette on top, at a cocktail party.

Serves 4 as a main course, 8 as an appetizer

ACCEPT SUBSTITUTES

I've also made these with a mix of tilapia and salmon. You can use just about any fish except bluefish or mackerel.

FOR THE FISH
1 pound cod, cut into 1-inch pieces
Coarse salt

FOR THE COURT BOUILLON
8 cups water
1 onion, diced
1 carrot, diced
1 celery rib, diced
1 bay leaf
5 white peppercorns

FOR THE BRANDADE
2 tablespoons olive oil
1 medium onion, minced
3 garlic cloves, minced
1 cup heavy cream
Coarse salt and freshly ground white
    pepper

1 russet potato, peeled, cut into
    chunks, boiled until tender, and riced
2 tablespoons capers
½ teaspoon lapsang souchong tea,
    ground in a spice grinder

All-purpose flour for dredging
2 large eggs
2 cups dry bread crumbs
Vegetable oil for frying

FOR SERVING
A few handfuls of frisée, or
    Cauliflower Puree (page 455), or
    German-Style Potato Salad (page
    467)
Truffle Vinaigrette (page 434)

FOR THE FISH: Season the cod well with salt. Put it in a saucepan and leave it on the counter while you make the court bouillon.

FOR THE COURT BOUILLON: Combine the water, onion, carrot, celery, bay leaf, and white peppercorns in a saucepan. Bring to a simmer over medium-high heat, then reduce the heat and simmer for 20 minutes.

Crank up the heat and bring the court bouillon to a boil. Strain it over the cod and stir. Cover the pan and let the cod sit for 20 minutes. Drain.

FOR THE BRANDADE: Heat a wide saucepan or large skillet over medium-high heat. Add the oil and onion and sauté until the onion is translucent, 2 to 3 minutes. Add the garlic and sauté for 1 minute. Add the cream, season with salt and white pepper, and bring to an active simmer. Simmer until reduced by half.

Flake the cod and add it to the pan. Stir, breaking up the fish more, and bring back to a simmer. Stir in the potato, capers, and tea. Cook, stirring often, until the brandade is very thick and dry. When you scrape a spoon across the center of the pan, you should leave a valley, with no liquid seeping into it. Check for salt and pepper. Scrape the brandade into a bowl and cool it completely.

Form the cooled brandade into 8 cakes (flour your hands if you need to). Set them on a plate or small baking sheet, cover with plastic, and refrigerate for at least 2 hours. You can make the cakes to this point a day in advance.

Set a rack over a baking sheet. Spread some flour on a plate. Beat the eggs in a shallow bowl. Spread the bread crumbs on another plate. Dredge the cakes in flour, patting off the excess, then dip them in the egg and coat in the bread crumbs. Pat all over to make sure the crumbs adhere. Set the cakes on the rack as you finish them.

Heat about ½ inch oil in a skillet over medium-high heat to 350 degrees. Fry the cakes in batches until golden brown, about 2 minutes per side. Drain on the rack.

TO SERVE: If using the frisée, toss it with some of the vinaigrette and divide it among four plates. Top with the cakes and drizzle more vinaigrette around the plates.

If you're serving the cauliflower, make a bed of the puree on four plates and set the cakes on top. Drizzle a ring of vinaigrette around the puree and pass the rest.

If you're serving the potato salad, spoon some vinaigrette onto four plates. Set the cakes on top and the salad on the side. Pass the remaining vinaigrette.

JUMBO LUMP CRAB CAKES

This recipe looks a lot longer and more complicated than most of the others in this book. It is. But I made my name on these crab cakes, and they are worth every moment of effort you expend in making them. You can make both the base and the cakes well in advance of serving. (The photo is on page 151.)

The only out-of-the-ordinary ingredients are the fish sauce and the panko (Japanese bread crumbs); you can get them both at Asian markets or specialty food shops.

In the restaurant, I use a ring mold that's actually a piece of PVC pipe. For simplicity at home, use a dry measuring cup.

Serves 4 as a main course, 6 as an appetizer

ACCEPT SUBSTITUTES

Blue crab from Maryland is the sweetest, and it will make the best
cakes, but you can make these with most crab you find at the
fish counter. Dungeness crab would be fine, but canned crab is too dry
and the pieces too small to work in this recipe.

By the way, "jumbo" refers to the size of the pieces of crabmeat.

Here's a guide to crabmeat grades:
Jumbo lump: largest pieces of crab and least amount of shell
Lump: large pieces of crab, with more shell
Backfin: small pieces of crab and lots of shell

FOR THE BASE
1½ cups vegetable oil
1 large onion, cut into ⅓-inch dice
1 green bell pepper or large poblano chile, seeded and cut into ⅓-inch dice
1 red bell pepper, cut into ⅓-inch dice
4 large egg yolks
2 tablespoons fresh lime juice
2 tablespoons Dijon mustard
1 tablespoon fish sauce
2 teaspoons Tabasco sauce
Freshly ground white pepper
Coarse salt

FOR THE CAKES
12 ounces jumbo lump crabmeat
1 tablespoon *each* finely chopped fresh dill, chives, and parsley (no coarse stems)
4 slices white sandwich bread (something like Pepperidge Farm), crusts removed, processed into crumbs
About 1 cup panko (Japanese bread crumbs)
Vegetable oil for sautéing

Cucumber salad (page 458 or 459)
Chipotle Sauce (page 425)

FOR THE BASE: Combine the oil, onion, green pepper or poblano, and red pepper in a saucepan and bring to a simmer over medium heat; simmer until the vegetables are tender, 7 to 8 minutes.

Meanwhile, combine the egg yolks, lime juice, mustard, fish sauce, Tabasco, and white pepper to taste in a large stainless steel bowl. (Setting the bowl on a damp kitchen towel on the counter will help keep it steady while you whisk.) Have ready a larger bowl filled with ice and some cold water.

When the vegetables are tender, remove the pan from the heat and immediately start drizzling the hot oil into the yolk mixture, whisking constantly. Begin by pouring in small splashes, incorporating the oil completely each time before adding more. This is just like making a mayonnaise, only a bit quicker. The heat of the oil will cook the yolks as you go, and when all the oil has been added, you should have a thick sauce. Scrape in any of the vegetables left in the pan and whisk vigorously for 30 seconds or so.

Set the bowl of sauce into the bowl of ice water and whisk it, spinning the bowl over the ice as you whisk, to cool the crab cake base down quickly. Season with salt and white pepper, taste, and correct the seasoning if necessary; a lot of pepper is nice. You can let the base sit on ice, whisking once in a while, for 30 minutes to 1 hour, or cover it with plastic and put it in the refrigerator.

FOR THE CAKES: Spread the crabmeat out on a small baking sheet — gently, so you don't break up the lumps — and pick over it to remove any pieces of shell or cartilage. Transfer the crab to a large bowl. Sprinkle the herbs over the crab, add 1 cup of the base and 1⅓ cups of the fresh bread crumbs, and fold together gently. Try not to break up the pieces of crab. This will start out wet, but the bread crumbs will soften, absorb moisture, and bind the cakes. Your goal here is to add as few bread crumbs as possible, so the crab flavor will rule. Let this mixture sit for about 10 minutes.

Take a bit of the crab mixture in your hand and try to shape it. If it holds together, great. If it's a bit loose, fold in a tablespoon or two more crumbs. Or, if it seems dry, fold in a bit more of the base. Leftover base will keep, tightly covered, for about a week in the refrigerator. See next page for an idea on using the leftovers.

Sprinkle some of the panko on a small plate. Fill a ¼-cup measure (for appetizers) or a ⅓-cup measure (for a main course or sandwich) with the crab mixture, pack it down, and flop it out into your palm. Press it firmly with your hands to compact it and shape into a cake. Set the cake on the panko, sprinkle the top with more panko, and tamp the crumbs onto the top and bottom of the cake; try not to get crumbs on the sides of the cake. Set the cake on a clean plate. Continue forming cakes, adding more panko to the plate as you need it. When you've formed all the cakes, set them in the refrigerator for 30 minutes. You can prepare the cakes well in advance; they will keep, covered with plastic, for 12 hours in the refrigerator.

Heat the oven to 250 degrees.

Heat a film of vegetable oil in a sauté pan or skillet over medium heat until it shimmers. Working in batches, brown the crab cakes on both sides, about 2 minutes per side. Add more oil to the pan if necessary. Transfer the cakes to an ovenproof platter as they're done. Then slide the platter into the oven for about 5 minutes, until the cakes are heated through.

For fancy serving, pile some cucumber salad on each plate; nestle 2 crab cakes next to it, and add a spoonful of the chipotle sauce. The salad's a great palate cleanser, cooling after the heat of the chipotle sauce, and a fine foil for the cakes. But I won't say that a big green salad and some tartar sauce aren't great accompaniments too.

VARIATION

Leftover grilled or broiled salmon makes delicious cakes. You'll need 2 cups of flaked cooked salmon, ¾ cup of the base, and ⅔ cup fresh bread crumbs. Let your taste be your guide for the herbs. I like the mixture of fresh dill, parsley, and chives. Use a ⅓-cup measure for shaping. This will make 6 cakes.

MAKE A SANDWICH

There are few things better than a good crab cake sandwich. Shred some lettuce and toss it with a little extra virgin olive oil and salt. Split open a soft roll, slather it with Green Tartar Sauce (page 417), and pile on the lettuce. Top it with a crab cake and a slab of ripe tomato.

CATFISH SLOPPY JOES

These are just as sloppy and delicious as you could hope for. Soft, tender potato rolls are my choice for serving, but any hamburger bun will do. (The photo is on page 159.)   Serves 8

ACCEPT SUBSTITUTES

Sloppy Joes are great made with tilapia, but you could try
skinless salmon, char, or trout too.

½ pound catfish fillet (bloodline
    trimmed; see page 37), cut into ⅓-
    inch dice
Coarse salt
¼ cup vegetable oil
1 cup diced onion
1 cup diced green bell pepper
2 teaspoons paprika
Barbecue Sauce for Fish (page 437)

FOR SERVING
8 hamburger buns
Softened butter
Potato chips

Season the catfish with salt. Let sit on the counter.

Heat a medium saucepan over medium-high heat. When the pan's hot, add the oil, onion, and bell pepper. Sauté, stirring often, until the onion starts to soften, about 3 minutes. Stir in the paprika and sauté, stirring, for 1 minute. Add the catfish and sauté for 1 minute. Stir in the barbecue sauce and bring to a simmer. Reduce the heat to low and simmer for 6 to 7 minutes, until thick.

Meanwhile, heat a griddle or cast-iron skillet over medium-high heat. Butter the buns and toast them on the griddle.

Fill the buns with the catfish mixture and pile some potato chips on top for crunch. Serve these Joes while they're hot.

PASTA AND RICE

PASTA WITH SHRIMP AND GINGER CREAM

The sweet heat of ginger is what makes this rich dish so fabulous. It's also quick and simple to make.   Serves 4

1 (4-inch) knob fresh ginger, peeled and cut into very thin matchsticks

1 cup dry white wine or dry vermouth

Olive oil

1 pound large (21–30) shrimp, shelled and butterflied (see page 41)

Coarse salt and freshly ground white pepper

2 tablespoons unsalted butter

¼ cup minced shallots

¼ cup champagne vinegar

2 cups heavy cream

¾ pound thin spaghetti

½ pound snow peas, tipped, strings pulled, and cut on an angle into thin julienne

½ pound plum tomatoes, seeded and chopped

Soak the ginger in the wine for about 15 minutes.

Put a large pot of salted water on to boil for the pasta.

Heat a large skillet over high heat. When the skillet's hot, pour in a slick of olive oil. Add the shrimp, season with salt and white pepper, and add the butter. Sauté the shrimp until pink and cooked through, about 3 minutes. Transfer to a bowl and cover to keep warm.

Put the skillet back on the heat and add the ginger and wine, the shallots, and champagne vinegar. Bring to a boil and boil to reduce the liquid to about 3 tablespoons. Pour in the cream, season with salt and white pepper, and bring to a boil. Reduce the heat so the cream simmers actively and cook until the cream has reduced by one third. Add the shrimp and any juices from the bowl.

Meanwhile, cook the pasta. When it is al dente, add the snow peas to the boiling pasta and then drain.

To serve, make a mound of the pasta in the center of four dinner plates. Spoon some of the sauce on the pasta and the rest around it. Arrange the shrimp in a circle around the pasta. Garnish with the tomatoes and serve immediately.

PASTA WITH SHRIMP AND ROASTED TOMATO SAUCE

You could think of this as a deconstructed pasta puttanesca. Rather than cooking the capers and olives in the sauce, I use them as a garnish. The result is a dish that's cleaner and fresher tasting. Roasting the tomatoes intensifies their flavor.   Serves 4

ACCEPT SUBSTITUTES

Sixteen sea scallops would stand in nicely for the shrimp. So, too, would 2 pounds of mussels or cockles; when the sauce has thickened, add them, cover, and simmer until they open, 4 to 5 minutes.

1 cup diced onion

4 large garlic cloves, cut into thin slices

6 anchovy fillets

2 pounds ripe summer tomatoes, cored and cut in half through the equator

6 tablespoons olive oil, plus additional for frying the capers

Coarse salt and freshly ground white pepper

4 kalamata olives, pitted and minced

2 tablespoons capers

¾ pound thin spaghetti

1 pound large (21–30) shrimp, shelled and butterflied (see page 41)

¼ cup chopped fresh parsley

Heat the oven to 500 degrees.

Combine the onion, garlic, and anchovies in an ovenproof skillet. Top with the tomatoes, cut side down. Drizzle on 4 tablespoons olive oil and season with salt and white pepper. Roast until the juices are bubbling and the tomato skins have blistered, wrinkled, and browned in spots, about 15 minutes. Remove the pan from the oven and let cool slightly.

When the tomatoes are cool enough to touch, pull off the skins and mash the tomatoes roughly with a potato masher. Set the pan over medium heat and simmer the sauce until thickened and reduced to about 2 cups. Check for salt and pepper. Keep the sauce warm.

Meanwhile, bring a large pot of salted water to a boil for the pasta.

Combine the olives and 1 tablespoon olive oil in a small bowl. You'll be garnishing with this later.

Heat ½ inch olive oil in a very small skillet. Blot the capers very dry on paper towels. When the oil is hot enough for frying (check by touching the bottom of the skillet with the handle of a wooden spoon; you should see bubbles around it immediately), fry the capers until they brown lightly and open up (they'll look like whole cloves), about 30 seconds. Remove with a slotted spoon and drain on paper towels.

Cook the spaghetti until al dente. Drain and toss with the sauce.

While the spaghetti is cooking, heat a large skillet over medium-high heat. When the skillet's hot, pour in the remaining 1 tablespoon olive oil. Add the shrimp and season with salt and white pepper. Sauté the shrimp until pink and cooked through, about 3 minutes.

Divide the pasta among four dinner plates and scatter the fried capers over it. Arrange the shrimp around the pasta and drizzle them with the olive garnish. Shower with chopped parsley and serve right away.

LOBSTER FRA DIAVOLO

Here's a classic recipe from the Italian-American kitchen—lobster cooked in a devilishly hot tomato sauce and served over linguine. (The photo is on page 154.)

Serves 4

5 tablespoons olive oil

2 lobsters (each about 1½ pounds), dispatched and prepared for pan-roasting (see page 47)

Coarse salt and freshly ground white pepper

1½ cups chopped onions

3 tablespoons chopped garlic

1 teaspoon chopped fresh thyme

1 teaspoon dried oregano, crumbled

1 teaspoon crushed red pepper

½ cup dry white wine

1 (28-ounce) can chopped tomatoes (or one 26-ounce box Pomì Chopped Tomatoes)

¾ pound linguine

¼ cup chopped fresh parsley

2 tablespoons chopped fresh basil

Heat a large (12-inch) skillet over high heat. When the pan's hot, spoon in 4 tablespoons olive oil. Season the lobster with salt and white pepper and add to the pan. Sauté until the shells are bright red all over, about 4 minutes. Remove the lobster with tongs and keep it warm in a bowl on the back of the stove.

Reduce the heat to medium-high and add the onions to the skillet, along with the remaining 1 tablespoon oil, and sauté until the onions start to soften, about 2 minutes. Add the garlic, thyme, oregano, and crushed red pepper and sauté for 1 minute. Pour in the wine and let it bubble up for 2 minutes, scraping the bottom of the pan to dissolve any browned bits.

Add the tomatoes, season with salt and white pepper, and bring to a boil. Reduce the heat so the sauce is at an active simmer, and cook for 10 minutes.

Meanwhile, bring a large pot of salted water to a boil. Cook the pasta to almost al dente. You'll finish cooking it in the sauce.

Stir the parsley and basil into the sauce and add the lobster. Simmer for about 4 minutes to heat the lobster through and finish the cooking.

Scoop out about 1 cup of the pasta water, then drain the pasta. Remove the lobster from the skillet and add the pasta. Cook, tossing the pasta in the sauce and adding some pasta water if needed, until the pasta has married with the sauce, about a minute.

Divide the pasta among four large plates, top with the lobster, and serve right away.

SHRIMP FRA DIAVOLO

I like Lobster Fra Diavolo so much that I had to adapt the recipe for shrimp. The sauce is enriched with shrimp stock to compensate for all the flavor you would otherwise get from the lobster shells.   Serves 4

1½ pounds extra-large (16–20 count)
   shrimp in the shell
5 tablespoons olive oil
½ cup dry white wine
2 cups water
Coarse salt and freshly ground white
   pepper
1½ cups chopped onions
3 tablespoons chopped garlic
1 teaspoon fresh thyme leaves

1 teaspoon dried oregano, crumbled
1 teaspoon crushed red pepper
1 (28-ounce) can chopped tomatoes
   (or one 26-ounce box Pomì Chopped
   Tomatoes)
¼ cup chopped fresh parsley
2 tablespoons chopped fresh basil
¾ pound linguine

Shell the shrimp—leave the tails on—and refrigerate them. You want the shells for the stock.

Heat a medium saucepan over medium-high heat. When the pan's hot, add 1 tablespoon olive oil and the shrimp shells and sauté until the shells turn red, about 1 minute. Add the wine and water and bring to a boil. Reduce the heat and simmer the stock for 30 minutes.

Turn off the heat and let the stock sit for 30 minutes for the flavor to deepen.

Line a strainer with cheesecloth, set the strainer over a bowl, and pour in the stock. Lift up the corners of the cheesecloth and squeeze to make sure you extract all the liquid from the solids.

Heat a large (12-inch) skillet over high heat. When the pan's hot, spoon in 2 tablespoons olive oil. Season the shrimp with salt and white pepper and add to the pan. Sauté, stirring, until the shrimp are curled and pink but not quite cooked through, about 2 minutes. Remove the shrimp with a slotted spoon and place in a bowl.

Reduce the heat to medium-high and add the onions to the skillet, along with the remaining 2 tablespoons olive oil. Sauté until the onions start to soften, about 2 minutes. Add the garlic, thyme, oregano, and crushed red pepper and sauté for 1 minute. Pour in the shrimp stock and bring it to a boil. Reduce to about ½ cup, scraping the bottom of the pan to dissolve any browned bits that may be there.

Add the tomatoes, season with salt and white pepper, and bring to a boil. Reduce the heat so the saucc is at an active simmer and cook for 10 minutes. Add the parsley, basil, and shrimp (with any juices in the bowl), cover, and turn off the heat.

Meanwhile, bring a large pot of salted water to a boil. Cook the pasta to al dente.

Drain the pasta and add it to the sauce. Toss well. Divide the pasta and shrimp among four large plates and serve right away.

LINGUINE WITH CLAMS

There's a really good hit of garlic in this dish, complementing the ocean brininess of the clams. It's not for the faint of heart.   Serves 4

ACCEPT SUBSTITUTES
Littleneck clams are fine for this; you'll need 4 dozen.

1 cup water
24 topneck clams, scrubbed
⅓ cup chopped garlic
⅓ cup olive oil
½ teaspoon crushed red pepper

½ teaspoon dried oregano, crumbled
Coarse salt
¾ pound linguine
½ cup chopped fresh parsley

Bring the water to a boil in a large pot. Drop in the clams, cover the pot, and steam until the clams open (see page 301).

Drain the clams in a strainer set over a bowl. When the clams are cool enough to handle, remove them from the shells—over the strainer so you capture all the juice. Chop the clams coarsely. Reserve the clams and juice separately.

Meanwhile, put the garlic and oil in a medium saucepan over medium heat. When the garlic starts to sizzle, reduce the heat to very low and let the garlic infuse into the oil for 15 minutes. Take it slow; you don't want the garlic to color.

Add the crushed red pepper and oregano to the garlic oil and heat for 5 minutes. Add the reserved clam juice, crank the heat to high, and reduce by half. Keep the sauce warm on the back of the stove.

While the sauce simmers, bring a large pot of salted water to a boil. Cook the linguine until al dente. Drain and return it to the pot.

Add the sauce, clams, and parsley to the pasta and toss well. Serve right away.

LINGUINE WITH TUNA SAUCE

I actually love this cold too, when the pasta has really absorbed the sauce. You might want to make the dish a day ahead, let it cool, and refrigerate it, then serve it as a pasta salad. Just toss it well.   Serves 4

½ cup plus 1 tablespoon olive oil

4 garlic cloves, minced

4 anchovy fillets, chopped

1 (6-ounce) can tuna packed in olive oil, drained

1 (28-ounce) can plum tomatoes in juice, pureed in a blender or food processor

¼ teaspoon cayenne or a pinch of crushed red pepper

Coarse salt

¾ pound linguine

½ cup chopped fresh parsley, plus additional for garnish (optional)

Put a large pot of salted water on to boil.

Heat a large skillet over medium-high heat. Add ½ cup olive oil and the garlic and cook until fragrant, about 1 minute. Add the anchovies and cook, stirring, until they start to fall apart. This, too, will take just a minute or two. Add the tuna and cook, stirring to break up the tuna, for 2 minutes. Add the tomatoes and cayenne or crushed red pepper and bring to a boil, then reduce the heat so the sauce is at an active simmer.

Meanwhile, cook the pasta until it's just shy of being al dente. Scoop out about 1 cup of the pasta water, then drain the pasta and toss it with the remaining 1 tablespoon olive oil.

Add the parsley and pasta to the sauce. Toss, still over the heat, for about 1 minute, adding some pasta water if the sauce is too tight.

Serve right away, with some chopped parsley on top if you'd like.

VARIATIONS

If you want to be bold, reconstitute some sun-dried tomatoes, chop them, and add with the tomato puree. Or add some drained capers along with the parsley. Or both.

THIN SPAGHETTI
WITH MUSSELS AND ANCHOVIES

I used to make this dish at Chelsea Central restaurant in New York. It was a crowd-pleaser there, and you'll find it will please the crowd at your dinner table too.

Serves 4

3 large garlic cloves, chopped

12 anchovy fillets (nice fat ones), chopped

Coarse salt

2 pounds mussels, scrubbed and debearded

1 tablespoon olive oil

Crushed red pepper

1½ cups heavy cream

¾ pound thin spaghetti

3–4 tablespoons chopped fresh parsley

Combine the garlic and anchovies in a mini food processor and pulse and process for about 1 minute to make a thick paste. Measure out ¼ cup of the paste and reserve the rest for another day. Alternatively, you can chop the garlic and anchovies to a paste on a cutting board or pound in a mortar and pestle.

Put a large pot of salted water on to boil for the pasta. Have ready a colander set over a bowl.

Heat a large deep heavy skillet over high heat. When the pan is very hot, add the mussels to the skillet, and cover immediately. Shake the pan two or three times and let the mussels cook. They should all be open in about 2 minutes—you're cooking on high heat. Drain the mussels in the colander over the bowl so you capture all the juices.

Return the skillet to the heat and add the olive oil, the ¼ cup anchovy paste, and a pinch of crushed red pepper. Cook, stirring, for about 1 minute to melt the anchovies, then add 1 cup cream and the juices from the mussels. Bring to an active simmer, lower the heat, and cook, stirring or whisking often, to reduce the sauce by half.

Meanwhile, cook the pasta until al dente. Remove the mussels from their shells.

Add the remaining ½ cup cream to the sauce and bring to a simmer. Stir in the mussels.

Drain the spaghetti and add it to the skillet. Toss over heat for about 30 seconds, then divide the pasta among four dinner or soup plates. Sprinkle with the parsley and serve right away.

RED CURRY SHRIMP

This dish combines the nutty/popcorn taste of shrimp with the heat of red curry. Add to that the cleansing coolness of the herbs, and you have a dish that will make you glow inside.

Take a little care making the tiniest dice of the bell peppers, so they'll look like confetti.

Serves 4

1 (14-ounce) can coconut milk

2 teaspoons red curry paste (see Note)

4 tablespoons vegetable oil

1½ pounds jumbo (11–15 count) shrimp, shelled, with tails left on

Coarse salt

1 onion, quartered and cut into very thin slices

Half a red bell pepper, cut into tiny dice

Half a green bell pepper, cut into tiny dice

3 garlic cloves, minced

⅓ cup sake

2 tablespoons fish sauce

2 scallions, cut into thin slices

4 teaspoons chopped fresh mint

4 teaspoons chopped fresh cilantro

Juice of 1 lime

Jasmine rice for serving

Pour the coconut milk into a small saucepan. Whisk in the red curry paste and bring to a simmer over medium heat. Turn off the heat and leave the pan on the back of the stove.

Heat a large skillet over high heat. When the pan's hot, add 2 tablespoons oil and the shrimp. Season with salt and cook, stirring, for 2 minutes. The shrimp should be barely cooked. Remove them with a slotted spoon.

Add the remaining 2 tablespoons oil to the skillet, along with the onion and peppers, and sauté for 1 minute. Add the garlic and sauté for 30 seconds, or until it's fragrant. Pour in the sake and bring to a boil, stirring to deglaze the pan. Add the coconut milk and the fish sauce, bring to a simmer, and simmer for 1 minute. Stir in the shrimp and bring to a boil, then turn off the heat and stir in the scallions, herbs, and lime juice.

Serve spooned over the rice.

NOTE: Red curry paste is available in the Asian section of many grocery stores.

SHRIMP RISOTTO

Shrimp flavors every bite of this creamy risotto.

Don't be afraid of making risotto. The process is so easy and satisfying; it's just something you can't walk away from while you're cooking.

(The photo is on page 155.)   Serves 4

4 cups Shrimp Stock (page 323)
¼ cup olive oil
⅓ cup minced shallots
2 tablespoons minced garlic
1 cup Arborio rice
1 cup dry white wine

Coarse salt and freshly ground white pepper
1 pound shrimp, shelled and cut into bite-sized pieces
1 cup grape tomatoes, quartered
Basil Oil (page 436)

Bring the stock to a simmer in a medium saucepan; keep at a gentle simmer.

Meanwhile, heat a wide saucepan or deep skillet over medium heat. Add the olive oil, shallots, and garlic and cook until the shallots have softened, about 2 minutes. Pour in the rice and cook, stirring pretty much constantly, for 2 to 3 minutes, so the rice can drink up the oil. When it's ready for the next step, the rice will make a different sound as you stir it, almost as if you are stirring tiny pebbles.

Pour in the wine and stir. Season with salt and white pepper and bring to a simmer. Now's the time to start monitoring the heat. You want the liquid at a steady simmer, moving but not bubbling away like a lunatic. Stir often, scraping the bottom of the pan. When most of the wine has been absorbed—when you scrape across the center of the pan, you'll leave a moat—ladle in 1 cup of the shrimp stock. Keep at a simmer, stirring away until the rice drinks up most of this liquid. Continue the process, adding stock by the cupful, until you've added 3 cups of stock.

Add the shrimp and tomatoes with the last cup of stock and simmer until the rice is al dente and still saucy.

Divide the risotto among four soup plates. Spoon a ribbon of basil oil around the risotto in each bowl. Serve immediately.

LEEK AND ASPARAGUS RISOTTO WITH SEA SCALLOPS

When you think about it, you're just making rice for dinner. But the asparagus puree and the scallops turn the rice into something fancy, something elegant.

Serves 4

ACCEPT SUBSTITUTES

Shrimp, shelled, but with tails left on

1 pound sea scallops, tough bits
   removed
⅓ cup plus 4 teaspoons olive oil
Coarse salt and freshly ground white
   pepper
3–4 sprigs thyme
1 bunch (about 1 pound) asparagus
4 ice cubes
5 cups Quick Vegetable Stock
   (page 476)

2 garlic cloves, minced
2 shallots, minced
1 cup Arborio rice
3 small leeks (about 8 ounces), white
   parts only, cut into very thin slices
1 cup dry white wine (Sauvignon Blanc
   is particularly nice in this dish)
4 tablespoons unsalted butter

Put the scallops in a bowl. Drizzle with 3 teaspoons olive oil, season with salt and white pepper, and toss with the thyme sprigs. Cover and refrigerate for at least an hour, or as long as overnight.

Bring a large saucepan of water to a boil. Salt the water very well, so it's as strong as or even stronger than seawater—say, 3 tablespoons for 4 quarts of water. The salt will coax all the flavor out of the asparagus.

Cut the tips from the asparagus and refrigerate them until you need them. Chop the stalks. Add the stalks to the boiling water, return to a boil, and blanch for 1 minute. Drain in a sieve or colander, refresh the asparagus in cold water, and drain again.

Put the stalks in a blender with the ice cubes and blend to make a smooth, thick puree. You can make this puree ahead if you want. Scrape it into a container and refrigerate it, covered. Just take it out of the refrigerator before you start making the rice.

Bring the stock to a simmer in a medium saucepan; keep at a low simmer.

Heat a wide saucepan or deep skillet over medium heat. Add ⅓ cup olive oil with the garlic and shallots and cook until they are softened, about 2 minutes. Pour in the rice and cook, stirring pretty much constantly, for 2 to 3 minutes, so the rice can drink up the oil. When it's ready for the next step, the rice will make a different sound as you stir it, almost as if you are stirring tiny pebbles. Add the leeks and cook, stirring, for another minute or two, so the leeks start to melt into the rice.

Pour in the wine and stir. Season with salt and pepper and bring to a simmer. Now's the time to start monitoring the heat. You want the liquid at a steady simmer, moving but not bubbling rapidly. Stir often, scraping the bottom of the pan. When most of the wine has been absorbed—when you scrape across the center of the pan, you'll leave a moat—ladle in 1 cup of the vegetable stock. Keep at a simmer, stirring away until the rice drinks up most of this liquid. Continue the process, adding stock by the cupful, until you've added 4 cups of stock.

Add the asparagus tips with the last cup of stock and simmer until the rice is just shy of al dente and still saucy. Stir in the asparagus puree and 3 tablespoons butter, cut into pieces. When the butter is melted, turn off the heat and let the risotto rest while you cook the scallops.

Heat a skillet over high heat. Add the remaining 1 tablespoon butter and 1 teaspoon oil. When the butter stops bubbling, add the scallops. Cook for about 2 minutes, until the bottoms of the scallops are caramelized. Turn them over, then transfer the scallops to a plate with a slotted spoon.

Divide the risotto among four soup plates. Top with the scallops. Serve immediately.

PAELLA

There must be as many variations on paella as there are cooks. I love the ocean flavors that clams and mussels add to this one.

You don't need a special paella pan, though it certainly is a nice pan to cook and serve the paella in. I designed it to be made in a 12-inch skillet.   Serves 4

ACCEPT SUBSTITUTES

You could replace the sea bass with rouget, striped bass, dorade, or even sea scallops.

4 chicken thighs (about 1¾ pounds)

Coarse salt and freshly ground white pepper

2 tablespoons olive oil

½ pound Spanish chorizo, casings removed, chopped

1 large onion, chopped

3 tablespoons chopped garlic

½ teaspoon saffron threads

1½ cups long-grain rice (don't use converted)

1 bouillon cube (optional)

1 ripe tomato, chopped

2 cups water

12 littleneck clams, scrubbed

4 (3-ounce) pieces black sea bass, about 1 inch thick, skin on

1 pound mussels, scrubbed and debearded

1 cup frozen peas, rinsed under hot water to defrost

⅓ cup chopped fresh parsley

Season the chicken with salt and white pepper.

Heat a large (12-inch) skillet over medium-high heat. When the pan's hot, add the oil and chicken. Brown the chicken well on both sides. Remove the chicken to a plate. If the chicken has released a lot of fat, spoon some out; you want about 3 tablespoons left in the pan.

Add the chorizo and sauté, stirring, until it browns, about 4 minutes. Add the onion and sauté, stirring, until it becomes translucent, about 3 minutes. Add the garlic and saffron and sauté, stirring, for about 1 minute, until fragrant. Add the rice and stir. Crumble in the bouillon cube, if using, add the tomato, and pour in the water. Stir, return the chicken to the skillet, and bring to a simmer.

Bury the clams in the rice, hinge down. Reduce the heat to low, cover the pan, and cook for 10 minutes.

Meanwhile, season the fish with salt and pepper. Add the mussels to the pan, pushing them hinge down into the rice, then add the fish, skin side up. Cover the pan and cook for 10 minutes. Scatter the peas over the rice, cover again, and cook for 2 minutes. Turn off the heat and let the paella rest for 5 minutes.

Garnish with the parsley and serve right from the skillet.

VARIATION

Lobster rocks in paella. You'll need 2 lobsters, each about 1½ pounds, prepared for pan-roasting (see page 47).

Leave all the fat in the skillet after you brown the chicken. Add the lobster pieces and sauté until the shells turn bright red. Set the lobster aside with the chicken and proceed with the recipe. Add the lobster to the rice along with the clams.

SALSAS AND RELISHES

SIMPLE SALSA

You can make this basic salsa year-round since you're using cherry or grape tomatoes. A mix of red and yellow tomatoes will give you a prettier salsa. And season with sea salt if you've got some.   Makes about 3½ cups

1 onion, cut into medium dice
1 red bell pepper, cut into medium
    dice
1 pint cherry or grape tomatoes,
    quartered or halved, depending on
    their size

1 garlic clove, minced
⅓ cup olive oil
2 tablespoons fresh lime juice
¼ cup chopped fresh basil and cilantro
Coarse salt

Combine all the ingredients in a bowl, seasoning well with salt. Cover with plastic and let the salsa sit for at least an hour for the flavors to develop.

This will keep, covered, in the refrigerator for 2 days.

MANGO SALSA

I love this with fish tacos. It's *picante*: to tame it, cut back on the serrano.
                    Makes about 3 cups

1 ripe mango, peeled, pitted, and cut
    into tiny dice
½ cup minced red onion
½ cup minced red bell pepper
2 tablespoons minced serrano chile
    (with seeds)

½ cup fresh orange juice
Juice of 1 lime
2 tablespoons olive oil
2 tablespoons chopped fresh cilantro
Coarse salt

Toss the mango, onion, bell pepper, and chile together in a bowl. Add the juices, oil, and cilantro and stir. Season with salt to taste.

Refrigerate for 1 hour before serving.

SALSA CRUDA

This is the salsa you want when you've grilled. Feel free to spice it up with more hot peppers or make it sharper with lime juice or salty capers.   Makes about 3 cups

½ cup diced red onion
¾ cup diced bell peppers (use a mix
   of red, yellow, and green)
1 ear corn, grilled (see box)
1 beefsteak tomato (or 3 plum
   tomatoes), seeded and diced
3 tablespoons drained capers
2 tablespoons chopped fresh basil

2 tablespoons fresh lime juice
⅓ cup olive oil
Coarse salt and freshly ground black
   pepper
1 jalapeño chile, seeded and minced
   very fine
Green Tabasco sauce

Combine all the ingredients except the Tabasco sauce in a bowl. Add a shot or two of Tabasco, toss, and taste. Add more Tabasco if you like.

Let the salsa sit at room temperature for at least an hour before serving.

It will keep, covered, in the refrigerator for 2 days.

ABOUT GRILLING CORN

Prepare a charcoal or gas grill.

Peel back the husks of the corn, without removing them, and remove the silk. Wrap the husks back around the ears. Submerge the corn in a bucket of cold water and leave it to soak for 15 minutes.

When the grill is hot, shake the excess water from the corn and lay it on the grill. Grill for 5 minutes, turning a few times. Don't worry when the husk chars.

Let the corn cool, then peel back the husks and cut the kernels off the ears. Or serve the corn hot, on the cob.

CHARRED PINEAPPLE AND MANGO SALSA

You control the heat in this sweet salsa. It all depends on how much chili powder you add.   Makes about 3 cups

3 slices fresh pineapple, each about ¼ inch thick
1 ripe mango
Grated zest and juice of 2 limes
1 small red onion, diced
1 small red bell pepper, diced
1 small green bell pepper, diced

2 scallions, chopped
1 garlic clove, minced
¼ cup chopped fresh cilantro
2 teaspoons extra virgin olive oil
Coarse salt
Chili powder

Prepare a charcoal or gas grill.

When the grill is hot (you can hold your hand 5 inches above the fire for just 5 seconds), place the pineapple slices on the grill. Cook until they appear charred — dark in color, with nice grill marks, but not blackened — on the first side. Turn them over and char the other side. Take them off the grill and let cool.

You can also heat a ridged cast-iron grill pan on the stovetop over high heat until very hot, about 3 minutes, and grill the pineapple as above.

Meanwhile, peel the mango and slice the flesh from the pit. Cut the slices into medium dice and drop into a medium bowl. Toss with the lime zest and juice.

When the pineapple has cooled to room temperature, cut it into medium dice and add to the bowl, along with the red onion, bell peppers, scallions, garlic, and cilantro, and stir well. Add the olive oil and season with salt and chili powder (taste to determine how much you like). Cover with plastic and refrigerate for a few hours until ready to serve. This is best the day it's made.

SKORDALIA

This garlicky Greek potato dip, combined with some Basic Beets (page 450), will transform a piece of sautéed or fried fish into something truly special. With 8 cloves, the garlic flavor is very intense — which I like — but you can cut it back to 6 if you're timid.   Serves 4 to 6

1 russet potato, scrubbed

Coarse salt

6–8 garlic cloves

¼ cup white vinegar

½ cup vegetable oil

¼ cup seltzer or club soda

Freshly ground white pepper

Put the potato in a small saucepan, cover with cold water by at least an inch, add a big pinch of salt, and bring to a boil over high heat. Reduce the heat to medium-high, cover partway, and boil gently until the potato is tender, about 20 minutes. Drain.

Meanwhile, chop the garlic in a food processor by dropping the cloves down the feed tube with the motor running. Scrape down the sides, pour in the vinegar, and process to make a smooth paste. Leave the paste in the processor.

When the potato is still warm but cool enough to handle, peel it and cut into chunks. Add to the processor and pulse a few times to make a rough puree. Scrape down the sides. Add the oil and pulse 6 to 8 times to combine. The puree will become smoother. Scrape again and add the seltzer or club soda. Process for about 2 seconds. Check for salt and season with white pepper.

This can sit at room temperature for a couple of hours. Or cover it and refrigerate for later. Bring back to room temperature before serving.

GUACAMOLE

The thing that makes the most difference in guacamole is the ripeness of the avocado. Squeeze the avocado with your palm, not your fingers, which would bruise it; it should yield but not feel mushy. Hass avocados—the ones with dark green, pebbly skin—have the best flavor.

Makes about 2 cups

½ cup diced red onion
2 small garlic cloves, minced or put
 through a press
2 serrano chiles, minced (with seeds),
 or 1 teaspoon minced habanero
 chile

¼ cup chopped fresh cilantro
Juice of 1 lime
2 ripe avocados
Coarse salt

Put the onion, garlic, chiles, cilantro, and lime juice in a bowl.

Cut an avocado lengthwise in half and twist the halves to separate. Hold the half with the pit in your palm and give the pit a whack with your chef's knife, then pivot the knife and lift up. You'll have the pit stuck to your knife and out of the avocado. (Grab the pit in a kitchen towel to take it off the knife.) Use a table knife to make a series of diagonal cuts through the avocado down to the skin. Make another series of cuts in the opposite direction so you have diamonds of avocado. Use a big spoon to scoop the avocado out of the skin and into the bowl. Repeat with the other half and the other avocado.

Season with salt and stir the guacamole well. Taste and adjust the seasoning if you need to.

TZATZIKI

The Greeks serve this cucumber dip as a *meze*, with bread for dipping, but I like combining it with fish, especially tandoori (see pages 162 and 188). Serves 4

2 cucumbers
1 garlic clove, minced
Coarse salt
1 cup Greek yogurt (see Note)

2 tablespoons chopped fresh mint
  or dill
1 tablespoon fresh lemon juice

Peel and seed the cucumbers, then grate them on the big holes of a box grater. Toss the cucumber with the garlic and ½ teaspoon salt and transfer to a strainer. Set the strainer over a bowl and refrigerate for at least 1 hour and up to 3 hours.

Squeeze the cucumber in the strainer, then turn it out into a clean kitchen towel and squeeze it again. You want to get as much of the liquid as possible out of the cukes so your tzatziki isn't runny.

Put the yogurt in a medium bowl and stir in the cucumber, mint or dill, and lemon juice. Check for salt. Cover and refrigerate for at least 1 hour before serving. It will keep for a few days, but the cucumber will weep and thin the tzatziki.

NOTE: Thick, tangy Greek yogurt has the consistency you need for tzatziki. I like Fage yogurt, which I've found in stores like Whole Foods. If you can't find Greek yogurt, get a pint of regular whole-milk yogurt and put it in a strainer lined with damp paper towels. Set the strainer over a bowl and refrigerate for 3 hours or so to drain the excess liquid.

PICKLED ONIONS

I developed this quick pickle specifically for Niçoise Salad (page 336), but use it wherever you want the clean bite of an onion pickle. Serves 4

1 cup red wine vinegar
1 cup water
2 teaspoons coarse salt
2 teaspoons sugar
1 teaspoon mustard seeds

1 teaspoon coriander seeds
2 allspice berries
1 bay leaf
1 large red onion, cut into
   thick half-moons

Combine the vinegar, water, salt, sugar, mustard and coriander seeds, allspice, and bay leaf in a heavy nonreactive saucepan. Bring to a simmer over medium heat and simmer for 3 minutes.

Add the onion and crank the heat up to high. Stir to separate the onion, and bring to a full boil. Remove from the heat and transfer to a glass jar or bowl. Let cool to room temperature.

Cover the pickle and refrigerate overnight before serving.

MIXED PICKLED VEGETABLES

A mix of golden and red beets is nice, but blanch the golden beets before you do the red ones so you don't dye them red. Leave about an inch of the tops on both the carrots and beets when you clean them.   Serves 4 to 6

3 tablespoons coarse salt

2 tablespoons sugar

2 bunches (about 14) baby carrots

2 bunches (8–9) baby beets (see headnote)

2 cups water

1 cup white vinegar

1 cup champagne vinegar

1 tablespoon coriander seeds

1 teaspoon mustard seeds

1 bay leaf

Bring a large saucepan of water to a boil. Add 1 tablespoon salt and 1 tablespoon sugar. Blanch the carrots until just tender, and remove them with a slotted spoon. Blanch the beets until just tender, and drain them.

Wipe out the saucepan and add the 2 cups water, the vinegars, coriander and mustard seeds, bay leaf, and the remaining 2 tablespoons salt and 1 tablespoon sugar. Bring to a simmer over medium heat. Turn off the heat and add the vegetables. Let cool to room temperature, then transfer to a container (vegetables and brine together), cover, and refrigerate for 8 hours before serving.

SAUCES, VINAIGRETTES, AND SPICE MIXES

BASIC BUTTER SAUCE

This simple sauce is invaluable for the fish cook. It's light and creamy and adds a note of luxuriousness to the plate. You can season it with a good squirt of lemon juice and serve it on its own, but it's best as the base for some very delicious variations (see the following pages).

You do need an immersion blender to make the sauce.   Makes about 1 cup

½ cup sliced shallots
¾ cup water
1 sprig thyme

8 tablespoons (1 stick) unsalted butter,
     cut into pieces
Coarse salt

Put the shallots, water, and thyme in a small saucepan and bring to a boil over medium-high heat. Reduce the heat to medium and cook at a low boil until the shallots are very soft and the water has reduced to a generous ¼ cup.

Remove the thyme and turn the heat to very low. Use an immersion blender to start pureeing the shallots. Add a piece of butter and continue to puree, emulsifying the water and butter. Continue adding the butter piece by piece, incorporating each bit of butter before adding another. Tilt the pan as you work and keep it over the heat. The sauce will become light and very pale yellow.

Strain the sauce through a fine sieve, pushing down on any solids that remain with a wooden spoon. Return the sauce to the pan. Season with salt.

You can serve the sauce right away or keep it warm at the back of the stove for an hour or so, giving it a whisk once in a while. Add a few drops of water if the sauce becomes too thick.

Store any leftovers tightly covered in the refrigerator. To rejuvenate leftover sauce, put it in a saucepan over medium-low heat and bring to a simmer. The sauce will break (separate) at this point. Don't worry. Reduce the heat to low and re-emulsify the sauce with the immersion blender.

GARLIC BUTTER SAUCE

Turn to this sauce when you need a good dose of garlic. Think about dipping some shrimp in it. Or spoon it over grilled mackerel.   Makes about 1 cup

6 large garlic cloves, minced to a paste
    or put through a press
Basic Butter Sauce (page 404), just
    made

Coarse salt and freshly ground white
    pepper
Fresh lemon juice

Add the garlic to the butter sauce and use an immersion blender to puree the garlic completely into the sauce (you don't want to come across bits of garlic). Check for salt and season the sauce with white pepper and lemon juice. Serve, or keep warm at the back of the stove for up to 1 hour before serving. Add a few drops of water if the sauce becomes too thick.

CUMIN BUTTER SAUCE

In this sauce, the earthiness of cumin is mellowed by the richness of butter.
Makes about 1 cup

2½ teaspoons cumin seeds, toasted
    and ground
3 large garlic cloves, minced to a paste
    or put through a press
Basic Butter Sauce (page 404), just
    made

Coarse salt and freshly ground white
    pepper
Fresh lime juice

Add the cumin and garlic to the butter sauce and use an immersion blender to puree the garlic completely into the sauce (you don't want to come across bits of garlic). Season the sauce with salt and white pepper and a squirt of lime juice. Keep warm at the back of the stove until serving. Add a few drops of water if the sauce becomes too thick.

MUSTARD BUTTER SAUCE

This sauce provides a beautiful accent to poached halibut, turbot, and other flatfish.

Makes about 1¼ cups

2 teaspoons Dijon mustard
2 tablespoons plus 2 teaspoons
   whole-grain mustard
Basic Butter Sauce (page 404), just
   made

Coarse salt
Fresh lemon juice

Whisk the mustards into the sauce. Taste, season with salt and lemon juice, and whisk again. Serve, or keep warm at the back of the stove for up to 1 hour before serving. Add a few drops of water if the sauce becomes too thick.

WASABI BUTTER SAUCE

The lush buttery flavor of this sauce is lightened with the zing of wasabi — a Japanese horseradish-like condiment.

Makes about 1 cup

2 tablespoons wasabi powder
   (see Note)
2–3 teaspoons dry vermouth

Basic Butter Sauce (page 404), just
   made

Moisten the wasabi powder with the vermouth, stirring to make a smooth paste. Add the wasabi paste to the butter sauce and give it a zap with the immersion blender. Serve, or keep warm at the back of the stove for up to 1 hour before serving. Add a few drops of water if the sauce becomes too thick.

NOTE: You can find wasabi powder in the Asian section of many grocery stores.

RED WINE BUTTER SAUCE

The port balances the intense red wine reduction, giving you a taste that's jammy and almost plummy. Combine it with butter, and you've got a silky sauce that I think of as savory cream cheese and jelly.

Pair the sauce with Basic Leeks (page 462), for a combination that will highlight the flavors of rich fish like salmon, sturgeon, swordfish, and halibut.

Makes about 1¼ cups

1 cup sliced shallots
3 sprigs thyme
1½ cups dry red wine
½ cup ruby port
½ pound (2 sticks) unsalted butter,
    cut into pieces

Coarse salt and freshly ground white
    pepper
1 tablespoon balsamic vinegar

Put the shallots, thyme, and red wine in a small saucepan and bring to a boil over high heat. Lower the heat and simmer until the wine has reduced to about 2 tablespoons (just a coating on the bottom of the pan) and the shallots are very tender.

Add the port and reduce to about ⅓ cup.

Remove the thyme. Turn the heat to very low. Use an immersion blender to start pureeing the shallots. Start adding butter a piece or two at a time, tilting the pan and using the blender to emulsify the butter and liquid. Continue adding butter bit by bit, incorporating what you have in the pan before adding more.

Strain the sauce through a sieve, pressing down on any solids that remain. Return the sauce to the pan, season with salt and white pepper, and add the vinegar. Serve, or keep warm at the back of the stove for up to 1 hour—giving the sauce a whisk once in a while—until you're ready to serve.

SCAMPI BUTTER SAUCE

I've taken the flavors of shrimp scampi—that old-time Italian-American prepara-tion—and translated them into a sauce that's perfect for poaching any kind of crab.

Keep this butter on hand, and you can have a truly elegant meal on the table in a matter of minutes.   Makes about 1 cup

FOR THE SCAMPI BUTTER
8 large garlic cloves, cut in half
1 shallot, chopped
½ pound (2 sticks) unsalted butter,
   softened
½ teaspoon Tabasco sauce
Coarse salt and freshly ground white
   pepper

TO FINISH THE SAUCE
3 tablespoons dry white wine or dry
   vermouth

FOR THE SCAMPI BUTTER: Turn a food processor on and drop the garlic down the feed tube, then drop in the shallot. Scrape the sides of the bowl and add the butter and Tabasco sauce. Process until light and fluffy. Season liberally with salt and white pepper. Process to combine.

Pack the butter into a small bowl and cover with plastic. Refrigerate until firm. The butter will keep in the refrigerator for about 1 week.

TO FINISH THE SAUCE: Bring the wine to a simmer in a small saucepan. Simmer for about 2 minutes; you want to cook off the alcohol, but you don't want to reduce the wine. Whisk in the cold scampi butter about 1 tablespoon at a time, to make an emulsified sauce. Use right away.

COMPOUND BUTTERS

Fat—and butter in particular—is a great carrier of flavor. In these recipes, the butter transports the flavors of herbs and spices to a piece of fish. Use slices of these butters to moisten and season broiled fish, as a garnish for a piece of sautéed fish, or as a sauce for roast fish. You'll find that the butters are also welcome on boiled potatoes or some noodles.

They will keep for about 5 days in the refrigerator and 2 months in the freezer.

Each recipe makes about ½ cup

BASIL BUTTER

2 packed cups fresh basil leaves
8 tablespoons (1 stick) unsalted butter, softened
1 garlic clove, minced to a paste or put through a press
Coarse salt and freshly ground white pepper

Bring a saucepan of salted water to a boil. Stir in the basil leaves and blanch them for 30 seconds. Drain, then shock the basil in a bowl of ice water. This blanching process guarantees the basil will stay bright green. Drain again, and squeeze the basil very dry. Start squeezing with your hands, then transfer the basil to a clean kitchen towel or a few layers of paper towels and squeeze some more.

Give the basil a rough chop.

Combine the basil, butter, and garlic in a food processor and process until smooth. Season with salt and white pepper and give the butter another pulse or two.

Scrape the butter out onto a piece of waxed paper or aluminum foil and use a spatula to form it into a rough log. Wrap the paper or foil around the log, using it to form a uniform shape as you roll. Twist the ends and refrigerate until firm.

RED PEPPER AND TABASCO BUTTER

1 red bell pepper, roasted (see page 475), peeled, seeded, and blotted dry
8 tablespoons (1 stick) unsalted butter, softened
4 teaspoons Tabasco sauce
Coarse salt

Give the bell pepper a coarse chop, then put it in a food processor with the butter and process until smooth. Add the Tabasco, season with salt, and give the butter another pulse or two.

Scrape the butter out onto a piece of waxed paper or aluminum foil and use a spatula to form it into a rough log. Wrap the paper or foil around the log, using it to form a uniform shape as you roll. Twist the ends and refrigerate until firm.

PORCINI BUTTER

8 tablespoons (1 stick) unsalted butter, softened
¼ cup dried porcini, ground to a powder in a spice grinder
1 teaspoon truffle oil
½ teaspoon sherry vinegar
Coarse salt and freshly ground white pepper

Combine the butter, porcini powder, truffle oil, and vinegar in a food processor. Process until light and fluffy. Season with salt and white pepper and pack into a small bowl.

Leave the butter at room temperature for about an hour for the flavors to develop, then cover with plastic wrap and chill until firm.

TARRAGON BUTTER

8 tablespoons (1 stick) unsalted butter, softened
4 teaspoons chopped fresh tarragon
1 teaspoon grated lemon zest
1 teaspoon fresh lemon juice
Coarse salt and freshly ground white pepper

Combine the butter, tarragon, and lemon zest and juice in a food processor. Process until light and fluffy. Season with salt and white pepper and pack into a small bowl.

Leave the butter at room temperature for about an hour for the flavors to develop, then cover with plastic wrap and chill until firm.

BLACK OLIVE AND ANCHOVY BUTTER

8 tablespoons (1 stick) unsalted butter, softened
2 teaspoons store-bought black olive paste
2 anchovy fillets, minced
1 small garlic clove, minced to a paste or put through a press
1 teaspoon grated lemon zest

Combine the butter, olive paste, anchovies, garlic, and lemon zest in a food processor. Process until light and fluffy. Pack into a small bowl.

Leave the butter at room temperature for about an hour for the flavors to develop, then cover with plastic wrap and chill until firm.

CHILE CILANTRO BUTTER

3 garlic cloves, unpeeled
2 serrano chiles
8 tablespoons (1 stick) unsalted butter, softened
2 tablespoons chopped fresh cilantro
½ teaspoon fresh lime juice
Coarse salt

Heat a small cast-iron skillet over medium-high heat. When it's good and hot, add the garlic and chiles and cook, stirring occasionally, until charred, about 10 minutes. Cool completely.

Peel and mince the garlic. Mince the chiles (with the seeds). Combine the garlic, chiles, butter, cilantro, and lime juice in a food processor. Process until light and fluffy. Season with salt and pack into a small bowl.

Leave the butter at room temperature for about an hour for the flavors to develop, then cover with plastic wrap and chill until firm.

GINGER SOY BUTTER

8 tablespoons (1 stick) unsalted butter, softened
2 tablespoons minced fresh ginger
2 teaspoons dark soy sauce
½ teaspoon rice vinegar

Combine the butter, ginger, soy sauce, and vinegar in a food processor. Process until light and fluffy. Pack into a small bowl.

Leave the butter at room temperature for about an hour for the flavors to develop, then cover with plastic wrap and chill until firm.

LEMON DILL BUTTER

8 tablespoons (1 stick) unsalted butter, softened
2 tablespoons minced fresh dill
1 teaspoon grated lemon zest
1 teaspoon fresh lemon juice
Coarse salt

Combine the butter, dill, and lemon zest and juice in a food processor. Process until light and fluffy. Season with salt and pack into a small bowl.

Leave the butter at room temperature for about an hour for the flavors to develop. Cover with plastic wrap and chill until firm.

SUN-DRIED TOMATO BUTTER

4 sun-dried tomatoes (8 halves; *not* packed in oil)
½ packed cup fresh basil leaves
8 tablespoons (1 stick) unsalted butter, softened
1 small garlic clove, minced to a paste or put through a press
Coarse salt

Cover the tomatoes with very hot water and let them sit for about 20 minutes to re-constitute. Drain, blot dry, and chop.

Bring a saucepan of salted water to a boil. Stir in the basil leaves and blanch them for 30 seconds. Drain, then shock the basil in a bowl of ice water. Drain again, then squeeze the basil very dry. Start squeezing with your hands, then transfer the basil to a clean kitchen towel or a few layers of paper towels and squeeze some more.

Give the basil a rough chop.

Combine the tomatoes, basil, butter, and garlic in a food processor. Process until the tomatoes are almost pureed (there should still be visible flecks) and the butter is light and fluffy. Season with salt and pack into a small bowl.

Leave the butter at room temperature for about an hour for the flavors to develop, then cover with plastic wrap and chill until firm.

ROUILLE

Golden from saffron and redolent of garlic, this mayonnaise sauce is the classic accompaniment to the fish stews of the Mediterranean. Makes about ¾ cup

1 tablespoon white vinegar
1 tablespoon water
Big pinch of saffron threads
2 slices white bread (something like
  Pepperidge Farm), crusts removed,
  cubed
2 garlic cloves, minced or put through
  a press

2 large egg yolks
⅛ teaspoon cayenne
Coarse salt and freshly ground white
  pepper
½ cup olive oil

Bring the vinegar, water, and saffron to a boil in a tiny saucepan (or zap it in the microwave).

Put the bread in a small bowl and pour in the vinegar and water, scraping to make sure you add all the saffron. Stir to moisten all the bread cubes.

Scrape the bread into a food processor and add the garlic, egg yolks, and cayenne. Season with salt and white pepper. Pulse to make a smooth paste. Scrape down the sides. With the motor running, pour in the oil in a steady stream.

Scrape the sauce out into a bowl and serve.

SPICY MAYONNAISE

You'll want this in your refrigerator when the mood strikes for crispy calamari, or a fried fish sandwich, or poached halibut. It would make a roast beef sandwich sing too.

If you can't find crème fraîche, substitute 1¼ cups sour cream and add another tablespoon of fresh lemon juice.

Makes about 4 cups

2 cups mayonnaise

1½ cups crème fraîche (see headnote)

5 tablespoons chili sauce (I like Heinz)

1–2 tablespoons grated horseradish
    (fresh or prepared), drained

3 tablespoons chopped capers

5 teaspoons Tabasco sauce

4 teaspoons Worcestershire sauce

3 tablespoons fresh lemon juice

½ teaspoon curry powder

Coarse salt and freshly ground white
    pepper

Whisk the mayonnaise, crème fraîche, chili sauce, horseradish, capers, Tabasco, Worcestershire, lemon juice, and curry powder together in a mixing bowl. Season with salt and white pepper. Taste and correct the seasoning.

You can serve this right away or make it in advance. It will keep in an airtight container in the refrigerator for up to 6 weeks.

SPICY RÉMOULADE

A staple at my restaurants for years, this is a great dipping sauce for fried fish and ideal for any cold cooked shellfish.

Harissa — the Middle Eastern seasoning paste — varies in heat and intensity, so taste your rémoulade and adjust accordingly. Remember, it should be spicy and hot.

Make this a day in advance if you can, so the flavors will build.

Makes about 1¼ cups

1 cup mayonnaise

2–3 anchovy fillets, minced to a paste

2 tablespoons minced cornichons

1 tablespoon drained capers (use the small nonpareils)

Grated zest of ½ lemon

1½ teaspoons fresh lemon juice

1 teaspoon Dijon mustard

6 dashes Tabasco sauce

1 tablespoon chopped fresh chervil or parsley

2 teaspoons chopped fresh dill

1 teaspoon Harissa (page 443 or store-bought)

Coarse salt and freshly ground white pepper

Whisk the mayonnaise, anchovies, cornichons, capers, lemon zest and juice, mustard, Tabasco, chervil or parsley, dill, and harissa together in a bowl. Taste, and adjust the harissa for spiciness — keep in mind that the heat will develop as the sauce sits. Season with salt and white pepper.

Cover and refrigerate for at least 1 hour before serving. The rémoulade will keep for at least a week.

GREEN TARTAR SAUCE

This sauce is best made ahead. Letting it sit in the refrigerator for about 24 hours gives the flavors time to develop.

Makes about 2½ cups

¼ cup chopped cornichons

1 tablespoon chopped capers

1 medium shallot, coarsely chopped

2 cups mayonnaise

½ teaspoon Dijon mustard

1½ heaping tablespoons chopped fresh dill

2 heaping tablespoons chopped fresh chives

2 heaping tablespoons chopped fresh flat-leaf parsley

1 teaspoon fresh lemon juice

½ teaspoon freshly ground white pepper

¼ cup olive oil

Drop the cornichons, capers, and shallot into a food processor. Process for a few seconds just to combine. Add the mayonnaise, mustard, herbs, lemon juice, and white pepper and process for about 8 seconds to blend well. Scrape down the sides. With the motor running, add the oil in a slow, steady stream.

Scrape the tartar sauce out into an airtight container, cover, and refrigerate for 24 hours before using.

SWEET PICKLE RELISH SAUCE

Sometimes simple is just what you want. Serve with broiled or fried fish.

Makes about 1¼ cups

1 cup mayonnaise
¼ cup India relish or sweet pickle
   relish

2 heaped teaspoons mustard "caviar"
   (see box)

Stir the mayo, relish, and mustard together. You can serve this right away. It will keep, covered, in the refrigerator, for at least a week.

MUSTARD "CAVIAR"

What I call mustard caviar is simply "bloomed" mustard seeds. I just think they look like caviar, and the seeds do pop in your mouth like caviar.

Combine ⅓ cup yellow mustard seeds, ¼ cup champagne vinegar, and 1 tablespoon sugar in a tiny saucepan. Bring to a simmer over medium-low heat. Simmer for a few minutes, until all but about 1 tablespoon of the vinegar has been absorbed. Take the pan off the heat and let sit until cool; the mustard will continue drinking up the vinegar.

Transfer to a glass jar. This will keep in the refrigerator for months.

CILANTRO AÏOLI

Use this sauce as a foil for something marinated, something spicy, or something grilled.   Makes about 1 cup

1 small shallot, chopped
1 garlic clove, chopped
3 tablespoons fresh lime juice
1 cup chopped fresh cilantro (small
   stems are fine)

½ cup mayonnaise
1 large egg yolk
Coarse salt

Put the shallot, garlic, lime juice, and cilantro in a food processor and pulse a few times to make a paste. Add the mayonnaise and egg yolk and process to make a smooth sauce. Season with salt.

Scrape the aïoli into a container and refrigerate until you need it. You can make this a day ahead.

HORSERADISH CREAM

This is the sauce I want with anything smoked or with a cod boiled dinner, which has the smokiness of bacon. Making it the day before gives the flavors time to ripen.

Makes about 1½ cups

1 cup crème fraîche
½ cup grated horseradish (fresh or
    prepared), drained
1 teaspoon Dijon mustard

1 teaspoon chopped fresh dill
1 teaspoon fresh lemon juice
Coarse salt and freshly ground white
    pepper

Whisk the crème fraîche, horseradish, mustard, dill, and lemon juice together in a bowl. Season with salt and white pepper and whisk again.

Cover with plastic and refrigerate overnight, if you have the time, or for at least 30 minutes.

COCKTAIL SAUCE

This sauce is great for oysters, clams, shrimp—you know, it works with any shell-fish. The key is freshly grated horseradish, but you can substitute the stuff in the jar as long as you drain it first.

Makes about 1 cup

½ cup chili sauce (I like Heinz)

¼ cup ketchup

2 tablespoons horseradish (fresh or prepared), drained

2–3 teaspoons fresh lemon juice

1 tablespoon gin

7–8 dashes Tabasco sauce

Coarse salt and freshly ground white pepper

Whisk the chili sauce, ketchup, horseradish, lemon juice, gin, and Tabasco together in a bowl. Season with salt and white pepper.

Cover and refrigerate until you're ready to use it. Stored in an airtight container, the sauce will keep for up to 6 weeks.

ABOUT GRATING HORSERADISH

The easiest way to grate a small amount of horse-radish—say, the 2 tablespoons you need for the Cocktail Sauce—is to peel the root and grate it on a Microplane. If you like, add a few drops of white vinegar and a pinch of salt. You'll be amazed at how the vinegar will release the pungent aroma of the horseradish.

For larger quantities, peel the horseradish and chop it relatively fine. Drop it into a food processor and process until you've got fine, even bits. Season with white vinegar, a teaspoon or two of water, and salt. This will keep for a couple of months, tightly sealed, in the refrigerator.

PARSLEY PESTO

Pesto doesn't have to be made with basil. And while usually you can use whatever parsley looks best at the store, for this recipe you do want flat-leaf; it's got deeper flavor.

Makes about ¾ cup

2 cups fresh flat-leaf parsley (tough stems removed; about 2 bunches)
2 garlic cloves, chopped
⅓ cup grated Parmesan cheese

2 tablespoons pine nuts
⅓ cup olive oil, plus a little more
Coarse salt

Put the parsley and garlic in a food processor and pulse until the parsley is finely chopped. Scrape down the sides as needed. Add the Parmesan and pine nuts and pulse once or twice. Then turn the processor on and pour in the oil in a steady stream. Process to a fine paste, scraping down the sides as you need to. Season with salt.

This will keep for about a week in the refrigerator. Pour a thin layer of olive oil on top before you cover the container, so the pesto won't discolor.

ARUGULA PESTO

Arugula gives this cheese-free pesto a peppery bite.   Makes about 1 cup

1 garlic clove, minced
⅓ cup pine nuts
6 ounces arugula, torn into pieces

¼ cup olive oil, plus a little more
Coarse salt

Put the garlic and pine nuts in a food processor and pulse until the nuts are coarsely chopped. Add the arugula by the handful, pulsing after each addition to make a paste. Then turn on the processor and add the oil in a steady stream. Season with salt.

Store this in the refrigerator in a jar. Pour a film of olive oil on top of the pesto before you cover it, to keep out the air and prevent it from discoloring. It will keep for about a week.

SOY-ORANGE SAUCE

I usually pair this sauce with Fennel Puree (page 460), another example of my love affair with the combination of fennel and orange—so good with fish. The sweet acidity of the sauce makes your mouth water, and I consider it a good sign when the food I'm eating makes my mouth water.

Makes about ⅔ cup

2 cups orange juice, preferably fresh
   (from about 6 oranges; see Note)
1 teaspoon soy sauce

4 tablespoons unsalted butter,
   cut into pieces

Pour the orange juice into a wide saucepan or skillet and bring to a boil over high heat. Lower the heat so the juice simmers actively and reduce to about ⅓ cup, scraping down the sides periodically.

Scrape the reduction into a small saucepan and add the soy sauce. Bring to a boil over medium-high heat, and whisk in the butter piece by piece to emulsify the sauce. Remove from the heat.

The sauce can sit at room temperature for an hour or so. Just give it a whisk once in a while.

NOTE: Try using blood oranges for this sauce when they're in season. You'll get a deeper color, but because blood oranges have a sharper acidity than navel oranges, you'll need to add more butter for balance. You're going for the sweetness of cream cheese and jelly.

CHIPOTLE SAUCE

Think smoky. Think spicy. Think delicious. I use this as a spread when I make fish burgers, but it could be a dip for fried fish too.

Chipotles in adobo are available canned in the Latin section of most markets. You're using only one of the chiles in this recipe, but leftovers will last forever in a jar in the refrigerator.

Makes about 1½ cups

1 large egg yolk
¼ cup rice vinegar
2 tablespoons fresh lime juice
¾ cup chopped fresh cilantro (use all but the toughest stems)
2 tablespoons chopped shallot

1 tablespoon chopped garlic
1 chipotle in adobo
¼ teaspoon adobo sauce (from the can)
1 cup vegetable oil
Coarse salt

Put the egg yolk, vinegar, lime juice, cilantro, shallot, garlic, chipotle, and adobo sauce in the jar of a blender. Blend on medium speed until you have a smooth paste.

With the blender still on medium, start drizzling in the oil slowly. When you've added about half the oil, crank the blender speed to high and pour in the rest of the oil in a steady stream. Taste, season with salt, and taste again.

This sauce keeps for at least a week, tightly covered, in the refrigerator.

TOMATILLO AND POBLANO SAUCE

This crisp and acidic sauce—a cooked salsa, really—is a great foil for brochettes and other grilled fish. It's also a terrific dip for fried oysters and, sure, for tortilla chips too.   Makes about 2 cups

2 tablespoons olive oil
2 poblano chiles, seeded and cut into
  chunks
1 serrano chile, cut into thin slices
  (optional)
8 garlic cloves, halved

¾ pound tomatillos, husked and
  rinsed in hot water
Coarse salt
1 cup fresh cilantro leaves
  (small stems are fine)
Juice of 1 lime

Heat a large skillet over high heat. Add the oil, chiles, and garlic and sauté, shaking the pan, for 1 minute. Add the tomatillos, season with salt, and continue to sauté, shaking the pan, for about 3 minutes. Reduce the heat to medium-low, cover the skillet, and cook—giving the pan a shake once or twice—until the tomatillos are tender and have started to slump, 7 to 10 minutes.

Turn off the heat and leave the skillet covered for about 20 minutes, so the ingredients steam.

Scrape the tomatillos, chiles, and garlic—along with any juices in the skillet—into a food processor and pulse a few times, until the sauce is chunky. Add the cilantro and lime juice and process again until pretty smooth. Taste for salt—it will need it.

Serve this chilled. It will keep in the refrigerator for a few days.

BELL PEPPER COULIS

Bring out this sauce whenever you want the flavor of bell peppers on your plate. Or put it on the table, along with one of the creamy sauces, like Spicy Rémoulade (page 416) as a dip for fried fish.

Make the coulis with red peppers, or yellow, or orange, depending on the color you want on your plate. Avoid green peppers; their flavor isn't right for this sauce.

Makes about ¾ cup

2 tablespoons olive oil

2 shallots, chopped

1 garlic clove, chopped

1 bell pepper (see headnote), chopped

Coarse salt

¼ cup dry white wine

2 teaspoons champagne vinegar

¼ cup vegetable oil

Heat a saucepan over medium-high heat. When the pan's hot, add the oil, shallots, and garlic. Sauté, stirring, for 1 minute. Add the bell pepper, season with salt, and sauté, stirring often, until the pepper is starting to get tender, about 10 minutes. Don't let the pepper brown.

Pour in the wine and cook until the pan is just about dry.

Scrape everything in the pan into a blender. Let cool for a couple of minutes, then process until smooth. Scrape the puree down. Turn the blender back on and pour in the vinegar and then the oil in a steady stream.

This will keep, covered, for about 3 days in the refrigerator.

TOMATO CONCASSÉ

Concassé may sound like something fancy, but it's just chopped tomatoes and some chopped onion, cooked down until very thick. It's another great companion for simply cooked fish.

You could make it with fresh tomatoes, but it's so much simpler to start with Pomì, the chopped tomatoes that come in a box. Canned chopped tomatoes are fine as well, but they're usually more watery, so the cooking time will be longer.

Makes about 1⅔ cups

2 tablespoons olive oil
½ cup chopped onion
2 teaspoons chopped garlic

2 cups chopped tomatoes (see headnote)
Coarse salt

Heat a saucepan over medium-high heat. Add the oil and onion and sauté until the onion is starting to soften, about 3 minutes. Add the garlic and sauté until the garlic is fragrant, about 30 seconds. Add the tomatoes, stir, and bring to a simmer. Lower the heat so the tomatoes just simmer, and cook until very thick and reduced, about 20 minutes. Season with salt.

You can serve this right away or refrigerate it for up to 3 days. Reheat it before serving.

HARISSA TOMATO SAUCE

No long simmering for this spicy sauce; you need cook it only long enough to wake up the spices.

Commercial harissa is often bland, at least to my taste. If you haven't made your own, you might want to use more or add a pinch of crushed red pepper. Taste it, and decide what you like. Makes about 2 cups

3 tablespoons olive oil

½ cup minced shallots

2 tablespoons minced garlic

2 tablespoons Harissa (page 443 or store-bought)

1 teaspoon Moroccan Spice Mix (page 440)

2 teaspoons red wine vinegar

2 cups chopped tomatoes (Pomì preferred; see Note)

Coarse salt

Heat a saucepan over medium-high heat. When the pan's hot, add the oil and shallots and sauté for 1 minute. Add the garlic and sauté for another minute. Add the harissa and Moroccan spice and sauté for 1 to 2 more minutes, stirring constantly, until the shallots are translucent.

Add the vinegar and stir. It will bubble up and evaporate almost immediately. Stir in the tomatoes and season with salt. Bring to a simmer, reduce the heat to medium, and simmer for 5 minutes. And that's the sauce.

You can make this a day in advance; reheat it when you serve.

NOTE: Thick, flavorful Pomì tomatoes are important in this sauce because it cooks so quickly. If you can't find them in your local grocery, you can substitute canned chopped tomatoes. Start with 3 cups and let the tomatoes drain in a strainer set over a bowl to remove the excess liquid, then measure out 2 cups.

PUTTANESCA SAUCE

This pasta sauce is actually a great accompaniment to fish. It's the start of a fine fish casserole too.

Makes about 3 cups

¼ cup olive oil

1 cup chopped onion

¼ cup chopped garlic

8–10 anchovy fillets, chopped

Crushed red pepper

3 cups chopped tomatoes (Pomì preferred)

½ cup sliced kalamata or other black olives

¼ cup drained capers

Heat a medium saucepan over medium-high heat. When the pan's hot, add the oil and the onion and cook, stirring often, until the onion is translucent, about 7 minutes. Add the garlic and continue cooking until the onion is turning gold at the edges, another 3 to 4 minutes. Add the anchovies and a good pinch of crushed red pepper and cook, stirring, until the anchovies start to melt, about 1 minute. Add the tomatoes, olives, and capers and bring to a simmer. Reduce the heat and simmer the sauce for 15 minutes, or until thick and fragrant.

You can use the sauce now or refrigerate it, covered, for up to 1 week.

COCONUT AND GREEN CURRY SAUCE

Make this Thai-inspired sauce a day or two ahead. It will only get better.

When cooking with lemongrass, use just the more tender inner core of the stalk, and crush it with the back of your knife before chopping.   Makes about 1 cup

2 tablespoons peanut or vegetable oil

1 cup chopped fresh lemongrass

¼ cup chopped fresh ginger

2 fresh kaffir lime leaves (see Note)

1 tablespoon green curry paste
  (see Note)

½ cup dry white wine

1 (14-ounce) can coconut milk

Coarse salt

1 teaspoon sugar

1–2 teaspoons fresh lime juice

Heat a medium saucepan over medium-high heat. When the pan's hot, add the oil, lemongrass, and ginger. Sauté, stirring, until very fragrant, about 2 minutes. Stir in the lime leaves and curry paste and cook for 1 minute. Add the wine and bring to a boil, stirring to dissolve the curry paste. Reduce to an active simmer and cook until the wine is reduced to about 2 tablespoons, about 4 minutes.

Pour in the coconut milk, season with salt, and bring to a boil. Reduce the heat to low and simmer the sauce until it reduces and thickens enough to coat the back of a spoon, about 25 minutes.

Strain the sauce through a fine sieve, pushing down on the solids. Check for salt and add the sugar and lime juice.

The sauce can sit at room temperature for about an hour. Or cover and refrigerate; heat it gently before serving.

NOTE: You can get fresh kaffir lime leaves at specialty markets and stores like Whole Foods. Green curry paste is available in the Asian section of many grocery stores.

ASIAN "VINAIGRETTE"

This tangy dressing works well with all sorts of salads. It doesn't emulsify the way a French-style vinaigrette will; just give it a shake before you use it.

Vietnamese fish sauce (*nuoc nam*) can be found in most Asian markets and in many specialty food stores and grocery stores. Look for the Golden Boy brand. Thai chile peppers are what I prefer, but any hot pepper will work. Whatever you use, though, don't seed it. *Makes about 1¼ cups*

⅓ cup vegetable oil
⅓ cup fish sauce (see headnote)
¼ cup fresh lime juice
¼ cup rice vinegar

2 tablespoons sugar
1 tablespoon chopped garlic
1 teaspoon chopped hot pepper
  (see headnote)

Combine all the ingredients in a jar and give them a good shake.

Use as needed in a salad, and keep the leftovers in the refrigerator. This lasts forever.

BACON VINAIGRETTE

You'll find that a little of this delicious sauce packs a lot of flavor. I like pairing it with grilled fish, but just about everything tastes good with bacon.

Take your time chopping the bacon, so you have small pieces.

Makes about 1 cup

12 slices (½ pound) bacon, finely
  chopped
3 tablespoons vegetable oil
Coarse salt and freshly ground white
  pepper

¼ cup minced shallots
2 tablespoons sherry vinegar
2 tablespoons fresh lime juice

Put the bacon and oil in a saucepan over medium-low heat. Cook, stirring once in a while, until the fat is rendered from the bacon, about 5 minutes. Season with salt and white pepper, reduce the heat to low, and cook until the bacon begins to brown, another 5 to 6 minutes.

Add the shallots and cook, stirring often, until they have softened and are starting to take on some color, about 5 more minutes. Add the vinegar and lime juice and immediately remove from the heat. Stir to deglaze, scraping up any brown bits from the bottom of the pan, then scrape the vinaigrette out into a small bowl.

Serve immediately, or let sit at room temperature for a couple of hours. Refrigerate leftovers, and reheat gently before serving. The vinaigrette will keep for a day or two.

TRUFFLE VINAIGRETTE

This fluffy, creamy vinaigrette is fragrant with the heady aroma of truffle. I pair it with "Brandade" Cakes (page 368), but it's a delicious dressing for string beans too.

Makes about 1 cup

1 cup chicken stock
2 large shallots, cut into thin slices
2 tablespoons sherry vinegar

1 teaspoon soy sauce
½ cup vegetable oil
¼ cup truffle oil (see Note)

Combine the stock and shallots in a small saucepan and bring to a boil over medium-high heat. Then lower the heat so the stock simmers actively and cook until the shallots are very tender and the stock has reduced to about ⅓ cup.

Pour the stock and shallots into a blender and add the vinegar and soy sauce. Give it all a whir to puree the shallots. With the blender running, pour in the vegetable oil in a slow stream to start the emulsion, then slowly pour in the truffle oil. Keep the blender going for another 30 seconds.

You can serve this right away or keep it at room temperature for a few hours.

NOTE: Truffle oil is available in specialty markets. You could substitute porcini oil, but the vinaigrette won't be as rich and fragrant.

ORANGE-SOY VINAIGRETTE

Citrusy, creamy, and a bit earthy too, from the soy, this all-purpose sauce works with many different fish.   Makes about 1 cup

2 oranges
½ cup plus 1 tablespoon vegetable oil
⅓ cup thinly sliced fresh ginger
¼ cup thinly sliced shallots
1 tablespoon thinly sliced garlic
1 teaspoon soy sauce

1 tablespoon sherry vinegar
¼ cup Fumet (page 296) or chicken stock
1 teaspoon fresh lemon juice
Coarse salt

Juice the oranges. Tear or cut the rinds of 1½ oranges into pieces (discard the rest).

Heat a saucepan over medium-high heat. When the pan's hot, add 1 tablespoon vegetable oil and the ginger. Sauté, stirring, for 30 seconds. Add the shallots and garlic and sauté, stirring, until fragrant, another 30 to 45 seconds. Add the orange juice and rinds, soy, and vinegar. Bring to a boil, then lower the heat so you have an active simmer and cook, pressing down on the solids once in a while, until thick, syrupy and reduced by two thirds (there will be liquid hiding in the solids).

Add the fumet or stock and bring back to an active simmer. Then strain, pushing down on the solids to get out all the liquid. You should have ½ cup. If you have more than that, boil to reduce it.

Pour the liquid into a blender. With the blender running, pour in the remaining ½ cup vegetable oil in a slow, steady stream. Keep the blender running for 30 seconds. Add the lemon juice and a pinch of salt.

The vinaigrette will keep for a couple of days in the refrigerator. Reheat it in a double boiler, whisking.

BASIL OIL

Whirring blades in a blender create heat, which would cook the blanched basil as you pureed it and turn the herb an unappealing khaki color. Using icy-cold oil ensures that the basil stays bright green.

Makes about 1 cup

¾ cup canola or vegetable oil
1½ packed cups fresh basil leaves

Coarse salt

Put the oil (in the measuring cup or a bowl) in the freezer for at least 1 hour.

Bring a large saucepan of salted water to a boil. Drop in the basil, blanch for 30 seconds, and drain. Refresh the basil in a bowl of cold water and drain again. (This blanching process helps keep the basil very green.) Squeeze the basil until it's very dry. Start with just your hands, then put the basil into a triple thickness of paper towels and use the towels to help you get out all the moisture.

Put the basil in a blender with the oil and a pinch of salt. Puree until very smooth. The oil will be thick and light green; the color will deepen as the oil sits. Transfer the oil to a bottle or other container.

The oil can be refrigerated for up to 3 weeks. Shake well before using.

BARBECUE SAUCE FOR FISH

Fish deserves its own special barbecue sauce. This one isn't aggressive in the least, so it's perfectly suited to the soft nuances of seafood. The flavor of the clam juice wafts through the sauce. Makes about 1¾ cups

2 tablespoons vegetable oil
1 cup minced onion
2 large garlic cloves, minced
1 teaspoon fresh thyme leaves
Coarse salt
1 tablespoon sugar
2 tablespoons water

1 tablespoon red wine vinegar
½ cup clam juice
1 cup ketchup
1 teaspoon Tabasco sauce
1 teaspoon Worcestershire sauce
Freshly ground white pepper

Heat a medium saucepan over medium-high heat. When the pan is hot, add the oil, onion, garlic, thyme, and a pinch of salt and cook, stirring often, until the onion is softened but not browned, about 5 minutes.

Meanwhile, combine the sugar and water in a small skillet over medium-high heat. Cook, swirling the sugar in the skillet, until the sugar dissolves and the caramel is dark amber. Add the vinegar and clam juice and boil until the caramel has dissolved.

Add the caramel and clam juice mixture to the onion, along with the ketchup, Tabasco, Worcestershire, and white pepper to taste. Bring to a boil, then lower the heat and simmer the sauce for 20 minutes. Let cool.

You can make this well in advance. It will keep for days in the refrigerator.

CHARMOULA

This all-purpose Moroccan spice paste is terrific for flavoring a whole grilled fish.

Makes about ¾ cup

5 garlic cloves, cut in half
2 tablespoons fresh lemon juice
2 heaped teaspoons paprika
1 teaspoon cumin seeds, toasted and
ground

1½ cups fresh cilantro, coarsely
chopped
½ cup fresh parsley leaves, coarsely
chopped
¼ cup olive oil

Turn a food processor on and drop the garlic down the feed tube. Scrape down the sides and add the lemon juice, paprika, and cumin. Pulse a few times to combine. Add the herbs and pulse a few times to make a coarse puree. Scrape the bowl. Turn the processor on and pour in the oil in a steady stream. Transfer the sauce to a bowl.

The charmoula will keep, tightly covered, in the refrigerator for up to 1 week, though the bright color will fade.

HOISIN GLAZE

Sweet, spicy, and thick, hoisin sauce is often referred to as Chinese barbecue sauce or seafood sauce (though it's made with soybeans). Here I kick up the sweetness quotient by adding honey and thin the sauce with lime juice for a bit of tang.

This quick glaze turns a simple piece of grilled or sautéed fish into something special. Brush it on as soon as the fish is cooked. Makes about ¼ cup

2 tablespoons hoisin sauce
Juice of ½ lime
1 teaspoon honey
1 small garlic clove, minced or put
   through a press

1 tablespoon minced fresh cilantro
Coarse salt

Stir the hoisin, lime juice, honey, garlic, and cilantro together in a small bowl. Season with salt.

This can sit on the counter for a couple of hours; or store it, covered, in the refrigerator for 3 days.

MOROCCAN SPICE MIX

The combination of earthy flavors in this spice rub works very nicely with salmon, mackerel, and other oily fish.   Makes about 6 tablespoons

2 tablespoons coriander seeds

2 tablespoons fennel seeds

1 tablespoon cumin seeds

1 tablespoon cardamom pods

10 whole cloves

Toast the spices in a small heavy skillet over medium heat until they are fragrant and lightly colored, about 7 minutes. Scrape them out into a bowl and let cool completely. You're really giving the cloves a chance to cool — process them while they're hot, and they will release oils that you'll never get out of your grinder.

Put the spices in a spice grinder and process into a fine powder. Transfer to a small jar and keep, out of the light, for up to 6 months.

HOMEMADE CHESAPEAKE SEASONING

Here's my take on Old Bay seasoning. Double or triple this recipe to have on hand. Use it as a rub for shrimp or crabs before you steam them. Or mix it with mayonnaise to make a spicy spread for sandwiches or for coating fish that you'll be grilling.

Makes about 2½ tablespoons

1 tablespoon celery seeds

1 teaspoon yellow mustard seeds

1 teaspoon white peppercorns

1 large bay leaf, torn into a few pieces

½ teaspoon sweet paprika

About ¼ teaspoon freshly grated nutmeg

¼ teaspoon ground ginger

¼ teaspoon cayenne

Combine all the ingredients in a spice grinder. Process until finely ground.

Store out of the light in a glass jar for up to 6 months.

CAJUN SPICE MIX

Yeah, I know: there are a lot of ingredients here, but this is really a great mix, ideal for grilling and broiling fish. Plus, it takes just a minute or two to make, and it keeps for months.   Makes about 1 cup

4 teaspoons coriander seeds

1 tablespoon fennel seeds

2 teaspoons white peppercorns

2 teaspoons black peppercorns

1 teaspoon cayenne

4 teaspoons Hungarian paprika

4 teaspoons chili powder

2 teaspoons celery seeds

1 tablespoon dried oregano, crumbled

1 tablespoon dried thyme

2 tablespoons coarse salt

2 tablespoons dried onion

1 tablespoon garlic powder

Combine the coriander seeds, fennel seeds, and peppercorns in a spice grinder and process until you have a coarse grind. Combine with the rest of the ingredients and mix well.

Transfer to a jar and keep, out of the light, for up to 6 months.

HARISSA

This spicy paste is one of the staples of the North African kitchen. Sure, you can buy it in tubes in specialty markets and even in some grocery stores, but I have to say, nothing beats the flavor of homemade. The recipe is from my coauthor.

Makes about ⅔ cup

2 ounces dried Baklouti chiles, wiped clean, stemmed, and seeded (see Note)

4 teaspoons fennel seeds

2 teaspoons coriander seeds

1 teaspoon crushed red pepper (optional)

1 teaspoon coarse salt

3 garlic cloves, chopped

6 tablespoons olive oil, plus a little more

Put the chiles in a heatproof bowl and cover with simmering water. Let the chiles rehydrate for 15 to 20 minutes.

Meanwhile, put the fennel and coriander seeds in a spice grinder with the crushed red pepper, if using, and salt. Grind to a fine powder, and pour into a food processor. Add the garlic to the processor.

Spoon 2 tablespoons of the chile soaking water into the processor, then drain the chiles and add them. Pulse a few times to make a very coarse paste. Scrape the sides down, then turn on the processor and pour in the oil. Process until you have a thick paste—don't worry, it needn't be completely smooth.

Pack the harissa into a glass jar, cover with a film of olive oil, and refrigerate. It will keep for about 1 month.

NOTE: Baklouti chiles, the traditional Tunisian hot pepper for harissa, are available from Kalustyan's (www.kalustyans.com). But you can substitute other dried chiles—say, guajillos, mulattos, pasillas, or even chipotles or moritas, if you want a fiery harissa.

ESSENTIAL SIDES

STEWED BABY ARTICHOKES (BARIGOULE)

This traditional French stew will be even better the day after you make it, so plan ahead if you can. It's particularly good with branzino and black sea bass.

Baby artichokes, which have no hairy choke hidden inside them, are much easier to clean than the big adult version. Serves 6

2 cups dry white wine

Juice of 2 lemons

2 pounds baby artichokes

1 lemon, cut in half

3 medium onions, cut into slices

1 large fennel bulb, trimmed, cored, and cut into slices

2 carrots, cut into slices (on an angle, to make them pretty)

2 garlic cloves, cut into thin slices

A handful of parsley stems and 5–6 sprigs thyme, tied together with kitchen string for an herb bouquet

Coarse salt

⅓ cup olive oil

Chopped fresh parsley for garnish

Pour the wine and lemon juice into a bowl. This acidic bath will prevent the cut artichokes from oxidizing and turning black.

Clean the artichokes: cut off the stem from each one, pull off the tough outer leaves (go down to the light yellow green), and cut off the tip. Cut each artichoke lengthwise in half. Rub it all over with the cut side of the lemon and drop it into the bowl with the wine and lemon juice.

Put the onions, fennel, carrots, garlic, and herb bouquet in a large heavy nonreactive saucepan. Season with salt and toss. Lift the artichokes out of the wine (reserve the wine) and layer them on top of the other vegetables. Pour in the oil, cover the pan, and sweat the vegetables over medium heat for 15 minutes.

Stir the vegetables, strain in the wine, and cover the pan again. Bring to a boil, then reduce the heat to medium-low and simmer until the artichokes are tender, about 20 minutes.

Pour the stew into a strainer set over a bowl. Return the liquid to the pan and bring to an active simmer. Reduce the liquid to about 1 cup. Give the liquid a whirl with an immersion blender to emulsify it.

Discard the herb bouquet, transfer the artichokes and vegetables to a bowl, and pour in the reduced liquid. Toss, then let the stew cool to room temperature. The barigoule will keep, covered, in the refrigerator for a week, if you can keep your hands off it.

Serve the stew garnished with a shower of chopped parsley.

ROAST ASPARAGUS

I think of asparagus as an herb standing in as a vegetable. It's a light, neutral accompaniment to rich fish.

Serves 4

1 pound asparagus, tough ends
  trimmed
2 tablespoons olive oil

Coarse salt and freshly ground black
  pepper

Heat the oven to 500 degrees.

Toss the asparagus with the oil on a baking sheet (no need to dirty a bowl) and season with salt and pepper. Spread the asparagus spears out so they're in a single layer.

Roast for about 10 minutes, until tender and starting to brown.

You can serve these hot or at room temperature.

GREEN BEANS AND CHORIZO

This is the side to turn to when you want a hint of Spanish flavor on your plate.

Serves 4

1 pound green beans

6 ounces Spanish chorizo

Coarse salt

1 tablespoon olive oil

Top and tail the green beans. Cut them into quarters on a sharp diagonal. Remove the casings from the chorizo and cut it into pieces about the same size as the beans.

Bring a large pot of salted water to a boil. Have an ice bath at the ready.

Blanch the beans in the boiling water until crisp-tender, just over a minute. Drain, then dump the beans into the ice bath to stop the cooking. Drain well. You can blanch the beans early in the day or even the day before. Refrigerate them in a bowl, covered with damp paper towels.

Heat a large skillet over high heat. When it's good and hot, add the oil and chorizo. Sauté, stirring, until the chorizo starts to brown, about 1 minute. Add the beans and sauté, stirring and tossing often, until they are good and hot, about 2 minutes. Check for salt, and serve.

BASIC BEETS

When you cook beets this way, you're just about pickling them, so they'll keep in the refrigerator for weeks. They're a great accompaniment to all kinds of fish, and when you combine them with Skordalia (page 397), the Greek garlic and potato dip —well, it's a match made in heaven.   Serves 4

1 bunch beets (3 large)	2 tablespoons sugar
½ cup red wine vinegar	2 tablespoons coarse salt

Trim the tops from the beets and scrub well.

Put the beets in a medium saucepan and cover with cold water by about an inch. Add the vinegar, sugar, and salt and bring to a boil. Reduce the heat to keep the beets at a gentle boil and cook until they are tender, 40 minutes to 1 hour. Cool the beets in the cooking liquid.

When the beets are cool enough to handle, remove them from the liquid and peel them (under running water, to avoid staining your hands). You can serve them now or put them in a plastic container, cover with the cooking liquid, and refrigerate.

BASIC BOK CHOY (OR CABBAGE)

Bok choy—a mild and sweet Chinese cabbage—is a nicely unassertive partner to fish. A little green, a little crunchy, this is the kind of thing you can make early in the day (or even the day before) and reheat for dinner.

Small heads of bok choy are much more tender than the large, so look for them. You can use this same technique for cooking cabbage.   Serves 4

Coarse salt

4 small heads bok choy (about 1½
    pounds), cut lengthwise in half, or
    ½ large (2½-pound) head of
    cabbage, cut into 4 wedges

2 tablespoons unsalted butter

Bring a large saucepan of salted water to a boil. Have ready a bowl of cold water.

Add the bok choy or cabbage to the water and bring back to a boil. Cook bok choy for about 2½ minutes, until just tender; cook cabbage for about 7 minutes, until the core is crisp-tender. Drain and plunge the vegetables into the cold water to stop the cooking. Drain again. Squeeze out the water, keeping the shape of the vegetable as you squeeze. You can refrigerate the bok choy or cabbage for serving later or proceed.

To reheat, bring about ¼ cup water to a boil in a skillet. Whisk in the butter and season with salt. Add the bok choy or cabbage and heat it through, turning it once or twice. Bok choy will take about 3 minutes to heat; cabbage will take about 5 minutes. Drain well before serving.

WILTED CABBAGE

Sometimes you want something sweet and fairly neutral with fish. Well, you've got that here, and it couldn't be easier to make.

Tender savoy cabbage wilts quickly. You can make this with green cabbage, but you'll need to cook it longer.   Serves 4

2 teaspoons vegetable oil
⅔ pound savoy cabbage, shredded
4 scallions, cut into thin slices

2 teaspoons soy sauce
1 teaspoon water

Heat the vegetable oil in a large nonstick skillet over medium heat. When it's hot, turn the heat to high and add the cabbage and scallions. Stir-fry for 30 seconds. Add the soy sauce and water and stir-fry until the cabbage is starting to wilt, about 1 minute. Serve.

ASIAN SLAW

The flavors here are bright and clean, a nice contrast to fried fish. So even if you have a mayonnaisey coleslaw in your repertoire, try this one. Serves 4

1 pound cabbage, cored and shredded
1 cup grated carrots (use the large
  holes of a box grater or the
  shredding disk of a food processor)

½ cup Asian "Vinaigrette" (page 432)
2 tablespoons chopped fresh mint
Coarse salt

Toss the cabbage and carrots with the vinaigrette and mint. Season with salt, toss, and taste. Adjust the salt if necessary. Cover with plastic wrap and refrigerate for 1 hour before serving.

CARROT SLAW

This slaw has nice crunch and great color. It's a simple, clean foil to many fish dishes.

Serves 4 to 6

3 cups shredded carrots (use the large holes on a box grater or the shredding disk of a food processor)
1 tablespoon grated fresh ginger (use a Microplane)

3 tablespoons rice vinegar
1 tablespoon vegetable oil
½ teaspoon ground toasted coriander seeds
Coarse salt

Toss the carrots with the ginger, vinegar, oil, and coriander. Season with salt and toss again. Cover with plastic wrap and refrigerate for 1 hour before serving.

CAULIFLOWER PUREE

Cooking cauliflower in cream keeps it mild and makes it a great connector of flavors. Pair it with anything earthy, particularly mushrooms or truffles.   Serves 4

1 (2-pound) head cauliflower, trimmed	½ cup water
Coarse salt	½ cup half-and-half or heavy cream
	Freshly ground white pepper

Rinse the cauliflower in cold water, then sprinkle it all over with salt (the water helps the salt stick).

Pour the water and half-and-half or cream into a heavy saucepan just large enough to hold the whole cauliflower, and season with white pepper. Add the cauliflower, cover, and bring to a simmer over medium-high heat. Reduce the heat to keep the liquid just at a simmer and cook until the cauliflower is tender when pierced with a small knife, about 15 minutes.

Transfer the cauliflower to a food processor (leave the liquid in the pan) and process to a coarse puree.

Reduce the cooking liquid to about 3 tablespoons. Add the liquid to the cauliflower and process again until you have a smooth puree. Check for salt and pepper.

You can serve this right away or make it early in the day and reheat it.

CELERY ROOT AND POTATO PUREE

Adding celery root to a simple potato puree ups the ante and adds a quietly complex layer of flavor.   Serves 4

1 small (about ¾ pound) celery root
1 cup heavy cream
Coarse salt

¾ pound russet potatoes
1 tablespoon unsalted butter, softened

Peel the celery root and cut it into ½-inch sticks. Put it in a small saucepan with the cream and a good pinch of salt. Bring to a boil over high heat, then reduce the heat so you have an active simmer, cover, and cook until the celery root is tender, about 20 minutes.

Meanwhile, peel the potatoes and cut them into chunks. Cover with water by at least an inch in a small saucepan, and add a good pinch of salt. Bring to a boil over high heat, then reduce the heat to an active simmer, cover partway, and cook until the potatoes are tender, about 17 minutes.

Drain the potatoes and put through a food mill fitted with the medium disk. Put the celery root, with whatever cream is left in the pan, through the food mill and mix with the potatoes. Stir in the butter, check for salt, and serve.

CREAMY CORN

Simple and rich, this dish is best made with summer corn, but it will work with frozen in a pinch.   Serves 4

3 ears corn (or 2½ cups frozen corn,   Coarse salt and freshly ground white
   run under hot water to defrost)   pepper
1 cup heavy cream

Cut the corn kernels from the cobs. Scrape the cobs with the back of your knife to get out all the juice.

Combine the corn, with the juices, and cream in a deep skillet or wide saucepan and season with salt and white pepper. Bring to a simmer over medium heat. Reduce the heat to keep at an active simmer and cook for about 10 minutes, stirring frequently, until thick. (Frozen corn will take a bit longer.)

Serve right away.

ASIAN CUCUMBER SALAD

Cleansing, cooling, and crisp, this is a perfect palate refresher.

The salad will start to weep as soon as you combine the vegetables with the dressing, but you can prep everything well in advance. Just save the tossing for the last minute.

You'll need a mandoline or vegetable slicer to shred the vegetables. And now is the time to use big fat carrots, which are easier to control on the mandoline. Rotate them as you reach the woody center (which you'll discard). As for the cucumber: you can substitute a garden variety cuke as long as you seed it first. A Kirby will work too. If you can't find daikon, substitute icicle or breakfast radishes. You'll need 4 or 5.   Serves 4

FOR THE DRESSING
½ cup Asian "Vinaigrette" (page 432)
1 small red onion, sliced as thin as
   possible

FOR THE SALAD
1 (4-inch) piece daikon radish, peeled
1–2 large carrots
1 small seedless cucumber
3 tablespoons chopped fresh mint

FOR THE DRESSING: Combine the vinaigrette and onion and let sit for at least 30 minutes.

FOR THE SALAD: Shred the daikon and carrots on a mandoline. Toss together in a bowl, cover with a damp paper towel, and put in the refrigerator until you're ready to serve. Grate the cucumber on a box grater. Cover with a damp paper towel and refrigerate.

At the last minute, combine the daikon, carrots, cucumber, and mint in a salad bowl. Toss with the dressing and serve immediately.

MOM'S CUCUMBER SALAD

My mom made something like this when I was growing up, though with red wine vinegar and no herbs. I took her idea and played with it. The cucumbers keep crisp, like a great dill pickle.   Serves 4

2 cucumbers, peeled, seeded, and cut
    into ¼-inch slices
Coarse salt
1 small red onion, cut into very thin
    slices

1 tablespoon sugar
1 tablespoon chopped fresh dill
About 1 cup rice vinegar

Put the cucumbers in a colander with a generous teaspoon of salt and toss. Fill a sealable plastic bag with ice cubes and put it on top of the cukes to weight them and keep them very cold. Put the colander in a bowl and refrigerate for 1 hour.

Take the colander out of the bowl and shake the cucumbers well over the sink. Don't do anything like blotting them or rinsing them.

Put the cukes into a bowl with the onion, sugar, and dill. Toss to combine. Pour in the vinegar; it should just cover the cucumbers. Cover and refrigerate for at least 1 hour before serving.

This will keep for at least 5 days in the refrigerator.

FENNEL PUREE

Think of this side when you want a foil for fatty salmon or oily fish like mackerel.

Serves 4

1 large (1-pound) fennel bulb,
   trimmed and cut into ½-inch slices
Coarse salt and freshly ground white
   pepper

1 tablespoon fennel seeds, toasted and
   tied in cheesecloth
1 cup water
2 tablespoons unsalted butter

Put the fennel in a large skillet and season it with salt and white pepper. Bury the packet of seeds in the center of the skillet and pour in the water. Dot with the butter.

Cut a round of parchment the size of your skillet and cut a hole in the center to release steam. Cover the fennel with the parchment and bring to a simmer over medium heat. Reduce the heat to medium-low and simmer gently until the pan is just about dry and the fennel is very tender, about 40 minutes.

Discard the packet of seeds. Puree the fennel in a food processor until very smooth. Check for salt and pepper.

You can serve this right away or make it early in the day and reheat it.

FENNEL SALAD

This all-purpose salad is great with all kinds of fish dishes.   Serves 4

2 oranges, peeled and segmented (see
    page 474), juice reserved
1 fennel bulb, trimmed and sliced as
    thin as possible (use a mandoline or
    vegetable slicer)

½ red onion, sliced as thin as possible
Coarse salt
Juice of ½ lemon
2 tablespoons extra virgin olive oil
4 kalamata olives, pitted and minced

Toss the oranges, fennel, and onion together in a bowl with salt to taste, the lemon juice, 1 tablespoon olive oil, and the juice left from segmenting the oranges. Cover and refrigerate until very cold.

When you're ready to serve, toss the salad again. Toss the olives with the remaining 1 tablespoon olive oil and scatter over the salad.

VARIATION

While I love the combination of fennel and orange, sometimes I want the perfume of truffles.

Slice a fennel bulb on a mandoline or vegetable slicer. Season with salt and white pepper and dress with 3 tablespoons olive oil, 1½ teaspoons truffle oil, and the juice of half a lemon. Toss. Add ¼ cup freshly grated Parmesan and toss again.

If you'd like, add thinly sliced hearts of palm or thinly sliced raw baby artichokes.

BASIC LEEKS

This quick braise provides a fine counterpoint to sautéed or grilled fish. And it's one of those dishes you can make in advance and reheat at dinnertime.   Serves 4 to 6

5 large leeks (white and light green
   parts)
2 cups water

4 tablespoons unsalted butter
1 tablespoon coarse salt

Slice the leeks lengthwise in half and cut into thin half-moons. Drop into a bowl of cold water and swirl around. Let the leeks sit for a few minutes to let any grit settle to the bottom of the bowl, then lift them out into a colander and drain them.

Bring the water, butter, and salt to a boil in a large skillet. Cut a piece of parchment into a round the size of the skillet. Add the leeks, cover with the parchment, and bring back to a boil. Reduce the heat so the leeks simmer actively and cook for 5 minutes, or until just tender.

You can serve these now or refrigerate them for later, when you should reheat them in their liquid. Drain well before serving.

BASIC LENTILS

Lentils go well with fish—salmon in particular. And you really don't need to do much to prepare them. Keep a batch of these on hand to reheat and serve when you need them.   Serves 4 to 6

½ pound (1 cup) green or brown
   lentils
Coarse salt

3 tablespoons unsalted butter
1 tablespoon water

Put the lentils in a saucepan and cover with cold water by at least 2 inches. Season with salt and bring to a simmer over medium heat. Reduce the heat and simmer until the lentils are just tender, about 20 minutes. (If your lentils are very old, they will take much longer to cook, sometimes as long as 1 hour. Add boiling water to the pan if you need to, to keep the lentils covered.) Drain the lentils and spread them out on a baking sheet so they cool evenly.

To serve, melt the butter with the water in a saucepan over medium heat. Add the lentils and cook, stirring occasionally, until hot.

LENTIL SALAD

Lentils are one of those ingredients, like beets, that exemplify earthiness. The vinaigrette in this salad accents that earthiness, and the peppers add a touch of sweetness and heat.

Serve with striped bass or with turbot or other firm flatfish.   Serves 4 to 6

1 cup green or brown lentils	¼ cup olive oil
Coarse salt	½ cup chopped scallions
¼ cup red wine vinegar	½ cup diced red bell pepper
1 tablespoon Dijon mustard	2 tablespoons diced poblano chile
Freshly ground white pepper	2 tablespoons chopped fresh parsley

Put the lentils in a saucepan and cover with cold water by at least 2 inches. Season with a pinch of salt. Bring to a simmer over medium heat, then lower the heat and simmer until the lentils are just tender, about 20 minutes. (If your lentils are very old, they will take much longer to cook, sometimes as long as 1 hour. Add boiling water to the pan if you need to, to keep the lentils covered.) Drain, then spread the lentils out on a baking sheet to cool them quickly and evenly.

Whisk the vinegar and mustard together in a salad bowl with salt and white pepper to taste. Drizzle in the oil, whisking to make an emulsion. Add the scallions, bell pepper, poblano, and lentils and toss. Taste and adjust the salt and pepper. Sprinkle on the parsley.

You can serve this right away or refrigerate it for later, but bring it back to room temperature first.

These gently stewed peppers are a perfect foil for scallops and shrimp, but I also like them with oily fish, like mackerel or bluefish.

The Anaheim pepper adds a very subtle note of heat. You can substitute any other slightly hot pepper or use another bell pepper and a pinch of crushed red pepper.

Serves 4

¼ cup olive oil
1 medium onion, cut into thin slices
2 garlic cloves, minced
4 anchovies, minced
3 large bell peppers (yellow and red), cut into thin slices

1 Anaheim or Hungarian wax pepper (see headnote), seeded and cut into thin slices
Coarse salt and freshly ground white pepper
1½ cups chopped tomatoes
2 teaspoons fresh thyme leaves

Heat a wide deep skillet over high heat. When the pan is hot, add the oil and the onion. Sauté, stirring often, until the onion starts to soften, about 2 minutes. Add the garlic and anchovies and sauté, stirring, until the garlic is fragrant, about 30 seconds. Add the peppers, season with salt and white pepper, and sauté, stirring often, for 3 minutes. Add the tomatoes and thyme, cover, and reduce the heat to medium-low. Simmer for 30 minutes, or until the peppers are very tender.

Let the peperonata cool to room temperature before serving or storing. It will keep for about 4 days in the refrigerator. Check the seasoning before you serve it.

POTATO SALAD LOUIS

I love the dressing for Louis Salad so much that I had to see how it worked with potatoes. It's right on the money. This potato salad is an ideal accompaniment to grilled fish.   Serves 4

1 pound white or creamer potatoes, scrubbed

Coarse salt

3 large hard-cooked eggs

3 scallions, chopped

⅓ cup diced red bell pepper

Louis Dressing (page 339), *without* the heavy cream

1 teaspoon fresh lemon juice

½ teaspoon celery seeds

Freshly ground white pepper

Put the potatoes in a saucepan and cover with cold water by at least an inch. Add a hefty dose of salt and bring to a boil over high heat. Reduce the heat to a gentle boil, cover the pan partway, and cook until the potatoes are tender. Drain and cool to room temperature.

Cut the potatoes into small chunks. Chop the eggs. Combine them in a mixing bowl with the scallions, bell pepper, dressing, lemon juice, celery seeds, and salt and white pepper to taste. Fold well but gently to distribute the dressing without breaking up the eggs too much.

Transfer to a serving bowl, cover, and refrigerate for at least 1 hour before serving.

GERMAN-STYLE POTATO SALAD

This warm and tangy salad should be in the repertoire of every fish cook. My version is lighter than the standard, and it doesn't have bacon. The oregano and rice vinegar aren't traditional either, but they make the salad taste so fine.   Serves 4

1 pound creamer (or baby red-
    skinned) potatoes — the size
    of small eggs
4 cups cold water
Coarse salt
⅓ cup vegetable oil

¾ cup minced shallots
1 teaspoon dried oregano
1 tablespoon sugar
¼ cup rice vinegar
Freshly ground white pepper
⅓ cup chopped fresh chives

Put the potatoes and the water in a saucepan and add a hefty dose of salt. (I believe in cooking potatoes in very well-salted water.) Bring to a simmer over medium-high heat. Simmer the potatoes for 12 minutes, or until they are just tender. Drain and cool slightly.

When the potatoes are cool enough to handle, peel them and cut into ¼-inch rounds.

Heat a large sauté pan over medium heat. When the pan is hot, add the oil and shallots and crumble in the oregano. Cook, stirring often, until the shallots are tender, about 4 minutes. Add the sugar and vinegar and bring to a boil. Fold in the potatoes and season with salt and white pepper. Simmer to heat the potatoes through, about 1 minute. Fold in the chives and remove from the heat.

Serve this warm or at room temperature.

COCONUT RICE WITH CARROTS

Cooking rice in coconut milk not only packs it with flavor but gives the rice a creamy texture. Here that texture is nicely offset by the little crunch of the carrots. The nuttiness of jasmine rice highlights the coconut.

Pair this with spicy fish dishes or any seafood with a tropical marinade.   Serves 4

1 cup jasmine rice
1 (14-ounce) can coconut milk
¼ cup water

Coarse salt
1 cup grated carrots (use the large
   holes on a box grater)

Put the rice in a bowl and cover with cold water. Swirl the rice around in the bowl, then drain. Repeat washing the rice until the water in the bowl is clear when you swirl the rice.

Put the rice in a saucepan with the coconut milk, water, and a good pinch of salt. Bring to a boil over medium-high heat. Stir the rice with a fork, reduce the heat to the lowest possible, and cover the pan. Cook for 15 minutes.

Toss the carrots with a pinch of salt and cover the rice with them. Put the cover back on the pan and cook for another 5 minutes.

Remove the lid, cover the pan with a kitchen towel, put the lid back on, and leave the rice on the back of the stove for 10 minutes.

Stir the carrots into the rice with a fork and serve.

JASMINE RICE

I prefer the nutty notes of jasmine rice with fish, but you can use this technique for cooking any long-grain rice.   Serves 4

2 cups water   1 cup jasmine rice
1 teaspoon unsalted butter   Coarse salt

Bring the water and butter to a boil in a saucepan over medium-high heat. Add the rice and a pinch of salt, stir, cover, and reduce the heat to the lowest possible. Cook the rice for 17 minutes.

Turn the heat off, take the lid off, and cover the pot with a clean kitchen towel; replace the lid and let the rice rest for 10 minutes. Stir with a fork before serving.

RICK'S KEY LIME PIE

*Y*ou need something sweet to finish a meal, and there may be no better dessert for a fish dinner than Key lime pie.

Make this with tiny Key limes if you can find them. If not, regular Persian limes will be just fine.   Makes one 9-inch pie

FOR THE FILLING
4 teaspoons grated lime zest
   (use your Microplane here)
4 large egg yolks
1 (14-ounce) can sweetened
   condensed milk
½ cup strained fresh lime juice

FOR THE CRUST
1¼ cups fine graham cracker
   crumbs (from about 11 whole
   crackers)
3 tablespoons sugar
5 tablespoons unsalted butter,
   melted

FOR THE TOPPING
¾ cup heavy cream
¼ cup confectioners' sugar

Half a lime, cut into paper-thin
   slices
Granulated sugar

Set a rack in the center of the oven and heat the oven to 325 degrees.

FOR THE FILLING: Whisk the lime zest and egg yolks in a medium bowl until the yolks are light and tinted pale green, about 2 minutes. Whisk in the condensed milk, then whisk in the lime juice. Let this sit on the counter to thicken while you make the crust.

FOR THE CRUST: Mix the crumbs and sugar together in a bowl. Drizzle in the butter and stir well with a fork to moisten all the crumbs. Scrape into a 9-inch pie plate. Press the crumbs over the bottom and up the sides of the pan to make an even, firm crust.

Bake the crust until lightly browned and fragrant, about 15 minutes. Cool on a rack for 20 minutes; leave the oven on.

Pour the filling into the crust and bake for 15 to 17 minutes, until just set—the filling should still jiggle a bit in the center when you shake the pan. Cool the pie completely on a rack, then refrigerate for at least 3 hours. You want it good and cold. You can make the pie a day in advance. Spray a piece of plastic wrap lightly with pan spray (a flavorless one) and cover the pie before you refrigerate it.

FOR THE TOPPING: Whip the cream in a cold bowl until soft peaks form. Whip in the confectioners' sugar 1 tablespoon at a time, then continue to whip until you have just-stiff peaks. Pipe the cream decoratively over the pie, or just spread it evenly with a spatula.

Dip the lime slices into some granulated sugar to coat and use to garnish the pie. Serve very cold.

SOME HELPFUL TECHNIQUES AND BUILDING-BLOCK RECIPES

PEELING, MINCING, AND GRATING GINGER

The easiest way to peel this gnarly rhizome is with a spoon. You heard me, a spoon. Hold the ginger in one hand, the spoon in the other, with the bowl pointing down toward the ginger. Use the tip of the spoon and scrape toward you, and you'll find the peel coming right off, with a minimum of waste.

There are a couple of ways of mincing ginger. The classic is cutting the ginger into thin coins, stacking the coins and cutting them into strips, then turning the strips and mincing. Less "French" is cutting the coins, smashing the coins with the flat of your knife, and chopping until you have a fine mince.

Grating ginger on a Microplane gives a more intense flavor, but you can also use a porcelain ginger grater.

CLEANING LEEKS

Unless I tell you otherwise, here's the way I prepare leeks.

Cut off the root and pull off the tough outer layer of the leek. Cut away the darkest, toughest green top of the leek (I like the flavor of the light green part) and discard that as well or save for stock. Cut the leek in half lengthwise, then slice very thin.

Drop the sliced leek into a bowl of cold water. Swirl it around with your hand, then let it sit for a few minutes for any grit to settle at the bottom of the bowl. Lift the leek out by hand and drop into a colander to drain.

MAKING LEMON WEDGES

I cut lemons in half lengthwise, then cut out the central membrane (two cuts on the diagonal, and it's gone) and poke out any remaining seeds with the tip of my knife. Then I cut the pieces in half. Lemon wedges should be substantial.

PEELING AND SEGMENTING CITRUS

Cut off the top and bottom of your fruit with a thin sharp knife, to the point where you expose the flesh. Set it with one cut end down on your board and cut off the peel and white pith. Just follow the shape of the fruit, and then go back to trim off any bits of pith you've missed. Set a strainer over a bowl. Pick up that naked citrus and sit it in your palm. Working over the strainer, cut down along one membrane, then up along the other membrane that's holding the segment. You've got one seg- ment free. Now cut down the other side of the membrane, flip your knife so it points out, and cut up along the next membrane. Segments always come in differ- ent sizes. Sometimes it may be easier just to cut down on both sides, rather than doing the cut-down, cut-up thing.

Continue until you've freed all the segments, then squeeze the guts over the strainer so you get all the juice. When you're using segments as a garnish, you get to drink the juice or use it for some other purpose.

ROASTING PEPPERS

For me, the easiest method is to put bell peppers on a baking sheet and pop them into a 400-degree oven for about 30 minutes, until the skins are blistered all over. Then I put them in a plastic bag, or in a bowl covered tightly with plastic wrap, and let them steam for at least 15 minutes. When the peppers are cool, I pull off the skins, open up the peppers, pull out the seed pods and stems, and cut away the ribs.

FRESH BREAD CRUMBS

I use close-textured bread (something like Pepperidge Farm) that's a day or two old. Cut off the crusts, cut or tear the bread into smaller pieces, and put it in the food processor. Process to fine, fluffy crumbs.

If the bread is very fresh, spread the crumbs out on a baking sheet and slide them into a hot (400-degree) oven for 2 to 3 minutes to dry slightly. Let them cool completely.

Two slices of bread will give you about ½ cup of bread crumbs.

CROUTONS

These garlicky toasts are an important part of bouillabaisse, serving as a raft for rouille, but they're also what you want when you're serving Boquerones (page 351) or smoked fish.

Cut a baguette into slices that are about ⅓ inch thick; it's nice if you cut them on an angle, but please yourself. Heat a sauté pan over medium-high heat, and when the pan's hot, pour in 2 or 3 tablespoons olive oil. Fry the slices of bread until they're golden brown on both sides, adding more oil as you need it. Rub the toasts with the cut side of a garlic clove, paying particular attention to the edges, and drain on paper towels. You can serve these right away or hours later.

QUICK VEGETABLE STOCK

This very light stock will complement the flavors of fish and seafood but not compete with them. It is the kind of thing you should be able to make with bits and pieces you have in the refrigerator, but you'll notice that there are no carrots. I don't much care for the color they add to the stock. But if I have some fennel on hand, I will definitely add it to the pot.   Makes about 4 cups

Coarse salt
1 large onion, chopped
2 celery ribs, chopped
2 shallots, chopped
3 garlic cloves, chopped

1 cup dry white wine
4 cups water
A handful of parsley stems
2 sprigs thyme
1 bay leaf

Sprinkle a light layer of salt into the bottom of a stockpot. Add the onion, celery, shallots, and garlic, cover, and sweat the vegetables over medium heat for about 10 minutes, until they have softened some.

Add the wine, water, parsley, thyme, and bay leaf and bring to a simmer over high heat. Lower the heat so the stock simmers gently for 30 minutes. Strain.

The stock will keep in the refrigerator for 3 days, and it can be frozen for about 4 months.

ONLINE SOURCES FOR FISH AND SHELLFISH

I like being able to see and smell the fish I'm going to buy and to talk with the person selling it, but that's not always possible. There are, however, some merchants ready and willing to ship you some great fresh fish and shellfish. Careful packing, frozen gel packs, and overnight shipping ensure that the fish arrives in pristine condition. Here's a sampling.

Seafood Choices Alliance

Your best resource may be the Seafood Choices Alliance suppliers listing, which allows you to search by fish species for retailers across the country.

www.seafoodchoices.com

Browne Trading Company

In addition to a selection of fresh fish, Browne Trading Company also sells caviar and smoked fish. It doesn't always list all the available fish on the Web site, so you should call.

www.brownetrading.com
800-944-7848

Farm-2-market.com

A source for sturgeon, oysters and mussels, and other ocean products. Farm 2 Market also sells sweet shrimp in season and wild head-on Louisiana shrimp that has never been frozen.

www.Farm-2-market.com
800-663-4326

Great Alaska Seafood

Salmon, halibut, and sablefish. The fish is vacuum-packed and flash-frozen.

www.great-alaska-seafood.com
866-262-8846

Taylor Shellfish Farms

Oysters, Manila clams, mussels, and Dungeness crabs from the Pacific Northwest.

www.Taylorshellfishfarms.com
360-432-3300

INDEX

Page references in *italic* refer to color photographs of prepared recipes. Page references in **boldface** refer to notes on fish and shellfish varieties, including buying tips.

A

mustard *(continued)*
    Butter Sauce, Turbot Poached in
        Milk, with Noodles and, 88, *150*
    "caviar," 418
    Honey Sauce for Gravlax, 355

N

net-pen farming, 18
New England fare
    Clam Chowder, 302–3
    Steamed Dinner, 112–13
New Orleans fare
    Oyster Po'Boy, 275
Niçoise Salad, 336–37
North African flavors
    Charmoula, 438
    Harissa, 443
    Moroccan Spice Mix, 440
    Sautéed Char with Moroccan Spices,
        Lentils, and Harissa Tomato
        Sauce, 239
    Sautéed Rouget with Tunisian
        Sauce, 242–43
nut crusts, 248
    see also almond(s)

O

oil(s), 29
    Basil, 436
    brushing grill grate with, 141
    frying, disposing of, 259
    -Poached Halibut with Gribiche and
        Poached Eggs, 96–97, *202*
    poaching fish in, 95
    Salmon Preserved in, 99
    Tuna Preserved in, 98
okra, in Shrimp Gumbo, 324–26
Olive, Black, and Anchovy Butter, 411
olive oil, 29
    poaching fish in, 95
omega-3 fatty acids, 16
omega-6 fatty acids, 16

onion(s)
    Fennel Gravlax, *149*, 356
    Pickled, *206*, 400
online sources for fish and shellfish,
    14, 477
orange
    Chipotle Marinade, Swordfish Bro-
        chettes with, 168–69, *208*
    Cream for Gravlax, *149*, 357
    Fennel Salad, 461
    Soy Sauce, 424
    Soy Vinaigrette, 435
orange roughy, 17
orata, *see* dorade royale
oregano, dried, 30
overcooking, 24–26
overfishing, 17–19
    fish to avoid due to, 17
oyster(s), 16, **64–65**
    aquaculture (fish farming) and, 17
    Fried, 275
    grilling, 175
    Po'Boy, 275
    Shooters, *148*, 279
    shucking, 28, 44
    Steamed West Coast, 111
    Stew, 308
oyster knives, 28

P

packets (*en papillote* preparation), 220
    of Barramundi with Shrimp and
        Mushrooms, 220–21
    of Bluefish with Peperonata, 222
    drugstore wrap for, 39
    of Haddock with Zucchini, Toma-
        toes, and Parsley Pesto, 223
    Salmon, Steamed, with Peanut and
        Red Curry Sauce, 114–15
    of Scrod with Clams and Potatoes,
        224–25
Paella, 390–91
paillards
    cutting, 38

grilling, 165
    Mahi Mahi, Grilled, 164
    Salmon, Grilled, 164
    Sturgeon, Grilled, 164
panko, 30
pantry staples, 28–29
en papillote preparation, 39, 220
    see also packets
parsley, 32
    Pesto, 422
    Pesto, Broiled Fish Fillets with, 123
    Pesto, Packets of Haddock with
        Zucchini, Tomatoes and, 223
pasta, 375–85
    Crab Poached in Scampi Butter
        Sauce with, 94–95
    Linguine with Clams, 382
    Linguine with Tuna Sauce, 383
    Lobster Fra Diavolo, *154*, 379
    Puttanesca Sauce, 430
    with Shrimp and Ginger Cream, 376
    with Shrimp and Roasted Tomato
        Sauce, 377–78
    Shrimp Fra Diavolo, 380–81
    Thin Spaghetti with Mussels and
        Anchovies, 384–85
Peanut and Red Curry Sauce,
    Steamed Salmon Packets with,
    114–15
peanut oil, 29
Peas, Rice and, 91
pecan(s)
    -Crusted Turbot, 247
    as crust for fish, 248
Peperonata, 465
    Packets of Bluefish with, 222
pepper(corns), 29
    cracking, 29
    Tuna au Poivre with Fennel Salad,
    231
pepper(s) (bell)
    Coulis, *206*, 427
    Peperonata, 465
    Red, and Tabasco Butter, 410
    roasting, 475
peppers, hot, *see* chiles